BEST MUSIC WRITING

2009

PREVIOUS EDITIONS OF
BEST MUSIC WRITING:

BEST MUSIC WRITING
2009

Greil Marcus, *Guest Editor*

Daphne Carr, *Series Editor*

DA CAPO PRESS
A MEMBER OF THE PERSEUS BOOKS GROUP

Designed by Timm Bryson
Set in 10.5 point Warnock Pro by the Perseus Books Group
Cataloging-in-Publication data for this book is available from the Library of Congress

First Da Capo Press edition 2009
ISBN 978-0-306-81782-3

Published by Da Capo Press
A Member of the Perseus Books Group
www.dacapopress.com

Da Capo Press books are available at special discounts for bulk purchases in the U.S. by corporations, institutions, and other organizations. For more information, please contact the Special Markets Department at the Perseus Books Group, 2300 Chestnut Street, Suite 200, Philadelphia, PA, 19103, or call (800) 810-4145, extension 5000, or e-mail special.markets@perseusbooks.com.

10 9 8 7 6 5 4 3 2 1

CONTENTS

Introduction

Greil Marcus

In many ways, the piece here that bothers me the most is Jody Rosen's "Researchers Play Tune Recorded Before Edison," a straight New York Times report on a small technological breakthrough. Researchers had managed to translate the audio waves of a performance of "Claire de Lune," recorded visually on paper in Paris in 1860, into sound that could be played back.

One commentator wrote that the discovery opened the possibility that, someday, we might be able to hear for ourselves the greatest of all lost voices: Lincoln's. That was my first thought, too. There's a way in which "the mystic chords of memory"— which is what we are forced to rely on when imagining if the delivery of, say, the lines "until every drop of blood drawn with the lash, shall be paid by another drawn with the sword," from Lincoln's Second Inaugural Address, matches the words themselves, undercuts them, or leaves them even more on fire than, on he page, they already are—can never be as powerful as mere chords of memory and no more, no need for mysticism: *I was there.*

Lincoln is just a touchstone. Anyone else might think of Emily Dickinson, Frederick Douglass—or a version of the number one hit minstrel-show play, *Uncle Tom's Cabin* (for the time being we have to rely on the Firesign Theatre recreation from their 1974 *Everything You Know Is Wrong*), or real slavery-time secret ring shouts in the woods, not merely the handed-down accounts transcribed in the 1930s by WPA writers or recorded by Alan Lomax in the 1940s. In other words, if Édouard-Léon Scott de Martinville could invent the phonautograph in France in the 1850s, who knows what Americans, or Russians, or Japanese came up with at the same time, or even earlier? It's 2009, one-hundred-and-twenty-one years since the Edison Company achieved playback on a wax cylinder, and we have no idea what remains to be heard: what we don't know.

That sense of contingency and uncertainty hangs over many of the pieces in this book, from Carrie Brownstein's "Mystery Drain" ("the unknown elevates the art . . . Robert Johnson, Bob Dylan, Badfinger, Sam Cooke, Brian Jones, Syd Barrett, Jandek, Bjork and Prince are just a few of the names that come to mind for me") to John Jeremiah Sullivan's "Unknown Bards" to Jace Clayton's "Confessions of a DJ" ("I've died in more than two dozen countries") to Edwyn Collins's "This Much I Know" ("They did this routine where they mimed ripping up a piece of paper. Afterwards our manager was crying. He said, 'The big moments are never as good as you think they're going to be'"). But while a sense of time, eternity, and the vast catacombs of what-might-be-but-is-not-yet hangs over this book (David Remnick's "Bird-Watcher," William Hogeland's "American Dreamers"), that same sense brings on a certain impatience. Get it over with! Tell me what you think! Time? As Charlie Haas once wrote of why punk songs were so short, people can't stick around for stuff that takes ten minutes to read. People have to *be somewhere* in ten minutes.

So there's Carrie Brownstein again with "Your Trusted Source for Music Reviews" ("Bear in Heaven—*Red Bloom of the Boom*," with a rating of "Double Tall Sugar Free Vanilla Latte") and a selection from Paul Ford's heroic, or demonic, "Six-Word Reviews of 763 SXSW Mp3s." It's not simply that he runs through the heart, soul, blood, toil, tears, and sweat of musicians who've given everything they have in a few words, implicitly dismissing music and criticism at the same time. He has to do it in six words, no more, no less. It's a game, a challenge, a line in the sand. The Waco Brothers' "How Fast the Time"? "I need to wash a shirt." That makes sense, the Waco Brothers are a sweaty band. Followed by Watershed, "Obvious": "Wish I had a clothes dryer." Which may be cuteness, criticism as limerick without rhyme, unless "Obvious" is so dripping with sincerity you really do need to put it in the dryer. Then Wax Fang, "World War II (Pt. 2)": "But where would I put it?" *What, God help me, if I were still stacking discs?*

I don't think it's jadedness or fatigue that's running the show here. Writers are sensitive to the mountains of trash presented to the public as a glowing chest of perfectly individuated precious stones, but they're looking for the stones, not the trash, unless they can turn the trash into a precious stone, as Aidin Vaziri does with his review of Guns N' Roses' *Chinese Democracy*: a one-sentence review prefaced by one-sentence reviews of nine other albums released at the same time, all in a tone of such unrelenting cynicism that when Hall and Oates' *Live at the Troubadour* gets "Awesome, as usual," you figure it probably is.

Writers are trying to reinvent what music writing might be— or discover it. Among the pieces this book was drawn from were any number of first-class, completely professional fly-on-the-wall musician profiles; personal testimonies; critical analyses in which the writer seemingly tried to rise to the occasion that seemed to be taking place as he or she listened, as if it were the writer's job— let's say *task*—to put as much soul-force into the music as the musicians must have. They were so well done I was on the verge of including all of them, until again and again I realized I'd read it all before—the same scenes, the same idle banter framed for significance, the same irony rescued from the same closing bathroom door, the same passionate attempts to plumb the artist's motives, to amplify the biographical echoes, to wring truth from the singer's power. After a couple of hundred pages I wasn't even sure I hadn't read the same pieces before, years before, with all the same names. People are fighting their way out from under this killing legacy of critical institutionalization, cliché, banality, stupidity, and repetition, where it can come to seem that performance is a representation of another performance before it is anything else, every gesture made by any singer seems borrowed from another one, every word or angle borrowed from oneself.

This book is not an almanac. It is not a record of the best or worst or most important what-happened-in-music of 2008, the year from which all of the pieces here were drawn. I don't know what happened in 2008, outside of a few musical events that happened to speak to me—I'm Not Jim's uncanny "Walks Into," Bob Dylan on election night at the University of Minnesota making "The Time They Are A-Changin'" and "Blowin' in the Wind" into something they never quite were before, and those pieces here that I read as they appeared—and I don't care. I distrust those who do know what happened in 2008, because I distrust the notion that something has to happen in any given year that in the future we will look back upon as a portent of something or as an example of something else. I do trust Flipper: "Life is pretty cheap / It's sold a decade at a time."

That's why, perhaps, there is so much of the past in these pages: what's formally consigned as the past. People here are writing to open the past, to get a feel for how much remains unsolved and unresolved, for what mystifications still close questions or prevent them from even being asked. The past is not stable: as Joshua Clover reinhabits 1972, 1998, 2003, and 2007, the years can seem as distant, their languages nearly as forgotten, as Geeshie Wiley's 1930 and her language, which in John Jeremiah Sullivan's hands—in her hands, too—can seem more like 1830, just as David Ramsey's "I Will Forever Remain Faithful," a memoir about Lil Wayne and a year spent teaching in New Orleans Recovery School District, can seem antediluvian, and Vanessa Grigoriadis's "The Tragedy of Britney Spears" the damned last words of a story that ended long ago.

The love in these pieces doesn't gainsay the disrespect in so many others. The disrespect doesn't question the love—it envies it, just as the love can't fully trust its own heart. The greatest struggle a writer faces is to say what he or she truly means without fear of how it will make him or her look, to be willing to be fooled, and the form the writer chooses, or that chooses the writer, comes after that, if you're so lucky. I think the people here got very lucky.

Guns N' Roses, *Chinese Democracy*
Aidin Vaziri

Axl Rose is an idiot. He spent nearly 15 years, countless millions and a truckload of Slash replacements making *Chinese Democracy* only to finally put it out in the same week as just about every other major release of 2008 (and only at Best Buy stores, at that). Since he made us wait so long, it's only fair that we make Axl wait for our verdict on the new Guns N' Roses album after we address all the other important new stuff coming out this week. Here goes. The Killers, *Day & Age:* Even worse than their last album, if that's technically possible. Kanye West, *808s & Heartbreak:* Kanye can't sing, yet everybody involved neglected to inform him. Daryl Hall & John Oates, *Live at the Troubadour:* Awesome, as usual. Coldplay, *Prospekt's March* (EP): The lukewarm leftovers from *Viva La Vida,* with a wholly unnecessary Jay-Z cameo. Barry Manilow, *The Greatest Songs of the Eighties:* Oh really, Barry? Where's "Girlfriend in a Coma"? David Byrne and Brian Eno, *Everything That Happens Will Happen Today:* Great if you have a Ph.D. in being boring. The Fireman, *Electric Arguments:* The latest from Paul McCartney's alter ego, which at points sounds like old U2. Ludacris, *Theater of the Mind:* He's stepping it up with the lyrics, slowing it down with the beats—call it a draw. R.E.M., *Murmur* (Deluxe Edition): Came out 25 years ago and still capable of making knees tremble uncontrollably. Finally . . . Guns N' Roses, *Chinese Democracy:* It's a bit overproduced, isn't it?

I Will Forever Remain Faithful

*How Lil Wayne helped me survive
my first year teaching in New Orleans*

David Ramsey

1.

Complex magazine: What do you listen to these days?
Lil Wayne: Me! All day, all me.

2. LIKE A WHITE PERSON, WITH BLUE VEINS

In my first few weeks teaching in New Orleans' Recovery School District, these were the questions I heard the most from my students:

- "I gotta use it." (This one might sound like a statement, but it's a request—May I use the bathroom?)
- "You got an ol' lady?" (the penultimate vowel stretched, lasciviously, as far as it'll go).
- "Where you from?"

3

- "You listen to that Weezy?"

I knew that third question was coming. Like many RSD teachers, I was new, and white, and from out of town.

It was the fourth question, however, that seemed to interest my students the most. Dwayne Carter, aka Lil Wayne, aka Weezy F. Baby, was in the midst of becoming the year's biggest rapper, and among the black teenagers that made up my student population, fandom had reached a near-Beatlemania pitch. More than ninety percent of my students cited Lil Wayne on the "Favorite Music" question on the survey I gave them; about half of them repeated the answer on "Favorite Things to Do."

For some of my students, the questions Where are you from? and Do you listen to Lil Wayne? were close to interchangeable. Their shared currency—as much as neighborhoods or food or slang or trauma—was the stoned musings of Weezy F. Baby.

The answer was, sometimes, yes, I did listen to Lil Wayne. Despite his ubiquitous success, my students were shocked.

"Do you have the mix tapes?" asked Michael, a sixteen-year-old ninth grader. "It's all about the mix tapes."

The following day, he had a stack of CDs for me. Version this, volume that, or no label at all.

And that's just about all I listened to for the rest of the year.

3. MY PICTURE SHOULD BE IN THE DICTIONARY
NEXT TO THE DEFINITION OF DEFINITION

Lil Wayne slurs, hollers, sings, sighs, bellows, whines, croons, wheezes, coughs, stutters, shouts. He reminds me, in different moments, of two dozen other rappers. In a genre that often demands keeping it real via being repetitive, Lil Wayne is a chameleon, rapping in different octaves, paces, and inflections. Sometimes he sounds like a bluesman, sometimes he sounds like a Muppet baby.

Lil Wayne does his share of gangsta posturing, but half the time he starts chuckling before he gets through a line. He's a ham. He is heavy on pretense, and thank God. Like Dylan, theatricality trumps authenticity.

And yet—even as he tries on a new style for every other song, it is always unmistakably him. I think of Elvis's famous boast, "I don't sound like nobody." I imagine Wayne would flip it: "Don't nobody sound like me."

4.

Every few weeks, Michael or another student—for this piece, the names of my students have been changed—would have a new burned CD that was supposedly Tha Carter III, Lil Wayne's long-anticipated sixth studio album. "This one's official," they would say. I learned to be skeptical even as I enjoyed the new tracks. Nothing "official" would come around until school was out for summer, but Lil Wayne created hundreds of new songs in 2007 and the first half of 2008. Vibe magazine took the time to rank his best seventy-seven songs of 2007, and that was not a comprehensive list. These songs would end up on the Internet, which downloaders could snag for free. He also appeared for guest verses on dozens of other rappers' tracks. He thusly managed to rate as the "Hottest MC in the Game" (according to MTV) and the "Best MC" (according to Rolling Stone), despite offering nothing new at the record store.

While Wayne claimed to do every song "at the same ability or hype," the quality varied widely. He wrote nothing down (he was simply too stoned, he explained), rapping off the top of his head every time the spirit moved him, which was pretty much all the time. The results were sometimes tremendous and sometimes awkward, but that was half the fun. His oeuvre ended up being a sort of unedited reality show of his wily subconscious.

5. AIN'T 'BOUT TO PICK TODAY TO START RUNNING

During the first few days of school, Darius, one of my homeroom students, kept getting in trouble for leaving classes without permission. At the end of the second day, he pulled me aside to tell me why he kept having to use the bathroom: he had been shot in the leg three times and had a colostomy bag.

When I visited him in the hospital a few weeks later—he was there for follow-up surgery—he told me about the dealers who shot him. Darius's speaking voice is a dead ringer for Lil Wayne's old-man rasp. "I told them, Do what you need to do, you heard me? I ain't scared, you heard me?"

Then he leaned over and pointed, laughing, to Sponge Bob on the television.

6.

Lil Wayne, rumor has it, briefly went to the pre-Katrina version of our school. Same name and location, but back then it was a neighborhood high school. The building was wrecked in the storm. Our school, a charter school, is housed in modulars (my students hate this euphemism—they're trailers) in the lot in back. Sometimes I went and peeked in the windows of the old building, and it looked to me like no one had cleaned or gutted it since the storm. It was like a museum set piece. There was still a poster up announcing an open house, coming September 2005.

7.

I taught fifth-grade social studies, eighth-grade writing, ninth-grade social studies. Sometimes I felt inspired, sometimes deflated.

One time, a black student vehemently defended his one Arab classmate during a discussion about the Jena 6: "If you call him a terrorist, that's like what a cop thinks about us." Another day, when I was introducing new material about Africa, a student interrupted me—"I heard them niggas have AIDS!"

8. PAIN, SINCE I'VE LOST YOU—I'M LOST TOO

Our students are afraid of rain. A heavy morning shower can cut attendance in half. I once had a student write an essay about her experience in the Superdome. She wrote, without explanation, that she lost her memory when she lost her grandmother in the storm. I was supposed to correct the grammar, so that she would be prepared for state testing in the spring.

9. KEEP YOUR MOUTH CLOSED AND LET YOUR EYES LISTEN

Lil Wayne is five-foot-six and wiry, sleepy-eyed, covered in tattoos, including teardrops under his eyes. His two camera poses are a cool tilt of the head and a sneer. He means to look sinister, I think, but there is something actually huggable about him. He looks like he could be one of my students—and some of my students like to think they look like him.

The other day, I saw Cornel West on television say that Lil Wayne's physical body bears witness to tragedy. I don't even know what that means, but I do think that Wayne's artistic persona is a testament to damage.

10.

One of my favorite Lil Wayne hooks is the chorus on a Playaz Circle song called "Duffle Bag Boy." In the past year, he started singing more, and this was his best turn. He sounds a little like the neighborhood drunk at first as he warbles his way up and down the tune, but his singing voice has an organically exultant quality that seems to carry him to emotional delirium. After a while, he's belting out instructions to a drug courier with the breathy urgency of a Baptist hymn. By the end of the song, the standard-order macho boast, "I ain't never ran from a nigga and I damn sure ain't 'bout to pick today to start running," has been turned by Lil Wayne into a plea, a soul lament.

11.

On New Orleans radio, it seems like nearly every song features Lil Wayne. My kids sang his songs in class, in the hallways, before school, after school. I had a student who would rap a Lil Wayne line if he didn't know the answer to a question.

An eighth grader wrote his Persuasive Essay on the topic "Lil Wayne is the best rapper alive." Main ideas for three body paragraphs: Wayne has the most tracks and most hits, best metaphors and similes, competition is fake.

12. MY FLOW IS ART, UNIQUE—MY FLOW CAN PART A SEA

Once I witnessed a group of students huddled around a speaker listening to Lil Wayne. They had heard these songs before, but were nonetheless gushing and guffawing over nearly every line. One of them, bored and quiet in my classroom, was enthusiastically, if vaguely, parsing each lyric for his classmates: "You hear that? Cleaner than a virgin in detergent. Think on that."

Pulling out the go-to insult of high schoolers everywhere, a girl nearby questioned their sexuality. "Y'all be in to Lil Wayne so much you sound like girls," she said.

They just kept listening. Then one of the boys was simply overtaken by a lyrical turn. He stood up, threw up his hands, and began hollering. "I don't care!" he shouted. "No homo, no homo, but that boy is cute!"

13.

Lil Wayne on making it: "When you're really rich, then asparagus is yummy."

Lil Wayne on safe sex: "Better wear a latex, cause you don't want that late text, that 'I think I'm late' text."

Lil Wayne on possibly less safe sex: "How come there is two women, but ain't no two Waynes?"

14.

Okay, but it's not any one line, it's that voice. Just the way he says "car in park" in his cameo on Mario's "Crying Out for Me" remix; it's a soft growl from another planet. It sounds like a threat and a comfort and a come-on all at once.

15. I AM JUST A MARTIAN, AIN'T NOBODY
ELSE ON THIS PLANET

Right before you become a teacher, you are told by all manner of folks that it will be 1) the hardest thing you've ever done, and 2) the best thing you've ever done. That seems like a recipe for recruiting wannabe martyrs. In any case, high stakes can blind you to the best moments. One day, I was stressing over what I imagined was my one-man quest to keep Darius in school and out of jail, and missed that a heated dispute between two fifth graders was escalating. Finally, I asked them what was wrong.

"Mr. Ramsey," one of the boys pleaded, "will you please tell him that if you go into space for a year and come back to Earth that all your family will be dead because time moves slower in space?"

16. AND TO THE KIDS: DRUGS KILL.
I'M ACKNOWLEDGING THAT.

But when I'm on the drugs, I don't have a problem with that.

On one of his best songs, the super-catchy "I Feel Like Dying," Lil Wayne barely exists. He always sounds high, but on this song he sounds as though he has already passed out.

A lot of the alarmism about pop music sending the wrong message to impressionable youth seems mostly overwrought to me, but I'll cop to feeling taken aback at ten-year-olds singing, "Only once the drugs are done, do I feel like dying, I feel like dying."

First time I heard a fifth grader singing this in falsetto, I said: "What did you say?"

He said: "Mr. Ramsey, you know you be listening to that song. Why you tripping?"

My students always ask me why I'm tripping at precisely the moments when the answer seems incredibly obvious to me.

17.

After Michael cussed out our vice principal, I did a home visit. Michael was one of the biggest drug dealers in his neighborhood, and also one of my best students.

His mother was roused from bed. She looked half-gone, dazed. Then she started crying, and hugged me, pulled my head into her body. "No one's ever cared like this," she said. "Bless you. Thank you."

Michael smiled shyly. "I just want to get in my right grade," he told me.

"We'll find a way to make that happen," I told him.

A few weeks later, I gave him a copy of a New Yorker piece on Lil Wayne.

"Actually, that was good," he said, later. "You teach me to write like that?"

18. BORN IN NEW ORLEANS, RAISED IN NEW ORLEANS . . .

You live here as a newcomer and locals are fond of saying "this is New Orleans" or "welcome to New Orleans" by way of explanation. They use it to explain absurdity, inefficiency, arbitrary disaster, and transcendent fun. Enormous holes in the middle of major streets, say, or a drunken man dressed as an insect in line behind you at the convenience store.

Our challenge in the schools is to try to reform a broken system (the "recovery" in Recovery School District doesn't refer to the storm—the district was created before Katrina, when the state took over the city's failing schools) amidst a beautiful culture that is sometimes committed to cutting folks a little slack.

I have heard the following things speciously defended or excused by New Orleans culture: truancy, low test scores, drug and alcohol addiction, extended families showing up within the hour to settle minor school-boy scuffles, inept bureaucracy, lazy teachers, students showing up hungover the day after Mother's Day. . . .

19.

Once, a girl's older sister looked askance at one of my best students after school, and about five minutes later there was a full-on brawl in the parking lot. I lost my grip on the student I was holding back and she jumped on top of another student's mother and started pounding.

On the pavement in front of me was a weave and a little bit of blood. One of my ninth graders was watching the chaos gleefully while I tried to figure out how to make myself useful. He was as happy as I've ever seen him. He shrugged beatifically. "This is New Orleans!" he shouted, to me, to himself, to anyone who might be listening.

20.

Sometimes my students tell me they are sick of talking about the storm. Sometimes it's all they want to talk about. Might be the same student. Some students have told me it ruined their lives, some students have told me it saved their lives. Again, sometimes the same student will say both.

21.

From an interview in early 2006:

AllHipHop.com: On the album, did you ever contemplate doing a whole track dedicated to the Hurricane Katrina tragedy?

Lil Wayne: No, because I'm from New Orleans, brother. Our main focus is to move ahead and move on. You guys are not from New Orleans and keep throwing it in our face, like, 'Well, how do you feel about Hurricane Katrina?' I f—king feel f—ked up. I have no f—king city or home to go to. My mother has no home, her people have no home, and their people have no home. Every f—king body has no home. So do I want to dedicate something to Hurricane Katrina? Yeah, tell that b—h to suck my d—k. That is my dedication.

22. I AM THE BEAST! FEED ME RAPPERS OR FEED ME BEATS.

Lil Wayne mentions Katrina in his songs from time to time. He has a track that rails against Bush for his response to the storm. But, to his credit, he doesn't wallow in his city's famous tragedy.

The world needs to be told, and reminded, of what happened here. But New Orleans is bigger and more spirited than the storm. So its favorite son can be forgiven for refusing to let it define him. For my students, Lil Wayne is good times and good memories, and enduring hometown pride. All they ask of him is to keep making rhymes, as triumphant and strange as the city itself.

23. EVER SINCE I WAS LITTLE, I LIVED LIFE NUMB

Michael stopped coming to school. His mother told me, "He's a man now. There's nothing more I can do."

Darius got kicked out for physically attacking a teacher.

I have lots of happy stories, so I don't mean to dwell on these two, but I guess that's just what teachers do in the summer months, replay the ones that got away.

24.

I read over this, and I got it all wrong. I fetishize disaster. I live in the best city in the world and all I can write about is hurricanes and dropouts.

25.

One time, after they finished a big test I gave them last period, my students started happily singing Lil Wayne's "La La La" on their way outside.

"Come on, Ramsey, sing along, you know it."

And so I did. "Born in New Orleans, raised in New Orleans, I will forever remain faithful New Orleans. . . ."

That I wasn't from New Orleans didn't much matter, so long as I was game to clap and dance and sing. It was a clear and sunny day, Lil Wayne was the greatest rapper alive, and school was out. It was time to have fun.

Terrorflu

Joshua Clover

RING ROAD

("Roadrunner," Jonathan Richman and the Modern Lovers, original version [1976 release], 4'06")

We begin on Route 128 when it's late at night. That's where the Modern Lovers begin, and the greatest American song of that era. The Modern Lovers are from Massachusetts. Joni Mitchell is from Canada and Bob Dylan is from myth.

Route 128 is a beltway around Boston. Such roads are less common in the United States than in Europe, Asia, South America. They tend to encircle dense cities of the older style, giving them a sense of order, of boundedness, or at least the promise that one might navigate around their labyrinthine cores. Younger typologies like grid cities have less use for such designs; sprawl cities almost none at all.

Boston has the road originally called the *Circumferential Highway*, the first of its kind in the U.S., now a curving high-tech run, a silicon ralley optimistically dubbed "America's Technology

Highway"—but in 1972, when "Roadrunner" was first recorded, it was a scungy corridor of doughnut shops and furniture stores, déclassé towns like Dedham and Lynnfield, nicer burbs like Newton and Milton, and then Natick, where Jonathan Richman was born. I used to take the bus to play miniature golf in Natick, and on the way you passed a butcher called Mr. Meat. That pretty much sums it up.

1972 matters. 1972 matters because it is almost 1973, the year of the oil crisis and gas rationing. It is almost 1973 but not quite and Jonathan Richman is driving the suburban ring road, faster miles an hour, and the price of gas is the farthest thing from his mind, he has the radio on and he's going around and around, the guitar is going around and around, the lyrics are going nowhere and that's the point, there's no particular place to go, just around and around, and he passes the spirit of 1956. 1956 is the commanding heights of the postwar boom, and the homely suburbs are in full bloom, and though it's *close* to the birth of rock'n'roll, it's the *exact* year of the largest public works project in American history, which is of course the *Federal Highway Act*, all 25 billion if it, the birth of the Interstate System, *fucking infrastructure* just like the Stop'n'Shop and the Howard Johnson's and the radio towers are fading remnants from the world of *stuff*, and this is why it's the greatest song of the era, because rock'n'roll is the last great invention of industrial capitalism and "Roadrunner" is a love song for industrial capitalism when it's late at night, and then Jonathan passes the spirit of 1957, he turns around in the night and is consumed by neon.

THE MAIN STREETS AND THE CINEMA AISLES
("Brimful of Asha," Cornershop, Norman Cook
Remix Single Version, 1998, 4'04")

And then it's 1972 again, leaking into 1973: the tilt from the long boom to the long bust, from the ascent to the decline of the American age, modernity to postmodernity, industrial to finance capital. There's a red thread that runs from 1973 through 1979's conservative counterrevolution. The thread runs through to 1989, year of the "Washington Consensus," when the collapse of the Second World briefly promises a respite from the narrative of decline. That same thread runs through 1997–98 when the global financial crisis known as the Asian Flu spread its contagion from Thailand to Malaysia to Singapore, the Philippines, Indonesia, Hong Kong, South Korea, Russia, Brazil, Argentina, landing on U.S. shores with the collapse of Long Term Capital Management, a hedge fund so heavy that it has to be bailed out to stem the global crisis, or so we're told. Long Term Capital Management was founded by the guys who developed the mathematical model that made the trading of *non-stuff* a viable and lucrative market. Derivatives, mutual funds, arbitrage, the whole sea-change known as "financialization": these guys brought that to life. Their instrument was called the Black-Scholes Equation, a mechanism so powerful that economic historians have called it an "epistemological rupture," and it was published in 1973, so maybe it's not a red thread but a ring road that runs through history, going around and around.

This is not to argue for something like just desserts, or karma, or other moralizing ideas of the *what-comes-around-goes-around* variety. This is just to name a fact about circulation. When you build the ring road, or the global economy, it becomes possible that something tossed out into the traffic will come back your way again, almost unrecognizable, monstrous, beautiful, who knows? In fact it becomes increasingly likely this will happen, because the circuits are more closely connected, faster, less regulated, the kind of thing that makes Thomas Friedman stain his khakis, and if you toss something catchy out there it's coming back around like the Roadrunner. It feels like freedom but it cuts both ways, sometimes it's the freedom of Jonathan going around and around in his car, and sometimes the Asian Flu going around and around in the markets. And the song itself is not just wheeling through its chord changes but through global culture, and it circulates through the relays of Sex Pistols and Greg Kahn, the Feelies and Yo La Tengo and Joan Jett, and inevitably something really interesting happens: it lands on the second track of an album by a British South Asian band except it's a little hard to recognize because it has different words and a different melody and isn't about the radio and Massachusetts, but about vinyl 45s and "playback singers" and especially Asha Bhosle, who recorded over 12,000 songs for Bollywood cinema. For all these reasons it's a little hard at first to hear that "Brimful of Asha" is Tjinder Singh's version of "Roadrunner" come back around as a global idea, the main streets are cinema aisles and Route 128 is the cultural circuit from Hollywood to South Asia to London and back again, and he suggests "we don't care . . . about the dams they're building," those IMF-mandated building blocks of globalization tearing India apart, and of course it turns out to be Cornershop's first global hit, but it doesn't really accelerate until the next year, as the Asian Flu is spreading to Russia and South America, when the song is remixed by Norman Cook and this is surely one of the greatest remixes in history, because it brings out the genius of the song without fucking it up, shows how the song is infinitely deep, it goes around and around like a 45, a repetitive structure filled with endless possibility, "from the morning past the evening to the end of the light"—and at the same time Norman Cook makes a *critical reading* of the song, he speeds up the crude jangle and pushes it forward, and he extends the final breakdown into the middle of the night, until you can hear, it's *obvious*, that "*forty-five*" is "*radio on!*" and that Cornershop is the Postmodern Lovers and the guitar goes around and around and the remix goes to #1.

FINANCE CAPITAL POP
("Galang," M.I.A., 2003 Showbiz Records version, 3'34")

So you have these songs making circular sounds and it turns out they are trying to think about circulation, about records on turntables and cars on ring roads and sounds in the transnational flow of culture: the relaying of sonic contagions through the system and around the globe and often returning to where they began but different, mutated. There's probably no better example than Rihanna's Stargate's Michael Jackson's Quincy Jones' Manu Dibango's "Soul Makossa," which is from 1972. And influence and pastiche and the import-export business are nothing new but such contagions and mutations intensify and accelerate within the regimes of mobile capital and mobile labor and globalization, until they become inseparable from the *very idea* of pop music: *finance capital pop*. But these conditions are not just the history of pop, they are the *history of history*, they are conjoined with the development of what we now call "the world-system," and *this*—not what anyone says in a song—is why pop music is political.

So it is only to be expected that some of the most interesting pop musicians would take this as pop's *representational problem*, the way the 19th century novel took the social order of industrial urbanization as its representation problem, its *formal* problem. And I am telling you that M.I.A. is a great pop artist, because this is her project: the same way that we work on music and literature and history and dance, M.I.A. works on circulation and she gets around. She's crafty.

Somewhere on *Arular* she seems to be talking back to the song actually called "Pop Muzik," by M, "London Paris New York Munich everybody talk about pop music," but M.I.A. says "London, quieten down, I need to make a sound. New York, quieten down, I need to make a sound." And Kingston and Brazil: hip-hop, grime, reggae, baile funk, but these aren't her *sounds*, they're what's going around on the big ring road; her sound is the big ring road itself. She is in no particular place. Her sound is globalization. But even before then, her very first release begins "London calling" and tosses the hook right into the space of flows and the song starts circling, sinister and joyous, West Indian slang and the chorus-chant going around like jump rope and someone is driving around London and M.I.A. is around London sort of like Tjinder Singh except this time by way of Sri Lanka and you can hear that too, and you know her father is a Tamil freedom fighter slash terrorist in a civil war that goes around and around, twenty-five years during which they perfect the craft of suicide bombing which shortly goes around the world like a contagion, and maybe you know that Sri Lanka was once Ceylon and that the war is much older than 25 years, that the local is the global, that the island has been divided for centuries, and was occupied by the Portuguese and conquered by the United Provinces because it was of interest to the Dutch East India Company, and then the British because it was of interest to their cover version, the *British* East India Company—what you might call *Double Dutch*—and the companies go around and around the globe and we learn to call this geopolitics and now we circle back around to London and *who the hell is hunting you in your BMW* and the song goes around and around, galang-a-lang-a-lang. It is 2003.

BALM ON GILEAD
("Bird Flu," M.I.A., 2007, 3'24")

2003 matters, and by now you hear the pattern. 2003 matters because of the re-emergence of Influenza A virus subtype H5N1. I say "re-emergence" because it first leapt from waterfowl to humans, killing six in Hong Kong, in 1997, the year of the Asian Flu economic crisis. H5N1 is often called "avian influenza," or more commonly, "bird flu." Among many contagions, contagion itself.

Bird flu is pure pop; it goes *around* the world. In 2004, Shigeru Omi, Regional Director of the World Health Organization, forecast "at least seven million deaths, but maybe more—10 million, 20 million, and in the worst case, 100 million." This is still in the future, but is not unlikely; it is perhaps the most predictable of epidemics. It's predictable because we built the situation ourselves: "Human-induced shocks—overseas tourism, wetland destruction, a corporate "Livestock Revolution," and the Third World urbanization with the attendant growth of mega slums," lists Mike Davis in *Monster at Our Door*, putting oarticular emphasis on the last, which has the effect of "shifting the burden of global poverty from the countryside to the slum peripheries of new megacities. Ninety-five percent of future world population growth will be in the poor cities of the South, with immense consequences for the ecology of disease." These are the cities in M.I.A.'s song "World Town," places in which particularity fights a losing battle against the role of the relay, part of the condition, the situation, in which contagions circulate.

It is this that loops through the song "Bird Flu," a disturbing sound that goes around and around, the loop self-produced and mesmerizing and comparable to nothing in pop music except maybe Timbaland's gurgling-baby loop in "Are You That Somebody": it's an ominous bird squawk against an even more ominous clatter of drums, but it's also the whole situation of pop music, in which cars and sounds and economic disasters and epidemics circulate, and the song is terrifying like pop songs rarely go out of their way to be.

It is very hard to say where bird flu comes from. The 2003 outbreak isolated in Hong Kong flared a month earlier in China, where "a strange contagious disease had killed more than a hundred people in Guangdong in a single week." No one is surprised that the radical industrialization of South China might prove an incubator for a pandemic. But the global driver of the "Livestock Revolution" is Tyson Foods, which kills 2.2 billion chickens annually and is, in Davis's words, "globally synonymous with scaled-up, vertically integrated production; exploitation of contract growers; visceral antiunionism; rampant industrial injury; downstream environmmental dumping; and political corruption." The Legoes of neoliberalism; Global Fried Chicken with an Arkansas accent. When bird flu arrives in Little Rock, it will be very hard to say it came from somewhere else.

As it happens, there is a single effective treatment for avian influenza: trade name Tamiflu. There is not very much of it; the patent-holder, Gilead Sciences, has gone to great lengths to prevent its inexpensive reproduction in the World Towns. Between George W. Bush's inauguration and 2007, Gilead stock increased in value more than 800 percent. And as it happens, the former chairman and still major stakeholder of Gilead is also signatory to the neoliberal Magna Carta, the "Statement of Principles" of the Project for a New American Century. The document is from 1997. The former Gilead chair is Donald Rumsfeld; you may know him as an apostle of the War on Terror. And M.I.A. writes, "I CALLED THIS BIRD FLU BECAUSE THIS BEAT GON KILL EVERYONE!!"

WELCOME TO THE TERRORFLU
("Bamboo Banger," M.I.A., 2007, 4'58")

So this is one thing you can say about *Kala*: M.I.A. is talking to Donald Rumsfeld. They are talking about blowback, and chickens coming home to roost; they are talking about circulation and contagion and neoliberalism. They are talking about bird flu and about terror: "Hands up—guns out—represent now world town." And the conversation goes around and around the globe, but it doesn't begin in some war zone or some necrojungle but on Route 128 when it's late at night. "Roadrunner Roadrunner, going hundred miles per hour" are her first words and she has the radio on and she's banging on the door of his Hummer Hummer, and we can assume she's listening to Modern Lovers except the beat is from a Tamil movie soundtrack, it's by a guy named Ilaiyaraaja, a prolific Indian film composer whose songs tend to be very difficult to sing and as a result fall to the best playback singers, foremost among them Asha Bhosle. *Forty-five.* Small world. No, it's a big world but M.I.A. gets around, everything gets around, because we have built the world that way. And the song has some hilarious moments, she's "hungry like the wolves" and instantly we remember the Duran Duran video with the beautiful pale boys in their South Asian fantasia, and isn't Duran Duran originally from that movie with the 50-foot Terrorist, *Barbarella?* . . . and it isn't ten seconds before Maya says "Barbarella look like she my dead ringer" as if to make sure *we* know *she* knows, knows she is riding this incredibly elaborate circuit, and she says "I'm a Roadrunner, a world runner" just to clarify things, she is in your system and she is trying to *become* the system like Wintermute at the end of *Neuromancer* except it's not the future it's now, represent now world town, and already she has said "now I'm *sit*ting down *chill*in' on *gun* powder, *strike* match *light* fire, *who's* that girl *called* Maya?" and then the refrain, "M.I.A. coming back with power power."

People like to worry about whether or not M.I.A. advocates political violence, and whether she has a right or a capacity to do so in any real way. The figure of the "terrorist pop star" is, for a certain kind of person, impossibly sexy; for another, entirely offensive; and for a third, conceptually impossible. But any of this is to miss the point almost entirely. The indexing of M.I.A. to the romanticized figure of the lone terrorist, even one draped in Third World nobility, tells us much more about the listener than the singer. Much more about habits of thought than about the music. There are always stories to be told about individuals, and about particular places, and these are stories we like to tell. But what would it mean to really *think* "the local is the global," and to fold the idea that "the personal is the political" back into the awful, exhausting, thrilling knowledge that *the political* is the political? What would it mean to find a sound for the situation?

That is exactly the thing that M.I.A. is trying to grasp, the representational problem for pop music, pop music which is not *in* London, Paris, New York, Munich any more than bird flu is *in* Hong Kong or Guangdong, economic contagion is *in* Thailand or Brazil, terrorism is *in* Baghdad or Colombo or Beirut. All of these things are in a *situation*, all of these things have *conditions of possibility* and they are the same conditions, and the structures that carry pop music around and around carry the others as well, they are riders in the space of flows that was built by people, in history, the great ring road that we built for reasons, that profit some and not others, all of these things are Roadrunners and it is very hard to say where they come from or where they are going, faster miles an hour, and they go around and around in the night.

Mystery Drain
Carrie Brownstein

Right now, I'm reading Francine Prose's *Goldengrove,* with this wonderful passage toward the beginning of the book:

"Nico . . . with her chalky, disappointed voice. It was strange how she sounded . . . hollow and checked out, and with a foreign accent that made it seem she was learning the words as she sang them."

Aside from reminding me how much I love stumbling upon pop-music asides in the middle of a non-music-themed novel, it also got me thinking about mystery and the mysterious. Nico is a perfect example. No matter how much you've demystified her persona with hagiography, she remains wraith-like and dimly lit, at least in one's imagination.

The notions of myth and mystery have always been crucial to the worship of music. The unknown elevates the art, removing it from the terrestrial realm, deeming it untouchable and holy. Sometimes, it's the musicians themselves who nurture the oblique; they are frustratingly ambiguous, spouting double-speak, peddling caprice. Or it can be their death that foments the uneasiness, leaving too many questions unanswered. Perhaps strange events befell the band. Some entire lives remain mysteries.

Robert Johnson, Bob Dylan, Badfinger, Sam Cooke, Brian Jones, Syd Barrett, Jandek, Bjork and Prince are just a few of the names that come to mind for me.

But where is the mystery now, and who embodies it? Certainly, in a time of relentless self-amplification, being mysterious could be a liability. With fans' attention spans being so short, and new music pouring in by the hour, bands (whether on their own or with pressure from their labels or managers) must feel the need to be available and present in order to stay relevant; the pursuit of relevance is a constant and exhausting endeavor. Yet updating your MySpace page on a daily basis, posting photos of your recording session on Flickr and writing a tour diary doesn't leave much to the imagination.

Maybe the definition of "mysterious" has changed to be more akin to "enigmatic." That allows for Jack White, M.I.A or Lil Wayne to be "mysterious," even though we can read about their comings and goings in the tabloids and on blogs.

Or we can think of mystery as a superficiality or costume. Then we get Marilyn Manson, Insane Clown Posse, Cher and Buckethead. But does makeup really cover anything other than self-consciousness? Certainly it doesn't mask intention. I mean, I'm pretty sure no one ever wondered what Kiss was about.

So maybe mystery isn't a requirement for loving music, for exalting it. Maybe it's the songs that we want to explore; for them to perplex us, not the artists themselves. But the age of overexposed musicians also means that the songs have to be better. If the artists are transparent, we need the songs to transcend what we know to be the authors' alternately pedestrian or outrageous lives.

That's when I go back to wanting a little more mystery overall, for there to be more elements to the music and to the musicians that leave me wondering, "Where did this come from?" And sometimes, I want the answer to be that I might not ever know.

Unknown Bards

The blues becomes transparent about itself

John Jeremiah Sullivan

Discussed in this essay:

American Primitive, Vol. II: Pre-War Revenants (1897–1939). Revenant Records.
$31.98

Escaping the Delta: Robert Johnson and the Invention of the Blues, by Elijah Wald.
Amistad. 368 pages. $14.95 (paper).

In Search of the Blues: The White Invention of Black Music, by Marybeth Hamilton.
Perseus Books. 309 pages. $24.95.

Late in 1998 or early in '99—during the winter that straddled the two—I spent a night on and off the telephone with a person named John Fahey. I was a junior editor at the *Oxford American* magazine, which at that time had its offices in Oxford, Mississippi;

Fahey, then almost sixty and living in Room 5 of a welfare motel outside Portland, Oregon, was himself, whatever that was: a channeler of some kind, certainly; a "pioneer" (as he once described his great hero, Charley Patton) "in the externalization through music of strange, weird, even ghastly emotional states." He composed instrumental guitar collages from snatches of other, older songs. At their finest they could become harmonic chambers in which different dead styles spoke to one another. My father had told me stories of seeing him in Memphis in '69. Fahey trotted out his "Blind Joe Death" routine at the fabled blues festival that summer, appearing to inhabit, as he approached the stage in dark glasses, the form of an aged sharecropper, hobbling and being led by the arm. He meant it as a postmodern prank at the expense of the all-white, authenticity-obsessed, country-blues cognoscenti, and was at the time uniquely qualified to pull it. Five years earlier he'd helped lead one of the little bands of enthusiasts, a special-ops branch of the folk revival, that staged barnstorming road trips through the South in search of surviving notables from the prewar country-blues or "folk blues" recording period (roughly 1925–1939).

Fahey was someone whose destiny followed the track of a deep inner flaw, like a twisted apple. He grew up comfortable in Washington, D.C., fixated from an early age on old guitar playing, finger-picking. After college he went west to study philosophy at Berkeley, then transferred at a deciding moment to UCLA's folklore program, a degree from which equipped him nicely to do what he wanted: hunt for old bluesmen. He took part personally in the tracking down and dragging back before the public glare of both Booker T. Washington "Bukka" White and, in a crowning moment, Nehemiah Curtis "Skip" James, the dark prince of the country blues, a thin black man with pale eyes and an alien falsetto who in 1931 recorded a batch of songs so sad and unsettling it's said that people paid him on street corners not to sing. Fahey and two associates found him in a charity hospital in Tunica, Mississippi, in 1964, dying with cruel slowness of stomach cancer. *We know you're a genius,* they told him. *People are ready now. Play for us.*

"I don't know," he supposedly answered. "Skippy tired."

I'd been told to get hold of Fahey on a fact-checking matter. The magazine was running a piece about Geeshie Wiley (or Geechie or Gitchie—and, in any case, likely only a nickname or stage moniker meaning that she had Gullah blood, or that her skin and hair were red-tinted). She's perhaps the one contemporary of James's who ever equaled him in the scary-beauty department, his spiritual bride. All we know about Wiley is what we don't know about her: where she was born, or when; what she looked like, where she lived, where she's buried. She had a playing partner named Elvie Thomas, concerning whom even less is known (about Elvie there are no rumors, even). Musicians who claimed to have seen Geeshie Wiley in Jackson, Mississippi, offered sketchy details to researchers over the years: that she could have been from Natchez, Mississippi (and was maybe part Indian), that she sang with a medicine show. In a sadistic tease on the part of fate, the Mississippi blues scholar and champion record collector Gayle Dean Wardlow (he who found Robert Johnson's death certificate) did an interview in the late Sixties with a white man named H. C. Speir, a onetime music-store owner from Jackson who moonlighted as a talent scout for prewar labels dabbling in so-called race records (meaning simply music marketed to blacks). Speir almost certainly met Wiley around 1930 and told his contacts at the Paramount company in Grafton, Wisconsin, about her—he may even have taken the train trip north with her and Elvie, as he was known to have done with other of his "finds"—but although at least two of Wiley and Thomas's six surviving songs (or "sides," in the favored jargon) had been rediscovered by collectors when Wardlow made his '69 visit to Speir's house, they were not yet accessible outside a clique of two or three aficionados in the East. Wardlow didn't know to ask about her, in other words, although he was closer to her at that moment than anyone would ever get again, sitting half a mile from where she'd sung, talking with a man who'd seen her face and watched her tune her guitar.

Not many ciphers have left as large and beguiling a presence as Geeshie Wiley. Three of the six songs she and Elvie Thomas recorded are among the greatest country-blues performances ever etched into shellac, and one of them, "Last Kind Words Blues," is an essential work of American art, sans qualifiers, a blues that isn't a blues, that is something other, but is at the same time a perfect blues, a pinnacle.

People have argued that the song represents a lone survival of an older, already vanishing, minstrel style; others that it was a one-off spoor, an ephemeral hybrid that originated and died with Wiley and Thomas, their attempt to play a tune they'd heard by a fire somewhere. The verses don't follow the A-A-B repeating pattern common to the blues, and the keening melody isn't like any other recorded example from that or any period. Likewise with the song's chords: "Last Kind Words Blues" opens with a big, plonking, menacing E but quickly withdraws into A minor and hovers there awhile (the early blues was almost never played in a minor key). The serpentine dual-guitar interplay is no less startling, with little sliding lead parts, presumably Elvie's, moving in and out of counterpoint. At times it sounds like four hands obeying a single mind and conjures scenes of endless practicing, the vast boredoms of the medicine-show world. The words begin,

> *The last kind words I heard my daddy say,*
> *Lord, the last kind words*
> *I heard my daddy say,*
> *"If I die, if I die, in the German War,*
> *I want you to send my money,*
> *Send it to my mother-in-law.*
> *"If I get killed, if I get killed,*
> *Please don't bury my soul.*
> *I cry, Just leave me out, let the buzzards eat me whole."*

The subsequent verse had a couple of unintelligible words in it, either from mumbling on Wiley's part or from the heavily crackling static that comes along with deteriorated 78-rpm discs. One could hear her saying pretty clearly, "When you see me coming, look 'cross the rich man's field," after which it sounded like she might be saying, "If I don't bring you flowers,/I'll bring you [a boutonniere?]." That verged on nonsense; more to the point, it seemed nonidiomatic. But the writer of the piece I was fact-checking needed to quote the line, and my job was to work it out, or prove to the satisfaction of my bosses that this couldn't be done. It was Ed Komara, in those days keeper of the sacred B. B. King Blues Archive at Ole Miss, who suggested contacting Fahey. Actually, what I think he said was, "John Fahey knows shit like that."

Finally a front-desk attendant agreed to put a call through to Fahey's room. From subsequent reading, I gather that at this time Fahey was making the weekly rent by scavenging and re-selling rare classical-music LPs, for which he must have developed an extraordinary eye, the profit margins being almost imperceptible. I pictured him prone on the bed, gray-bearded and possibly naked, his overabundant corpus spread out like something that only got up to eat: that's how interviewers discovered him, in the few profiles I'd read. He was hampered at this point by decades of addiction and the bad heart that would kill him two years later, but even before all that he'd been famously cranky, so it was strange to find him ramblingly familiar from the moment he picked up the phone. A friend of his to whom I later described this conversation said, "Of course he was nice—you didn't want to talk about *him*."

Fahey asked for fifteen minutes to get his "beatbox" hooked up and locate the tape with the song on it. I called him back at the appointed time.

"Man," he said, "I can't tell *what* she's saying there. It's definitely not 'boutonniere.'"

"No guesses?"

"Nah."

We switched to another mystery word, a couple of verses on: Wiley sings, "My mother told me, just before she died/Lord, [precious?] daughter, don't you be so wild."

"Shit, I don't have any fucking idea," Fahey said. "It doesn't really matter, anyway. They always just said any old shit."

That seemed to be the end of our experiment. Fahey said, "Give me about an hour. I'm going to spend some time with it."

I took the tape the magazine had loaned me and went to my car. Outside it was bleak north-Mississippi cold, with the wind unchecked by the slight undulations of flatness they call hills down there; it formed little pockets of frozen air in your clothes that zapped you if you shifted your weight. I turned the bass all the way down on the car's stereo and the treble all the way up, trying to isolate the frequency of Wiley's voice, and drove around town for the better part of an hour, going the speed limit. The problem words refused to give themselves up, but as the tape ran, the song itself emerged around them, in spite of them, and I heard it for the first time.

"Last Kind Words Blues" is about a ghost-lover. When Wiley says "kind"—as in, "The last kind words I heard my daddy say"— she doesn't mean it like we do; she doesn't mean *nice*; she means the word in its older sense of *natural* (with the implication that everything her "daddy" says afterward is unnatural, is preternatural). Southern idiom has retained that usage, in phrases involving the word "kindly," as in "I thank you kindly," which—and the *OED* bears this out—represent a clinging vestige of the primary, archaic meaning: not *I thank you politely and sweetly* but *I thank you in a way that's appropriate to your deed.* There's nothing "kind," in the everyday way, about the cold instructions her man gives for the disposal of his remains. That's what I mean about the blues hewing to idiom. It doesn't make mistakes like that.

Her old man has died, as he seems to have expected—the first three verses establish this, in tone if not in utterance. Now the song moves into a no-man's-land: she's lost. Her mother warned her about men, remember, "just before she died." The daughter didn't listen, and now it's too late. She wanders.

I went to the depot,
I looked up at the sun,
Cried, "Some train don't come,
Gon' be some walking done."

Where does she have to get to so badly she can't wait for another train? There's a clue, because she's still talking to him, or he to her— one isn't sure. "When you see me coming, look 'cross the rich man's field," if I don't bring you *something*, I'll bring you *something else*, at least that much was clear—and part of an old story: If I don't bring you silver, I'll bring you gold, etc.

Only then, in the song's third and last movement, does it get truly strange.

The Mississippi River, you know it's deep and wide,
I can stand right here,
See my baby from the other side.

This is one of the countless stock, or "floating," verses in the country blues—players passed them around like gossip, and much of the art to the music's poetry lay in arrangement rather than invention, in an almost haiku-like approach, by which drama and even narrative could be generated through sheer purity of image and intensity of juxtaposition. What has Wiley done with these lines? Normally they run, "I can see my baby [or my "brownie"]/from this other side." But there's something spooky happening to the spatial relationships. If I'm standing *right here*, how am I seeing you *from* the other side? The preposition is off. Unless I'm slipping out of my body, of course, and joining you *on* the other side. Wiley closes off the song as if to confirm these suspicions:

What you do to me, baby, it never gets out of me.
I believe I'll see ya,
After I cross the deep blue sea.

It's one of the oldest death metaphors and would have been ready to hand, thanks to Wiley's non-secular prewar peers. "Precious Jesus, gently guide me," goes a 1926 gospel chorus, "o'er that ocean dark and wide." *Done gone over.* That meant dead. Not up, over.

Greil Marcus, the writer of the piece I was fact-checking, mentioned the extraordinary "tenderness" of the "What you do to me, baby" line. It can't be denied. There's a tremendous weariness too. "It never gets out of me," and part of her wishes it would—this long disease, your memory. ("The blues is a low-down achin' heart disease," sang Robert Johnson, echoing Kokomo Arnold echoing Clara Smith echoing a 1913 sheet-music number written by a white minstrel performer and titled "Nigger Blues.") There's nothing to look forward to but the reunion death will bring. That's the narrow, haunted cosmos of the song, which one hears as a kind of reverberation, and which keeps people up at night.

I was having an intense time of it in the old Toyota. But when I got back onto the phone with Fahey, he was almost giddy. He'd scored one: *blessèd.* That's what her mother told her, "Lord, blessed daughter, don't you be so wild." I cued up to the line. It seemed self evident now, impossible to miss. I complimented his ear. Fahey cough-talked his way through a rant about how "they didn't care about the words" and "were all illiterate anyway."

A reflexive swerving between ecstatic appreciation and an urge to minimize the aesthetic significance of the country blues

was, I later came to see, a pattern in Fahey's career— the Blind Joe
Death bit had been part of it. It's possible he feared giving in to
the almost demonic force this music has exerted over so many—
or worried he'd done so already. I'm fairly certain his irony me-
ter hovered at zero when he titled his 2000 book of short stories
How Bluegrass Music Destroyed My Life. More than that, though,
the ability to flick at will into a dismissive mode was a way to
maintain a sense of expert status, of standing apart. You'll find the
same tendency in most of the other major blues wonks: when the
music was all but unknown, they hailed it as great, invincible
American art; when people (like the Rolling Stones) caught on
and started blabbering about it, they rushed to remind everyone
it was just a bunch of dance music for drunken field hands. Fahey had reached the point where he could occupy both extremes
in the same sentence.

He'd gotten as far as I had with "[a boutonniere?]," which remained the matter at hand, so we adjourned again. Came back,
broke off. This went on for a couple of hours. I couldn't believe he
was being so patient, really. Then at one point, back in the car, after many more rewindings, some fibers at the edge of my inner-
most ear registered a faint "L" near the beginning of that last
word: b-o-L-t? Boltered? A scan through the OED led to "bolt,"
then to "bolted," and at last to this 1398 citation from John de Tre-
visa's English translation of Bartholomeus Anglicus's ca. 1240
Latin encyclopedia, *De proprietatibusrerum* (*On the Order of
Things*): "The floure of the mele, whan it is bultid and departid
from the bran."

Wiley wasn't saying "flowers"; she was saying "flour." The rich
man's flour, which she loves you enough to steal for you. If she
can't get it, she'll get bolted, or very finely sifted, meal.

When you see me coming, look 'cross the rich man's field.
If I don't bring you flour,
I'll bring you bolted meal.

Fahey was skeptical. "I never heard of that," he said. But later, after saying goodbye for what seemed the last time, he called back with a changed mind. He'd rung up people in the interim. (It would be fun to know whom—you'd be tracing a very precious little neural pathway in the fin-de-siècle American mind.) One of his sources told him it was a Civil War thing: when they ran out of flour, they started using bolted cornmeal. "Hey," he said, "maybe we'll put you in the liner notes, if we can get this new thing together."

The new thing was still in development when he died. On the phone we talked about Revenant, the self-described "raw musics" label he'd co-founded in 1996 with a Texas lawyer named Dean Blackwood. Revenant releases are like Konstruktivist design projects in their attention to graphic detail, with liner notes that are de facto transcripts of scholarly colloquia. Fahey and Blackwood had thought up a new release, which would be all about prewar "phantoms" like Wiley and Thomas (and feature new, superior transfers of the pair's six sides). The collection's only delimiting criteria would be that nothing biographical could be known regarding any of the artists involved, and that every recording must be phenomenal, in a sense almost strict: something that happened once in front of a microphone and can never be imitated, merely re-experienced. They had been dreaming this project for years, refining lists. And I'd contributed a peck of knowledge, a little ant's mouthful of knowledge.

Almost six years passed, during which Fahey died in the hospital from complications following multiple-bypass surgery. I assumed, with other people, that he'd taken the phantoms project with him, but in October of 2005, with no fanfare and after rumors of Revenant's having closed shop, it materialized, two discs and a total of fifty songs with the subtitle *Pre-War Revenants (1897–1939)*.

Anyone interested in American culture should find a way to hear this record. It's possibly the most important archival release since Harry Smith's seminal *Anthology of American Folk Music* in 1952, and for the same reason: it represents less a scholarly effort to preserve and disseminate obscure recordings, indispensable as those undertakings are, than the charting of a deeply informed aesthetic sensibility, which for all its torment was passionately, selflessly in communion with these songs and the nuances of their artistry for a lifetime. Listening to this collection, you enter the keeping of a kind of Virgil.

To do it right entailed remastering everything fresh from 78s, which in turn meant coaxing out a transnational rabbit's warren of the so-called serious collectors, a community widespread but dysfunctionally tight-knit, as by process of consolidation the major collections have come into the keeping of fewer and fewer hands over the years. "The serious blues people are less than ten," one who contributed to *Pre-War Revenants* told me. "Country, seven. Jazz, maybe fifteen. Most are to one degree or another sociopathic." Mainly what they do is nurse decades-old grudges. A terrifically complicated bunch of people, but, for reasons perhaps not totally scrutable even to themselves, they have protected this music from time and indifference. The collectors were first of all the finders. Those trips to locate old blues guys started out as trips to canvass records. Gayle Dean Wardlow became a pest-control man at one point, in order to have a legitimate excuse to be walking around in black neighborhoods beating on doors. "Need your house sprayed?" Nah. "Got any weird old records in the attic?"

Something like 60 percent of the sides on *Pre-War Revenants* are SCO, single copy only. These songs are flashbulbs going off in immense darknesses. Blues Birdhead, Bayless Rose, Pigmeat Terry, singers that only the farthest gone of the old-music freaks have heard. "I got the mean Bo-Lita blues," sings the unknown Kid Brown ("Bo-Lita" was a poorly understood Mexican game of chance that swept the South like a hayfire about a hundred years ago and wiped out a bunch of shoebox fortunes). There's a guy named Tommy Settlers, who sings out of his throat in some way. I can't describe it. He may have been a freak-show act. His "Big Bed Bug" and "Shaking Weed Blues" are all there is of whatever he was, yet he was a master. Mattie May Thomas's astonishing "Workhouse Blues" was recorded a cappella in the sewing room at a women's prison:

> *I wrassle with the hounds, black man,*
> *Hounds of hell all day.*
> *I squeeze them so tight,*
> *Until they fade away.*

In what is surely a trustworthy mark of obscurantist cred, one of the sides on *Pre-War Revenants* was discovered at a flea market in Nashville by the person who engineered the collection,

Chris King, the guy who actually signs for delivery of the rein-
forced wooden boxes, put together with drywall screws and capable of withstanding an auto collision, in which most 78s arrive
for projects like this. The collectors trust King; he's a major collector himself (owner, as it happens, of the second-best of three
known copies of "Last Kind Words Blues") and an acknowledged
savant when it comes to excavating and reconstructing sonic information from the wrecked grooves of prewar disc recordings.
I called him a couple of years ago, looking for details of how this
project had come to life. Like Fahey, King graduated college with
degrees in religion and philosophy; he can wax expansive about
what he does. He described "junking" that rare 78 in Nashville,
the Two Poor Boys' "Old Hen Cackle," which lay atop a stack of
45s on a table in the open sun. It was brown. In the heat it had
warped, he said, "into the shape of a soup bowl." At the bottom
of the bowl he could read the word PERFECT, a short-lived hillbilly label. "Brown Perfects" are precious. He took it home and
placed it outside between two panes of clear glass—collector's
wisdom, handed down—and allowed the heat of the sun and the
slight pressure of the glass's weight slowly to press it flat again, to
where he could play it.

Sometimes, King told me, he can tell things about the record's
life from how the sound has worn away. The copy of Geeshie Wiley's "Eagles on a Half" (there's only one copy) that King worked
with for *Pre-War Revenants* had, he realized, been "dug out" by
an improvised stylus of some kind—"they used anything, sewing
needles"—in such a manner that one could tell the phonograph
it spun on, or else the floor underneath the phonograph, was
tilted forward and to the right. Suddenly you have a room, dancing, boards with a lot of give, people laughing. It's a nasty, sexy

song: "I said, squat low, papa, let your mama see./I wanna see that old business keeps on worrying me." King tilted his machine back and to the left. He encountered undestroyed signal and got a newly vibrant mastering.

Strangest of the songs is the very oldest, "Poor Mourner" by the duo Cousins & DeMoss, who may or may not have been Sam Cousin and Ed DeMoss, semi-famous late-nineteenth-century minstrel singers—if so, then the former is the only artist included on *Pre-War Revenants* of whom an image has survived: a grainy photograph of his strong, square face appeared in the *Indianapolis Freeman* in 1889. These two performed "Poor Mourner" for the Berliner Company in 1897. (Emile Berliner had patented disc, as opposed to cylinder, recording; discs were easier to duplicate.)

Dual banjos burst forth with a frenetic rag figure, and it seems you're on familiar if excitable ground. But somewhere between the third and fourth measure of the first bar, the second banjo pulls up, as if with a halt leg, and begins putting forward a drone on top of the first, which twangs away for a second as if it hadn't been warned about the imminent mood change. Then the instruments grind down together, the key swerves minor, and without your being able to pinpoint what happened or when, you find yourself in a totally different, darker sphere. The effect is the sonic equivalent of film getting jammed in an old projector, the stuck frame melting, colors bleeding. It all takes place in precisely five seconds.

It is unaccountable. Chris King said, "That is not a function of some weird thing I couldn't fix." I asked if maybe the old machines ran slightly faster at the start. He reminded me that the song didn't start with music; it started with a high voice shouting, "As sung by Cousins and DeMoss!"

When this song comes up I invariably flash on my great-grandmother Elizabeth Baynham, born in that same year, 1897. I touched that year. There is no degree of remove between me and it. I barely remember her as a blind, legless figure in a wheelchair and afghan who waited for us in the hallway outside her room. Knowing that this song was part of the fabric of the world she came into lets me know I understand nothing about that period, that very very end of the nineteenth century. We live in such constant closeness with the abyss of past time, which the moment is endlessly sucked into. The Russian writer Viktor Shklovsky said art exists "to make the stone stony." These recordings let us feel something of the timeyness of time, its sudden irrevocability.

If *Pre-War Revenants* marks the apotheosis of the baroque aestheticization of early black southern music by white men, which has brought you such sentences as these, then it's only proper that the collection appear now, as we're finally witnessing the dawn of a new transparency in blues writing: the scholarship of blues scholarship. Two good books in this vein have been published in the past few years: Elijah Wald's *Escaping the Delta: Robert Johnson and the Invention of the Blues* and Marybeth Hamilton's *In Search of the Blues* (subtitled, in its first, British edition, *Black Voices, White Visions*, and in the American, *The White Invention of Black Music*). Both are engaging and do solid, necessary work. I approached them with something like defensiveness, expecting to be implicated, inevitably, in the creepy racial unease that shadows the country-blues discourse, which has always been, with a couple of extremely notable examples (Zora Neale Hurston and

Dorothy Scarborough), white guys talking to one another about black music, and about a particular period in the music, one that living black American artists mostly consider quaint.

Both new books replace hoary myths with researched histories of far greater interest. Both seek to deconstruct the legend of the "Delta bluesman," with his crossroads and hellhounds and death by poison, his primal expression of existential isolation. Both end up complicating that picture instead. Wald's book takes away the legend of Robert Johnson's "inexplicable" technical ability, for which, rivals whispered, he sold his soul, and gives us instead Johnson the self-aware craftsman and student of other people's records, including those of Skip James, from whom Johnson lifted the beautiful phrase "dry long so," meaning indifferently, or for the hell of it. I don't think the reviews of *Escaping the Delta* that appeared at the time of its publication went far enough in describing its genius. Partly this owed to the book's marketing, which involved a vague suggestion that Robert Johnson would therein be exposed as a mere pop imitator. What *Escaping the Delta* really does is introduce us to a higher level of appreciation for Johnson's methods.

Wald puts you inside Johnson's head for the San Antonio and Dallas sessions, and takes you song by song, in an extremely rigorous way (he's another lifelong student of the music); he shows you what Johnson decided to play and when and puts forward convincing reasons why, shows you what sources he was combining, how he changed them, honored them. Wald is especially good at comparing the alternate takes, letting us hear the minutiae of Johnson's rhythmic and chordal modifications. These become windows onto the intensity of his craftsmanship. By picking up certain threads, you can track his moves. Blind Lemon

Jefferson sang, "The train left the depot with the red and blue light behind/Well, the blue light's the blues, the red light's the worried mind." That was a good verse. That was snappy. Eddie and Oscar, a polished, almost formal country-blues duo out of North Carolina (Eddie was white, Oscar was black), had already copied that. Johnson probably heard it from them. But when he went—

> *When the train, it left the station,*
> *With two lights on behind,*
> *Ah, when the train left the station,*
> *With two lights on behind,*
> *Well, the blue light was my blues,*
> *And the red light was my mind.*
> *All my love's in vain.*

—that was something else. Johnson knew it was something else. He knew how good it was, knew the difference between saying "the red light's the worried mind" and saying "the red light was my mind." After all, he's the same person who wrote the couplet, "From Memphis to Norfolk is a thirty-six hours' ride./A man is like a prisoner, and he's never satisfied." Part of hearing the blues is taking away the sociological filter, which with good but misguided intentions we allow to develop before our senses, and hearing the self-consciousness of the early bluesmen—hearing that, as Samuel Charters put it in the liner notes to Henry Townsend's *Tired of Bein' Mistreated* (1962), the "blues singer . . . feels himself as a creative individual within the limits of the blue style."

It's an extraordinary thought movie Wald creates for a hundred pages or so. If the jacket copy primed me to come away disabused

.of my awe for Johnson's musicianship, instead it was doubled. Everything Johnson touched he made subtler, sadder. He took the mostly comical ravings of Peetie Wheatstraw the Devil's Son-in-Law and smoothed them into Robert Johnson's devil, the melancholy devil who walks like a man and looks like a man and is much less easily laughed off.

Whereas Wald wants to educate our response to the country blues away from nostalgia and toward a more mature valuation—by reminding us that all folk was once somebody's pop—Marybeth Hamilton, an American cultural historian who teaches in England, looks back instead at the old sense of aura, asking where it came from. *In Search of the Blues* traces white fascination with the country blues to its roots in the mind of one James McKune, a weedy, closeted, alcoholic *New York Times* rewrite man turned drifter who kept his crates of 78s under his bunk at a YMCA in Brooklyn. Until now his tale has been known only to readers of the *78 Quarterly*. McKune came from North Carolina and in 1971 died squalidly after a sexual transaction gone wrong. In the early Forties he was among the first to break from the world of hardcore New Orleans jazz collecting, which developed in Ivy League dorms and was byzantine with specialisms by the late Thirties. Hamilton proves deft on the progression of McKune's taste. He started out an obsessive for commercial ethnographic material, such as regional dance songs from Spain on the Columbia label. He was interested, in other words, in culturally precious things that had been accidentally snagged and preserved by stray cogs of the anarchic capitalist machine.

One of McKune's few fellow travelers in this backwater of the collecting world was Harry Smith, who would go on in 1952 to create the *Anthology of American Folk Music*. Smith urged McKune

to send to the Library of Congress for a curious index, compiled
by Alan Lomax during his field-recording days and held in man-
uscript there, of "American Folk Songs on Commercial Records."
That list is the real DNA of the country blues as a genre. Hamilton writes:

> *What [McKune] read there confounded*
> *everything he had ever assumed*
> *about race records. The dizzying variety*
> *of musical styles, the sheer oddity*
> *of the song titles. . . . Most intriguing*
> *of all were Lomax's mentions of blues*
> *recordings [that] promised something*
> *undiluted and raw.*

A strangeness to notice here is that McKune's discovery happened in 1942. Robert Johnson, described on Lomax's list with the
notes "individual composition v[ery] f[ine], touches of voodoo,"
had been alive and recording just four years earlier. Already he existed for McKune as he exists for us, when we approach him
through the myth, at an archaeological remove. The country
blues has its decade or so and then is obliterated with a startling
suddenness, by the Depression, the Second World War, and the
energy of the Chicago sound. In 1938, John Hammond, an early
promoter of American folk music (later to become Bob Dylan's
first producer), put together a concert called "From Spirituals to
Swing." He intended it as a statement on the aesthetic legitimacy
of African-American music. Hammond sent off a cablegram
inviting Robert Johnson to come north and be in the show, to perform at Carnegie Hall. It's a hinge moment in blues historiogra-
phy—the second act, which would lead north and then to the fes-

tivals, reaches out to the first, which is disappearing with the onset of war, and tries to recognize a continuity. But Johnson had just
died, at twenty-seven, either of poison or of congenital syphilis. He
was employed to pick cotton at the time. At the concert they
wheeled a phonograph onto the stage and played two of his
records in the stillness. Even the *mediation* we think of as being
so postmodern, the ghostliness surrounding the recordings themselves as material objects, is present at the very beginning.

McKune undertook to search out these recordings, to know
them. Hamilton says he once rode a bus 250 miles from Brooklyn to the D.C. suburbs to hear Dick Spottswood's recently
turned-up copy of Skip James's "Hard Time Killin' Floor Blues."
He walked in, sat down, heard the record, and walked back out.
Those who knew him recall his listening "silently. In awe."

> *People are drifting*
> *From door to door*
> *Can't find no heaven,*
> *I don't care where they go.*

Spottswood was one in a circle of adepts who gathered around
McKune in the late Forties and Fifties. They went on to become
the Blues Mafia, the serious collectors. They didn't really gather
around McKune—he lived at the YMCA. But he visited their
gatherings and became the *chef du salon*. (This is the same Dick
Spottswood who a few years later would play Blind Willie Johnson's "Praise God I'm Satisfied" over the telephone for a young
John Fahey—who'd called up demanding it—causing Fahey to
weep and nearly vomit.)

McKune was never an object-freak: like Fahey—who went
looking for Skip James partly in hopes of learning the older man's

notoriously difficult minor-key tunings—he wanted the songs, the sounds, though he searched as relentlessly as any antiquarian. His early "want lists" in the *Record Changer* magazine are themselves now valuable collectibles. Hamilton includes the lovely detail that occasionally in his lists, he would issue a call for hypothetical records. For instance, he might advertise for "Blues on black Vocalion, any with San Antonio master numbers"; that is, records made in the same studio and during the same week as Robert Johnson's most famous sessions. (Goethe looking for the *Urpflanze!*)

What McKune heard when the records arrived transfixed him. Hamilton shows her seriousness and should earn the respect of all prewar wonks by not reflexively dismissing this something as an imagined "primitive" or "rough" quality. Indeed, those were the words that would have been used at the time by jazz collectors who for the most part dismissed this music as throwaway hick stuff, novelty songs made by people too poor to get to New Orleans. We can offer conjectures, as Hamilton does, intelligently, about the interior mansions of McKune's obscurantism— about whether, say, his estimation of Charley Patton as the greatest of the country-blues singers was influenced by the fact that Patton's records are the muddiest and least intelligible, allowing the most to be read into them—but the rigorous *attention* underlying all of McKune's listening stands as his defense.

Rarely did McKune attempt published aesthetic statements of any kind, and it's odd how he keeps repeating one word. Writing to *VJM Palaver* in 1960 about Samuel Charters's then recent book, *The Country Blues,* McKune bemoaned the fact that Charters had concentrated on those singers who'd sold the most records, such as Blind Lemon Jefferson and Brownie McGhee, whose respective oeuvres McKune found mediocre and slick. McKune's letter is sputtering in the arcane fury of its narcissism of minor difference, but the word he keeps getting stuck on is "great." As in "Jefferson made only one record I can call *great*" (italics McKune's). Or, "I know twenty men who collect the Negro country blues. All of us have been interested in knowing who the *great* country blues singers are" (his again), "not in who sold best." And finally, "I write for those who want a different basis for evaluating blues singers. This basis is their relative greatness . . . "

When I saw that letter in Hamilton's book, it brought up a memory of being on the phone with Dean Blackwood, John Fahey's partner at Revenant records, and hearing him talk about his early discussions with Fahey over the phantoms project. "John and I always felt like there wasn't enough of a case being made for these folks' *greatness*," he'd said. "You've got to have their stuff together to understand the potency of the work." Before dismissing as naive the boosterism of these pronouncements, we might ask whether there's not a simple technical explanation for the feeling being expressed or left unexpressed in them. I would submit that there is and it's this: The narrative of the blues got hijacked by rock 'n' roll, which rode a wave of youth consumers to global domination. Back behind the split, there was something else: a deeper, riper source. Many people who have written about this body of music have noticed it. Robert Palmer called it Deep Blues. We're talking about strains within strains, sure, but listen to something like Ishman Bracey's "Woman Woman Blues," his tattered yet somehow impeccable falsetto when he sings, "She got coal-black curly hair." Songs like that were not made for dancing. Not even for singing along. They were made for listening. For grown-ups. They were chamber compositions. Listen to Blind

Willie Johnson's "Dark Was the Night, Cold Was the Ground." It has no words. It's hummed by a blind preacher incapable of playing an impure note on the guitar. We have to go against our training here and suspend anthropological thinking; it doesn't serve at these strata. The noble ambition not to be the kind of people who unwittingly fetishize and exoticize black or poor-white folk poverty has allowed us to remain the kind of people who don't stop to wonder whether the serious treatment of certain folk forms as essentially highor higher-art forms might have originated with the folk themselves.

If there's a shared weakness to these two books, it's that they're insufficiently on the catch for this pitfall. "No one in the blues world was calling this music art," says Wald. Is that true? Carl Sandburg was including blues lyrics in his anthologies as early as 1927. More to the point, Ethel Waters, one of the citified "blues queens" whose lyrics and melodies had a funny way of showing up in those raw and undiluted countryblues recordings, had already been writing self-consciously modernist blues for a few years by then (e.g., "I can't sleep for dreaming . . . ," a line of hers I first heard in Crying Sam Collins and took for one of his beautiful manglings, then was humbled to learn had always been intentionally poetic). Marybeth Hamilton, in her not unsympathetic autopsy of James McKune's mania, comes dangerously close to suggesting that McKune was the first person to hear Skip James as we hear him, as a profound artist. But Skip James was the first person to hear Skip James that way. The anonymous African-American people described in Wald's book, sitting on the floor of a house in Tennessee and weeping while Robert Johnson sang "Come On in My Kitchen"—they were the first people to hear the country blues that way. White men "rediscovered" the blues, fine. We're talking about the complications of that at last. Let's not go crazy and say they invented it, or accidentally credit their "visions" with too much power. That would be counterproductive, a final insult even.

There's a moment on those discs of Gayle Dean Wardlow's interviews, the ones in Revenant's Patton set. Wardlow is talking with Booker Miller, a minor prewar player who knew Charley Patton. And you can hear Wardlow, who was a deceptively good interviewer—he just kept coming at a person in this *Rain Man* style that would have made anybody feel the less awkward one in the room—and you can tell he's trying to get Miller to describe the *ritual* of his apprenticeship to the elder Patton. "Did you meet him at a juke joint," asked Wardlow, "or on the street?" How did they find each other? It's the sort of question one would ask.

"I admired his records," answered Booker Miller.

Bird-Watcher

Thinking about Charlie Parker, every day

David Remnickk

Every weekday for the past twenty-seven years, a long-in-the-tooth history major named Phil Schaap has hosted a morning program on WKCR, Columbia University's radio station, called "Bird Flight," which places a degree of attention on the music of the bebop saxophonist Charlie Parker that is so obsessive, so ardent and detailed, that Schaap frequently sounds like a mad Talmudic scholar who has decided that the laws of humankind reside not in the ancient Babylonian tractates but in alternate takes of "Moose the Mooche" and "Swedish Schnapps."

For Schaap, Bird not only lives; he is the singular genius of mid-century American music, a dynamo of virtuosity, improvisation, harmony, velocity, and feeling, and no aspect of his brief career is beneath consideration. Schaap's discursive monologues on a single home recording—say, "the Bob Redcross acetate" of Parker playing in the early nineteen-forties over the Benny Goodman Quartet's 1937 hit "Avalon"—can go on for an entire program or more, blurring the line between exhaustive and exhausting. There is no getting to the end of Charlie Parker, and sometimes there is no getting to the end of "Bird Flight." The program is the anchor of WKCR's daily schedule and begins at eight-twenty. It is supposed to conclude at nine-forty. In the many years that I've been listening, I've rarely heard it end precisely as scheduled. Generations of Columbia d.j.s whose programs followed Schaap's have learned to stand clutching an album of the early Baroque or nineteenth-century Austrian yodelling and wait patiently for the final chorus of "I'll Always Love You Just the Same."

Schaap's unapologetic passion for a form of music half a century out of the mainstream is, at least for his listeners, a precious sign of the city's vitality; here is one obstinate holdout against the encroaching homogeneity of Clear Channel and all the other culprits of American sameness. There is no exaggerating the relentlessness of Schaap's approach. Not long ago, I listened to him play a recording of "Okiedoke," a tune that Parker recorded in 1949 with Machito and His Afro-Cuban Orchestra. Schaap, in his pontifical baritone, first provided routine detail on the session and Parker's interest (via Dizzy Gillespie) in Latin jazz, and then, like a car hitting a patch of black ice, he veered off into a riff of many minutes' duration on the pronunciation and meaning of the title—of "Okiedoke." Was it "okey-doke" or was it, rather, " 'okey-dokey,' as it is sometimes articulated"? What meaning did this innocent-seeming entry in the American lexicon have for Bird? And how precisely was the phrase used and understood in the black precincts of Kansas City, where Parker grew up? Declaring a "great interest in this issue," Schaap then informed us that Arthur Taylor, a drummer of distinction "and a Bird associate," had "stated that Parker used 'okeydokey' as an affirmative and 'okeydoke' as a negative." And yet one of Parker's ex-wives had averred otherwise, saying that Parker used "okeydoke" and "okeydokey" interchangeably. (At this point, I wondered, not for the first time, where, if anywhere, Schaap was going with this.) Then Schaap introduced into evidence a "rare recording of Bird's voice," in which Parker is captured joshing around onstage with a disk jockey of the forties and fifties named Sid Torin, better known as Symphony Sid. After a bit of chatter, Sid instructs Parker to play another number: "Blow, dad, go!"

Okeydoke, says Bird.

Like an assassination buff looping the Zapruder film, Schaap repeated the snippet several times and then concluded that Charlie Parker did not use "okeydoke" as a negative. "This," Schaap said solemnly, "tends to revise our understanding of the matter." The matter was evidently unexhausted, however, as he launched a rumination on the cowboy origins of the phrase and the Hopalong Cassidy movies that Parker might well have seen, and perhaps it was at this point that listeners all over the metropolitan area, what few remained, either shut off their radios, grew weirdly fascinated, or called an ambulance on Schaap's behalf. At last, Schaap moved on to other issues of the Parker discography, which begins in 1940, with an unaccompanied home recording of "Honeysuckle Rose" and "Body and Soul," and ends with two Cole Porter tunes, "Love for Sale" and "I Love Paris," played three months before his death, in 1955.

Schaap is not a musician, a critic, or, properly speaking, an academic, though he has held teaching positions at Columbia, Princeton, and Juilliard. And yet through "Bird Flight" and a Saturday-evening program he hosts called "Traditions in Swing," through his live soliloquies and his illustrative recordings, commercial and bootlegged, he has provided an invaluable service to

a dwindling art form: in the capital of jazz, he is its most passionate and voluble fan. He is the Bill James of his field, a master
of history, hierarchies, personalities, anecdote, relics, dates, and
events; but he is also a guardian, for, unlike baseball, jazz and the
musicians who play it are endangered. Jazz today is responsible
for only around three per cent of music sales in the United States,
and what even that small slice contains is highly questionable.
Among the current top sellers on Amazon in the jazz category are
easy-listening acts like Kenny G and Michael Bublé.

For decades, jazz musicians have joked about Schaap's adhe-
sive memory, but countless performers have known the feeling
that Schaap remembered more about their musical pasts than
they did and was always willing to let them in on the forgotten se-
crets. "Phil is a walking history book about jazz," Frank Foster, a
tenor-sax player for the Basie Orchestra, told me. Wynton
Marsalis says that Schaap is "an American classic."

In the eyes of his critics, Schaap's attention to detail and authenticity is irritating and extreme. He has won six Grammy
Awards for his liner notes and producing efforts, but his ency-
clopedic sensibility is a matter of taste. When Schaap was put in
charge of reissuing Benny Goodman's landmark 1938 concert at
Carnegie Hall for Columbia, he not only included lost cuts and
Goodman's long-winded introductions but also provided pro-
longed original applause tracks, and even the sounds of the stage
crew dragging chairs and music stands across the Carnegie stage
to set up for the larger band. His production work on a ten-disk
set of Billie Holiday for Verve was similarly inclusive. Schaap
wants us to know and hear everything. He seems to believe that
the singer's in-studio musings about what key to sing "Nice Work
If You Can Get It" in are as worthy of preservation as a bootleg

of Lincoln's Second Inaugural. Reviewing the Holiday set for the Village Voice, Gary Giddins called Schaap "that most obsessive of anal obsessives."

That's one way of looking at the matter. Another is that Schaap puts his frenzied memory and his obsessive attention to the arcane in the service of something important: the struggle of memory against forgetting—not just the forgetting of a sublime music but forgetting in general. Schaap is always apologizing, acknowledging his long-windedness, his nudnik tendencies. "The examination may be tedium to you," he said on the air recently as he ran through the days, between 1940 and 1944, when Parker might have overdubbed Goodman's "Chinaboy" in Bob Redcross's room at the Savoy Hotel in Chicago. ("His home was Room 305.") Nevertheless, he said, "my bent here is that I want to know when it happened because I believe in listening to the music of a genius chronologically where possible, particularly an improvising artist." The stringing together of facts is the Schaapian process, a monologuist's way of painting a picture of "events of the past" happening "in real time."

"I just hope the concept speaks to some," he said as his soliloquy unspooled. "It's two before nine. I'm speaking to you at length. I'm Phil Schaap."

On a recent Sunday morning, I met Schaap at the WKCR studios, at Broadway and 114th Street. (The station is at 89.9 on the FM dial; it also streams live online at wkcr.org.) Schaap is tall and lumbering and has a thick shock of reddish hair. It was March 9th, Ornette Coleman's seventy-eighth birthday. Schaap, his meaty arms loaded up with highlights and rarities in the Coleman discography, had come prepared for celebration. Nearly everything in his grasp was from his home collection. He does not consider collecting to be at the center of his life, but allowed that he does own five thousand 78s, ten thousand LPs, five thousand tapes, a few thousand hours of his own interviews with jazz musicians, "and, well, countless CDs." Schaap, who was married once, and briefly, in the nineties, lives alone in Hollis, Queens, in the house where he grew up. He admits that his collection, and his living quarters, could use some straightening.

"I've got to get things in order," he said. "I'm determined to do it. This is the year. If I didn't have a memory, I wouldn't know where anything is."

The WKCR studios are a couple of blocks south of the main entrance to the Columbia campus, and they tend to look as though there'd been a post-exam party the previous night and someone tried, but not hard, to clean up. The carpets are unvacuumed, the garbage cans stuffed with pizza boxes and crushed cans. Taped to the wall are some long-forgotten schedules and posters of John Coltrane and Charles Mingus. The visitor's perch—a red Naugahyde armchair—was long ago dubbed the "Dizzy Gillespie chair," after Gillespie, Parker's closest collaborator, sat there for hours of conversation with Schaap. Usually, the only person around at WKCR is the student host on the air. Schaap is Class of '73. He is fifty-seven. "Financially, I live, at best, like a twenty-five-year-old," he said. He has been broadcasting on WKCR, pro bono, since he was a freshman. The Parker-Tiny Grimes collaboration "Romance Without Finance" could be the theme for his income-tax form.

"Take a seat," he said, plopping his records down near his microphone. "I gotta get busy."

Conversation with Schaap in the studio, especially when the program features the breakneck tunes of early jazz or swing music—the soprano saxophonist Sidney Bechet playing "The Sheik of Araby" followed by Benny Carter and His Orchestra on "Babalu"—does not allow for Schaapian reflection. "Deadlines every three minutes!" he'll shout, throwing up his hands. "So many records!"

When he's working, Schaap concentrates hard, and not merely on his own solos. He takes pride in the art of the segue, paying particular attention to the "sizzling sonic decay" of a last cymbal stroke. ("You won't hear that again in your lifetime!" he boasted after one particularly felicitous transition.) But with Ornette Coleman, an avatar of extended improvisation, Schaap had more time. The first number he broadcast was "Free Jazz," Coleman's 1960 breakthrough, played with two quartets; "Free Jazz" is the Action painting of American music and lasts thirty-seven minutes and three seconds. The sound started to build, the quartets began their dissonant duel. Schaap smiled off into the distance. "Eddie Blackwell's right foot, man!" he said, then he remembered himself and turned the volume down. "So?" he said.

When I asked Schaap about his childhood, he turned morose, saying, "I may have gotten all my blessings in life up front." His parents, and nearly all his teachers and the scores of musicians he befriended from school age, were dead. "Everyone that raised me is gone."

Schaap was born to jazz. His mother, Marjorie, was a librarian, a classically trained pianist, and an insistent bohemian. At Radcliffe, she listened to Louis Armstrong records and smoked a corncob pipe. His father, Walter, was one of a group of jazz-obsessed Columbia undergraduates in the thirties who became professional critics and producers. In 1937, he went to France to study at the Sorbonne and work on an encyclopedia of the French

Revolution. While he was there, he collaborated with the leading jazz critics of Paris, Hugues Panassié and Charles Delaunay, on a bilingual edition of their pioneering magazine, *Jazz Hot*. He helped Django Reinhardt with his English and Dizzy Gillespie with his French. Back in New York, he earned his living making educational filmstrips, in partnership with the jazz photographer William P. Gottlieb.

"They lived for music, and the rest was making a check," Phil said. "Jazz was always playing in the house." By the time he was five, Schaap could sing Lester Young's tenor solo on the Count Basie standard "Taxi War Dance." When he was six, his babysitter rewarded him for doing her geometry homework by taking him to Triboro Records, in Jamaica, to buy his first 45s: Ruth Brown's "Mama, He Treats Your Daughter Mean" and Ray Charles's "(Night Time Is) The Right Time." Phil soon started buying discarded jazz 78s by the pound.

In his parents' living room and then on his own pushy initiative, Schaap met many first-rank jazz musicians and came to consider them his "grandfathers." Some, like the bassist Milt Hinton and the trumpet player Buck Clayton, lived around Hollis, which had become a bedroom community for musicians. Others came into his life, he said, "as if by magic."

"In August, 1956, I went to the Randall's Island Jazz Festival with my mother, and we saw Billie Holliday, Dizzy Gillespie, and a lot of others," he said. "At one point, we went backstage after the Basie band played. Remember, this is through the hazy recollections of a five-year-old, but I do recall someone trying to hit on my mother, and he asked her about Joe Williams, who was singing then for Basie. To brush the guy off, she said she preferred the earlier singer for the Basie band, Jimmy Rushing, and at that point another man, who turned out to be Basie's drummer, Jo Jones, said, 'Madame, I heard that—that was wonderful.' The two of them got to talking, and Jo asked me if I knew who Prince Robinson was. I said that he was a tenor player for McKinney's Cotton Pickers. I'd heard a Bluebird 78 that my father owned. Jo Jones was impressed. So he said, 'Madame, you've got yourself a new babysitter.'"

Jo Jones was arguably the greatest drummer of the swing era. When Jones was in New York, Walter Schaap would drop off his son at Jones's apartment and Phil and "Papa Jo" watched cartoons and played records. Inevitably, other musicians came over and took an interest in the kid with the unusual immersion in jazz. "That was when Jo was living at 401 East Sixty-fourth Street," Schaap said. "Later, he lived at 333 East Fifty-fourth Street and also at the Hotel Markwell, on Forty-ninth Street—lots of musicians lived there. He played a Basie record for me once in order to teach me about Herschel Evans, the great tenor player. It must have been 'Blue and Sentimental.' Jo called me 'Mister.' 'Mister, what does that sound like to you?' I blurted out, 'It sounds friendly to me.' And Jo said, 'That's right. The first thing to know is, Herschel Evans is your friend.'"

In first grade, Schaap pestered his schoolmate Carole Eldridge (and, when that failed, her mother) until he got an introduction to her father, the trumpeter Roy Eldridge. When he was fourteen, he hitched a ride into Manhattan with Basie during the 1966 subway strike. "When I started hearing that Phil was going around meeting all the jazz greats at the age of six, I wondered if it was all fantasy," his father told the Times not long before he died, two years ago.

The family became accustomed to their son's range of friendships. Phil once brought home the saxophonist Rahsaan Roland

Kirk, who was known for his ability to play three horns at once and for his heroic capacities at the dinner table. Schaap challenged Kirk to an eating contest. The event came to a halt when they had eaten, in Schaap's recollection, "one mince pie each baked by Herbie Hall's wife. You know Herbie? A major clarinet player."

Schaap's memory was almost immediately evident. He claims that at the age of two he recited the names of the American Presidents, in order, "while standing on a rocking chair." He was the kind of kid who knew the names and numbers of all the New York Rangers of the nineteen-sixties and, whether you liked it or not, recited them. He was the kind of kid, too, who wrote to the manager of the Baltimore Orioles to give him advice backed up by statistical evidence. He routinely beat all comers, including his older cousin the late sportswriter Dick Schaap, in the board game Concentration. At school, this was not a quality universally admired. "I guess some kids may have found it annoying," he allows. But musicians were generally fascinated by young Schaap. Count Basie was one of many who discovered that Schaap knew the facts of his life almost better than he did. "I think that kind of freaked Basie out," Schaap said. "I'd talk to him about a record date he did in the thirties, and he looked at me, like, 'Who . . . is . . . this . . . child?'"

By the time Schaap was established on the radio, nearly every musician who passed through New York was aware of his mental tape recorder. Twenty-five years ago, the bandleader, pianist, and self-styled space cadet Herman (Sonny) Poole Blount, better known as Sun Ra, swept by a night club and, before having to give a speech at Harvard, "kidnapped" Schaap. Sun Ra claimed that as a young man he had been "transmolecularized" to Saturn, and thereafter he expounded a cosmic philosophy influenced by ancient Egyptian cosmology, Afro-American folklore, and Madame Blavatsky. In order to prepare for his audience in Cambridge, Sun Ra insisted that Schaap fill him in on the details of his existence on Earth. Schaap obliged, telling Sun Ra that, according to his musicians' union forms, he was born in Birmingham, Alabama, in 1914. "I could tell him things like what 78s by Fletcher Henderson he was listening to in the thirties and about his time playing piano for the Henderson Orchestra later on," Schaap said. "He was vague about it all, but what I said made sense to him. I also knew that his favorite flavor of ice cream was the Bananas 'n Strawberry at Baskin-Robbins. It was a hot summer night, so I went up the block and bought him a quart, and we ate sitting in the car."

The urge to preserve, to collect, to keep time at bay, to hold on to the past is a common one. In this Schaap is kin to Henri Langlois, who tried to find and preserve every known film for the French Cinémathèque, kin to the classical-music fanatics who drift through thrift shops looking for rereleases of Mengelberg and Furtwängler acetates, kin even to Felix Mendelssohn, who helped revive the music of Bach for Germans. He is one with all the bibliophiles, cinephiles, audiophiles, oenophiles, butterfly hunters, fern and flower pressers, stamp and coin collectors, concert tapers, and opera buffs who put an obsession at the center of their lives. "There is no person in America more dedicated to any art form than Phil is to jazz," his friend Stanley Crouch, who is writing a biography of Charlie Parker, said. "He is the Mr. Memory of jazz, and, as with the Mr. Memory character in 'The Thirty-Nine Steps,' the Hitchcock movie, there are those who think he ought to be shot. He can get on your nerves, but, then, you can get on his."

The day after Ornette Coleman's birthday was the birthday—
the hundred and fifth—of the cornet player Bix Beiderbecke,
and Schaap returned to the studios for another marathon of
close attention. Along with Louis Armstrong and Sidney Bechet,
Beiderbecke was a pioneer of jazz as it moved from the all-in
polyphony of the earliest bands to a form of ensemble playing that
allowed for solo improvisation. The broadcast was a strange
time-tunnel transition, from Ornette's self-invented "harmolodic"
experiments to Bix's short solo flights on "Goose Pimples" and
"Three Blind Mice," but Schaap's taste is broad. As he queued up
his records, he said to me, "I remember March 10, 1985. I did 5
AM to 5 PM It was some birthday for Bix." Schaap was unshaved,
sleepy, complaining, as usual, of overwork. He felt as if he, too,
were a hundred and five.

Schaap is perpetually weary. He works hard: there are the radio shows, the classes he's teaching now at Juilliard and at Jazz at
Lincoln Center, and various producing projects. But it's not the
work, exactly. Schaap carries with him a burden of loss and a dis-
interest in the contemporary world. He is theatrically, adamantly,
old: "I haven't seen more than six movies since 1972. Three baseball games, maybe five. I think the last novel I read was 'Invisible
Man,' when I was at Columbia. I haven't seen any television after
the first husband in 'Bewitched.'" He never bothered to see "Bird,"
Clint Eastwood's Charlie Parker bio-pic. He does not own an
iPod. And unless you have a spare afternoon it is best not to ask
him what he thinks of digital downloads.

Before long, he was off on a Schaapian riff sparked by the
playing of "Wringin' an' Twistin'," recorded, as Schaap said,
"eighty-one years ago by OKeh records with Frankie Trumbauer
on C-melody saxophone and Eddie Lang on guitar." Eventually,

through the surface scratches, one could hear a voice say, "Yeah, that's it!" Schaap assured his listeners that there was "no doubt of the voice's identity." It was Trumbauer. But that was not enough to cool his curiosity. "Someone is also humming the passage," he went on. "Is it Eddie Lang or is it Trumbauer? I wonder about it. It's a test cut on the metal part before the passage begins. And then there's another voice that you can hear say, 'Yeah.' That 'yeah' is not Eddie Lang. It could be unidentified. Or it could be Bix's voice."

Schaap played the sequence again.

Yeah.

And again.

Yeah.

One more time.

Yeah.

Meanwhile, the earth warmed imperceptibly; glaciers plunged into the sea.

Yeah.

"There," Schaap said. "There! That's it! September 17, 1927. Not that it's the most important thing that ever happened to you. But, still. I'd like to know, if possible, what Bix's speaking voice was like."

These questions were of no less moment to Schaap than the Confederate maneuvers at Shiloh were to Shelby Foote. Such is the flypaper of his mind and the didactic turn of his personality. When, finally, Schaap played another Beiderbecke record—a twenty-minute string of tunes, to be fair—I asked him what possible interest he could have in the provenance of the ghostly "yeah"s of yesteryear.

"What can I say? I make no apologies. I'm interested," he said. "Did Bix have a Southern accent? A German accent? A Midwestern accent? Did he sound shy or did he speak with authority? I really do think it's him, that it's Bix who says, 'Yeah.'"

Schaap paused and listened to a passage in "Goose Pimples."

"O.K.," he said, "it may not be a great mystery. But it's a mystery, all the same. I do these things that are a turnoff, but it's my dime. I try very hard to make sure that everyone gets something out of all this. I guess for the first twenty years I was on the radio I was concerned about telling you absolutely everything about every tune. Then, in the nineties, I started concentrating on small issues, one at a time. Like that 'Okiedoke' thing. These days, I'm going for a little balance."

As a broadcaster, Schaap is unpoetic. He does not have the evocative middle-of-the-night gifts of a radio forebear like Jean Shepherd. Or take Jonathan Schwartz, whose specialty for both XM satellite radio and WNYC, in New York, is American singers. Schwartz is as obsessed with Frank Sinatra as Schaap is with Parker, but Schwartz, a brilliant storyteller with a café-society voice as smooth as hot buttered rum, conjures Sinatra's world: the stage of the Paramount, the bar at Jilly Rizzo's. Schaap is an empiricist, an old-fashioned historicist. Facts are what he has. His capacity to evoke Charlie Parker's world—Kansas City in the Pendergast era; the Savoy Ballroom scene uptown; Minton's, the Three Deuces, and Birdland; Bird's dissolution and early death— is limited to the accumulation of dates, bare anecdotes, obscure names. The emotional side of his broadcasts comes from his relationships with the musicians. His mental life can be spooky even to him. "Sometimes," he said, "I think I know more about what Dizzy Gillespie was thinking in 1945 than I do what I was thinking in 1967 or last week."

The precocious obsessive is a familiar high-school type, particularly among boys, but the object of Schaap's obsession was a

peculiar one among his classmates. "The lonely days were adolescence," he admitted. "My peer group thought I was out of my
mind. But, even then, kids knew basic things about jazz. Teddy
Goldstein knew 'Take the A Train.' But he kept telling me, 'Don't
you know what the Beatles are doing? Your world is doomed!'"

When he was in his teens, Schaap played the trumpet. He took
theory classes at Columbia. "I even got a lesson in high notes
from Roy Eldridge," he said. But his playing, especially his into-
nation, was mediocre. "I put my trumpet in its case and that was
it," he said. "March 11, 1974."

Schaap learned to serve the music anyway. In the wake of the
Columbia campus strikes in 1968, a group of students set out to
get rid of WKCR's "classroom of the air" gentility. "All of us were
listening to the Grateful Dead and Jimi Hendrix, but we knew that
all of that stuff was available elsewhere," Schaap told me over a
burger near Lincoln Center. "Jimi Hendrix didn't need WKCR."
And so the station began broadcasting jazz, including multi-day
festivals on Albert Ayler (1970), John Coltrane (1971), Charles
Mingus (1972), Archie Shepp (1972), and Charlie Parker (1973).
During the 1973 Parker festival, Schaap did two forty-eight-hour
work shifts, splitting his time between WKCR and his paying job,
at the university's identification-card office. "On Friday, August
31, 1973, I had to get to the I.D.-card office," he recalled. "The last
record I played was 'Scrapple from the Apple.' Recorded November 4, 1947. The C take. On Dial. But I think I played the English Spotlite label. Anyway, I entered the back stairwell and the
record was still playing in my head"—Schaap interrupted himself
to hum Parker's solo—"and then I was out on a Hundred and
Fourteenth Street and I could hear it playing from the buildings,
from the open windows. That was a turning point in the station's

history. The insight was that Charlie Parker was at least tolerable to all people who liked jazz. If you idolized King Oliver, you could tolerate Charlie Parker, and if you think jazz begins with John Coltrane playing 'Ascension' you can still listen to Bird, too."

Musicians were beginning to tune in. During a Thelonious Monk festival, one of the d.j.s went on about how Monk created art out of "wrong notes." Monk, who rarely spoke to anyone, much less a college student, called the station and, on the air, declared, "The piano ain't got no wrong notes." In 1979, Schaap was at the center of a Miles Davis festival at a time when Davis was a near-recluse living off Riverside Drive. Davis started calling the station, dozens and dozens of calls—"mad, foul, strange calls," Schaap recalled. Davis's inimitable voice, low and sandpapery, was unnerving for Schaap. But then one day—"Friday, July 6, 1979"—his tone changed, and for nearly three hours the two men went over the details of "Agharta," one of his later albums. Finally, after Schaap had clarified every spelling, every detail, Davis said, "You got it? Good. Now forget it. Play 'Sketches of Spain'! Right now!"

Just after starting as a d.j., Schaap began organizing musical programs, mainly at the West End, on Broadway at 113th Street. He managed the Countsmen—former sidemen for Count Basie—along with other groups made up of refugees from other big bands, and got them work. Older musicians, such as Jo Jones, Sonny Greer, Sammy Price, Russell Procope, and Earle Warren, who had known Schaap as an eccentric teen-ager now welcomed him as a meal ticket.

"When I was a child, I lived under the illusion that these performers, who put on such an excellent front, dressed to the nines and acting like kings, made real money," Schaap said. He lost that innocence about forty years ago, when he happened to glance at a check made out to Benny Morton, a trombonist who had been with the Fletcher Henderson and Basie bands. "It was for fifty-eight dollars, and it was for a gig at Carnegie Hall," Schaap recalled. Jazz reached its commercial peak in the mid-nineteen-forties, but by 1950 the ballrooms had closed down. The postwar middle class no longer went out dancing; they were watching television and listening to records at home. The clubs on Fifty-second Street—the Onyx, the Famous Door, the Three Deuces—disappeared. Eventually, rock and roll displaced jazz as America's popular music. World-class musicians were scrounging for work. Performers who had enjoyed steady employment took second jobs as messengers on Wall Street, bus drivers, and bank guards. For comradeship, they were hanging out at the Chock Full o' Nuts at Fiftieth and Broadway and at a few bars around town.

"Phil took these guys out of the Chock Full o' Nuts and put them on the stage of the West End," Loren Schoenberg, the executive director of the National Jazz Museum in Harlem, told me. "So for the young people who idolized them, and guys who'd never heard of them, Phil brought them to us." Screamin' Jay Hawkins, an early rhythm-and-blues star, used to call Phil Schaap's mother at home and beg her to get her son to do for him what he'd done for the horn players of the Basie band.

As "Bird Flight" became a fixture of the jazz world, Schaap began to get jobs teaching, but, even with the rise of academic jazz programs, no one has offered him a professorship. Some of his students—including Ben Ratliff, who is now the main jazz critic for the Times, and Jerome Jennings, a drummer for, among others, Sonny Rollins—swear by Schaap as a teacher, but some complain that his displays of memory can be tiresome and aimed at underscoring his students' cluelessness. This spring, I took Schaap's Charlie Parker course at Swing University, the educational wing of Jazz at Lincoln Center, and could see both sides. In four two-hour evening sessions, he provided an incisive, moving narrative of Parker's incandescent career, but he could also be oppressive, not least with his pointless occasional class "surveys." "Who knows 'Yardbird Suite'?" he'd ask. Then, moving from desk to desk, he'd poll the students, embarrassing those honest enough to confess their ignorance.

As a teacher, Schaap is less concerned about the tender sensibilities of his students than with developing knowledgeable and passionate listeners. "The school system is creating six thousand unemployable musicians a year—from the Berklee College of Music, Rutgers, Mannes, Manhattan, Juilliard, plus all the high schools," he said. "There are more and more musicians, and no gigs, no one to listen. So what happens to these kids? They work their way back to the educational system and help create more unemployable musicians. My rant is this: I'm not trying to teach you to play the alto sax. No. I'm trying to get you to learn how to listen to Charlie Parker. Louis Armstrong is the greatest musician of the twentieth century. But name twenty musicians today who really listen to Louis Armstrong. Go ahead: I'll give you a week."

There are many excellent young (and youngish) jazz musicians around, including the pianist Jason Moran and the sax player Joshua Redman, to say nothing of the extended family of players around Wynton Marsalis. In February, Herbie Hancock won an Album of the Year Grammy for his arrangements of Joni Mitchell songs. But, generally, a hit album in jazz means sales of ten thousand. Ornette Coleman, Sonny Rollins, and a few other giants of an earlier time still roam the earth, but even they cannot reliably sell out a major hall. Coleman's concert at Town Hall in March was as thrilling a musical event as has taken place this year in New York. The theatre was at least a quarter empty.

"In the fall of 1976, when Woody Herman was rehearsing for a forty-year-anniversary concert at Carnegie Hall, I was invited to watch," Schaap told me. "A saxophonist wasn't paying attention, and at one point Woody Herman crept up on him, put his face next to the musician's, and said, 'Son, what do you want to be?' And the guy said, 'I want to be the next Stan Getz.' And Woody Herman said, 'Son, there's not gonna be another Stan Getz!' In other words, people like Stan Getz and Woody Herman were pop stars! That's not going to happen again."

In the spring of 1947, around the same time that Charlie Parker was playing the Hi-De-Ho club, in Los Angeles, a young Bedouin herding goats along the northwest shore of the Dead Sea discovered several tall clay jars that contained manuscripts written in ancient Hebrew and Aramaic. Wrapped in linen, the manuscripts were part of a much larger cache of ancient texts, which came to be known as the Dead Sea Scrolls.

"For decades, there were rumors that jazz had its own Dead Sea Scrolls," Schaap told me more than once. "One was a cylinder recording of Buddy Bolden"—the New Orleans cornettist and early jazz pioneer who was committed to a mental institution before the rise of 78s. "But this will probably never be found. The second, of course, is called 'the Benedetti recordings.'"

All of Schaap's listeners have grown accustomed to his close attention to the "crucial" obscurities of the Parker discography: "the unaccompanied 1940 alto recording in Kansas City," "the paper disk of 'Cherokee,'" "the Wichita transcriptions," and "the lit-tle-known Clyde Bernhardt glass-based acetate demo disks." These recordings can be revelatory, but they also try the patience. Recently on "Bird Flight," Schaap showcased a home recording of Parker in February, 1943—important because he was playing tenor saxophone, not his customary alto—and the sound was so bad that you couldn't quite tell if you were hearing "Sweet Geor-gia Brown" or radio waves from the surface of the planet Uranus.

The Benedetti recordings, however, occupy a privileged place not only in Schaap's mental Bird cage but also in musical history. And Schaap helped bring them out of their urns.

For decades, stories circulated in the jazz world that Dean Benedetti, a saxophonist of modest distinction, upon hearing Parker play in the mid-forties, threw his own horn into the sea and pledged himself to follow Parker everywhere he went, record-ing his hero's performances. Benedetti was said to have obtained, through Army connections, a Nazi-era German wire recorder, and he carried out his mission at clubs, concert halls, and private apartments all over the world. In the meantime, he was rumored to be a drug dealer who supplied Bird, a longtime addict, with heroin. Many of the legends of Benedetti's devotions came from "Bird Lives!," an entertaining but iffy biography published in 1973 by a Los Angeles-based record producer, Ross Russell. Through the decades, no recordings surfaced. Ornithologists could not help but wonder: Had they been lost? Had they sunk, as rumored, along with a freighter in the Atlantic? Eventually, only the most committed, with their collections of 78s and back issues of Down Beat, spoke much of the matter. Like "the Bolden cylin-der," the Benedetti recordings seemed to have taken their eternal rest in the watery grave of jazz legend.

But then, in 1988, Benedetti's surviving brother, Rigoletto (Rick), got in touch with Mosaic, a small jazz outfit in Stamford, Connecticut, that specializes in reissues from the vaults of the major labels. It was true, Rick Benedetti informed the owner, Michael Cuscuna: there really were recordings. Was Mosaic interested?

"The real backstory was incredible," Cuscuna told me.

On July 29, 1946, Parker was in desperate shape: depressed, drinking, strung out, broke, and lonely in Los Angeles, he had struggled through an afternoon recording session with the trumpeter Howard McGhee. His recording that day of "Lover Man" was a technical mess—Parker was barely able to make it through the song—but it is a painful howl, as devastating to hear as Billie Holiday's last sessions. That night, at the Civic Hotel, Parker twice wandered into the lobby naked. Later on, he fell asleep while smoking, setting his mattress on fire. The police arrested him and a judge had him committed to the Camarillo State Hospital, a psychiatric facility. When he was released, six months later, he was off heroin for the first time since he was a teen-ager in Kansas City. His musician friends threw a jam-session party for him on February 1, 1947, at the home of a trumpet player named Chuck Copely. One of the guests was a handsome young man—pencil mustache, dark eyes, hipster clothes—named Dean Benedetti.

Benedetti went out and bought a Wells-Gardner 78-r.p.m. portable disk-cutter at Sears, Roebuck and, in March, recorded Parker playing with Howard McGhee's band at the Hi-De-Ho. (The historical bonus here is that Parker plays tunes from McGhee's repertory, and so we hear him soloing, for the first and last time, on Gus Arnheim's "Sweet and Lovely" and Al Dubin and Harry Warren's "September in the Rain.") Later that year, in

New York, Parker was back on drugs but still at the height of his musical powers. He formed what is now considered his "golden-era" quintet: Parker on alto sax, the twenty-one-year-old Miles Davis on trumpet, Max Roach on drums, Duke Jordan on piano, and Tommy Potter on bass. Benedetti recorded the quintet on March 31, 1948, at the Three Deuces, on Fifty-second Street, Parker's primary base of operations. By this time, Benedetti was using heroin and had no means of support; when the management realized that he didn't plan to spend any money, it provided him with what Schaap would call "the ultimate New York discourtesy"—it threw him out. In Schaap's terms, it is a "tragedy" that Benedetti was unable to record the rest of Parker's nights at the Three Deuces. And it is true that, of all the Benedetti recordings, these are the most significant. On "Dizzy Atmosphere," Parker plays with dangerous abandon, a runaway truck speeding down the highway into oncoming traffic, never crashing; and even the twenty-six-second passage from the ballad "My Old Flame" is memorable, a glimpse of human longing in sound.

Finally, in July, 1948, Benedetti recorded the Parker quintet for six nights at the Onyx, a rival club on Fifty-second Street. The sound from the Onyx sessions is the worst of all, mainly because Benedetti was forced by the club's management to place his microphone near Max Roach's drum kit. The effect is often like trying to hear a lullaby in a thunderstorm.

The recordings are not for casual listeners. Disks and tape were expensive commodities, and to save money Benedetti usually turned on the machine only when Parker was soloing. Many recordings are no more than a minute long. One morsel lasts precisely three seconds. There are no fewer than nineteen versions of "52nd St. Theme." But to the aficionado this is like complaining that the Dead Sea Scrolls were torn and discolored. One hears Parker on Coleman Hawkins tunes like "Bean Soup" and quoting everything from "In a Country Garden" to a bit from H. Klosé's "25 Daily Exercises for Saxophone."

Cuscuna said that, faced with stacks of cracking forty-year-old tapes and ten-inch acetate disks, he realized that "only Phil Schaap was brilliant enough—and insane enough—to do the job."

Schaap took the materials to the apartment where he was living at the time—a record-and-disk-strewn place in Chelsea—and "just stared" at them for "many, many hours." He felt an enormous sense of responsibility. "This increased the volume of live improvisations of a great artist by a third," he told me one morning after signing off from "Bird Flight." "Imagine if someone were to find a third more Bach, a third more Shakespeare plays, a third more prime Picasso."

When Schaap first tried to play a tape, it snapped. He tried hand-spinning the tape. It broke again. He realized that the tapes were backed with paper, not plastic. The paper had dried out, making the tape extremely fragile. The solution, Schaap decided, was to secure the most delicate spots with Wite-Out. And so he went through every inch of the Benedetti tapes—all eight miles—and did the job, the tape in his left hand, a tiny Wite-Out brush in his right.

"I guess the only thing I've ever done in jazz that was harder was when we did an eleven-day Louis Armstrong festival on WKCR, in July, 1980," he said. Schaap worked for more than two years on the Benedetti project. He and Cuscuna once figured out his remuneration. "I think it was approximately .0003 cents an hour," Schaap said. "But who's complaining?"

Mosaic has so far sold five thousand copies of "The Complete Dean Benedetti Recordings of Charlie Parker."

"That's triple platinum for us," Cuscuna said.

For Schaap, the fascinations and mysteries of the discography are unending, even though Parker's career lasted less than fifteen years. Parker died on March 12, 1955, at the Stanhope Hotel, while watching jugglers on Tommy Dorsey's television variety show. A doctor who examined the body estimated that Parker was in his mid-fifties. He was thirty-four.

On Easter Sunday, I met Schaap in the lobby of the Kateri Residence, a nursing home on Riverside Drive. He was there to visit one of the last of "the grandfathers who helped raise him."

We went to the twelfth floor and headed for a small room at the end of the hall. From the doorway, we could see a round old man slumped in a wheelchair, sleeping, a woollen scarf over his shoulders and a blanket on his lap. It was Lawrence Lucie. "I met Larry fifty-one years ago," Schaap said. He was six. Lucie played guitar for almost anyone worth playing for: from Jelly Roll Morton to Joe Turner. He played in the big bands of Fletcher Henderson, Benny Goodman, Lucky Millinder, Duke Ellington, and Benny Carter. When Coleman Hawkins recorded "Body and Soul," Lucie was in the band. Lucie not only played with Louis Armstrong; he was the best man at Armstrong's wedding. He is the last person alive to have played with Ellington at the Cotton Club. Lucie's father was a barber in Emporia, Virginia; he was also a musician, and Lawrence joined his father's band as a banjo player when he was eight. Now he is a hundred years old. No one alive is as intimately connected to the origins of jazz music as Lucie. His last gig, which he quit only a couple of years ago, was playing standards at Arturo's, a coal-oven-pizza joint on Houston Street in the Village.

"Larry, it's me, Phil."

Schaap gently shook the old man's shoulder.

Lucie opened his eyes and, very slowly, looked up at his visitor. As he brought Schaap into focus, he smiled and his eyes brightened.

"Phil! How nice!"

Not many people are still around to visit. A grandnephew is the closest relative that Schaap knows of, and he lives in California. Schaap and Lucie were clearly thrilled to see each other. Nearly all of Schaap's jazz grandfathers—Jo Jones, Roy Eldridge, Buck Clayton, Doc Cheatham, Max Roach—are gone. Lucie had not lost his elegance. Although he had no reason to expect a visit, he was wearing a tie, a smart silk one with an abstract blue-and-red pattern. On the other side of his bed was a guitar in a battered case and, above it, a poster of the Lucy Luciennaires, a quartet that featured his wife, the singer Nora Lee King, who died eleven years ago. In the seventies and eighties, Lucie and King used to perform weekly on a Manhattan public-access cable channel.

Lucie, who celebrated his centennial in December, was glad to hear Schaap talk about his days with Fletcher Henderson. And when Schaap asked him if he remembered the name of the song that Benny Carter opened with at the Apollo seventy-four years ago, Lucie said, "I know, Phil, but do you?"

"Sure, it was 'I May Be Wrong (But I Think You're Wonderful).'"

"That's right." Both men laughed.

"And you played the first notes," Schaap said. Indeed, they were the first notes played in the Apollo when, in 1934, the theatre opened under that name and began admitting African-American audiences.

Schaap wheeled Lucie to the elevator and up to a solarium on the penthouse floor, where they could look out over the Hudson

River and reminisce, a conversation that was more a matter of Schaap recalling highlights of Lucie's career and Lucie saying, over and over, "Phil Schaap knows me better than I know me. Phil Schaap knows his jazz."

Finally, Lucie asked to go down to the fifteenth floor, where a volunteer was playing piano and singing show tunes.

"You coax the blues right out of my heart."

Arrayed in front of the piano were fifty or sixty residents, some of them nearly as old as Lucie and many a great deal less healthy. A nurse passed out Easter cookies. Lawrence Lucie had heard better music in his time, but he was happy to stay and listen. "There's always something going on here," he said dryly. "The action never stops."

Schaap bent over and told his friend that he was off.

"What a delight," Lucie said. "It's always so good to see you."

"I'll be back soon," Schaap said. "You know I will."

Researchers Play Tune Recorded Before Edison

Jody Rosen

For more than a century, since he captured the spoken words "Mary had a little lamb" on a sheet of tinfoil, Thomas Edison has been considered the father of recorded sound. But researchers say they have unearthed a recording of the human voice, made by a little-known Frenchman, that predates Edison's invention of the phonograph by nearly two decades.

The 10-second recording of a singer crooning the folk song "Au Clair de la Lune" was discovered earlier this month in an archive in Paris by a group of American audio historians. It was made, the researchers say, on April 9, 1860, on a phonautograph, a machine designed to record sounds visually, not to play them back. But the phonautograph recording, or phonautogram, was made playable—converted from squiggles on paper to sound—by scientists at the Lawrence Berkeley National Laboratory in Berkeley, Calif.

"This is a historic find, the earliest known recording of sound," said Samuel Brylawski, the former head of the recorded-sound division of the Library of Congress, who is not affiliated with the research group but who was familiar with its findings. The audio excavation could give a new primacy to the phonautograph, once considered a curio, and its inventor, Édouard-Léon Scott de Martinville, a Parisian typesetter and tinkerer who went to his grave convinced that credit for his breakthroughs had been improperly bestowed on Edison.

Scott's device had a barrel-shaped horn attached to a stylus, which etched sound waves onto sheets of paper blackened by smoke from an oil lamp. The recordings were not intended for listening; the idea of audio playback had not been conceived. Rather, Scott sought to create a paper record of human speech that could later be deciphered.

But the Lawrence Berkeley scientists used optical imaging and a "virtual stylus" on high-resolution scans of the phonautogram, deploying modern technology to extract sound from patterns inscribed on the soot-blackened paper almost a century and a half ago. The scientists belong to an informal collaborative called First Sounds that also includes audio historians and sound engineers.

David Giovannoni, an American audio historian who led the research effort, will present the findings and play the recording in public on Friday at the annual conference of the Association for Recorded Sound Collections at Stanford University in Palo Alto, Calif.

Scott's 1860 phonautogram was made 17 years before Edison received a patent for the phonograph and 28 years before an Edison associate captured a snippet of a Handel oratorio on a wax cylinder, a recording that until now was widely regarded by experts as the oldest that could be played back.

Mr. Giovannoni's presentation on Friday will showcase additional Scott phonautograms discovered in Paris, including recordings made in 1853 and 1854. Those first experiments included attempts to capture the sounds of a human voice and a guitar, but Scott's machine was at that time imperfectly calibrated.

"We got the early phonautograms to squawk, that's about it," Mr. Giovannoni said.

But the April 1860 phonautogram is more than a squawk. On a digital copy of the recording provided to The New York Times, the anonymous vocalist, probably female, can be heard against a hissing, crackling background din. The voice, muffled but audible, sings, "Au clair de la lune, Pierrot répondit" in a lilting 11-note melody—a ghostly tune, drifting out of the sonic murk.

The hunt for this audio holy grail was begun in the fall by Mr. Giovannoni and three associates: Patrick Feaster, an expert in the history of the phonograph who teaches at Indiana University, and Richard Martin and Meagan Hennessey, owners of Archeophone Records, a label specializing in early sound recordings. They had collaborated on the Archeophone album "Actionable Offenses," a collection of obscene 19th-century records that received two Grammy nominations. When Mr. Giovannoni raised the possibility of compiling an anthology of the world's oldest recorded sounds, Mr. Feaster suggested they go digging for Scott's phonautograms.

Historians have long been aware of Scott's work. But the American researchers believe they are the first to make a concerted search for Scott's phonautograms or attempt to play them back.

In December Mr. Giovannoni and a research assistant traveled to a patent office in Paris, the Institut National de la Propriété Industrielle. There he found recordings from 1857 and 1859 that were included by Scott in his phonautograph patent application.

Mr. Giovannoni said that he worked with the archive staff there to make high-resolution, preservation-grade digital scans of these recordings.

A trail of clues, including a cryptic reference in Scott's writings to phonautogram deposits made at "the Academy," led the researchers to another Paris institution, the French Academy of Sciences, where several more of Scott's recordings were stored. Mr. Giovannoni said that his eureka moment came when he laid eyes on the April 1860 phonautogram, an immaculately preserved sheet of rag paper 9 inches by 25 inches.

"It was pristine," Mr. Giovannoni said. "The sound waves were remarkably clear and clean."

His scans were sent to the Lawrence Berkeley lab, where they were converted into sound by the scientists Carl Haber and Earl Cornell. They used a technology developed several years ago in collaboration with the Library of Congress, in which high-resolution "maps" of grooved records are played on a computer using a digital stylus. The 1860 phonautogram was separated into 16 tracks, which Mr. Giovannoni, Mr. Feaster and Mr. Martin meticulously stitched back together, making adjustments for variations in the speed of Scott's hand-cranked recording.

Listeners are now left to ponder the oddity of hearing a recording made before the idea of audio playback was even imagined.

"There is a yawning epistemic gap between us and Léon Scott, because he thought that the way one gets to the truth of sound is by looking at it," said Jonathan Sterne, a professor at McGill University in Montreal and the author of "The Audible Past: Cultural Origins of Sound Reproduction."

Scott is in many ways an unlikely hero of recorded sound. Born in Paris in 1817, he was a man of letters, not a scientist, who worked in the printing trade and as a librarian. He published a book on the history of shorthand, and evidently viewed sound recording as an extension of stenography. In a self-published memoir in 1878, he railed against Edison for "appropriating" his methods and misconstruing the purpose of recording technology. The goal, Scott argued, was not sound reproduction, but "writing speech, which is what the word phonograph means."

In fact, Edison arrived at his advances on his own. There is no evidence that Edison drew on knowledge of Scott's work to create his phonograph, and he retains the distinction of being the first to reproduce sound.

"Edison is not diminished whatsoever by this discovery," Mr. Giovannoni said.

Paul Israel, director of the Thomas A. Edison Papers at Rutgers University in Piscataway, N.J., praised the discovery as a "tremendous achievement," but called Edison's phonograph a more significant technological feat.

"What made Edison different from Scott was that he was trying to reproduce sound and he succeeded," Mr. Israel said.

But history is finally catching up with Scott.

Mr. Sterne, the McGill professor, said: "We are in a period that is more similar to the 1860s than the 1880s. With computers, there is an unprecedented visualization of sound."

The acclaim Scott sought may turn out to have been assured by the very sonic reproduction he disdained. And it took a group of American researchers to rescue Scott's work from the musty vaults of his home city. In his memoir, Scott scorned his American rival Edison and made brazen appeals to French nationalism. "What are the rights of the discoverer versus the improver?" he wrote less than a year before his death in 1879. "Come, Parisians, don't let them take our prize."

"Idol" Banter
Meet the boys

Ann Powers

Simon is already nervous. Not only did he trash adorably campy Danny Noriega simply because he raised the shadow of Sanjaya-that snap! Danny gave Mr. Crest Whitestrips after earning the honorific "hideous" was the best moment of the night-but he criticized the gang for not being current, over and over again. This contest is meant to discover a recording artist, Simon insisted, and please, male contestants, don't forget our former "Idols" are getting dropped from their labels left and right. Show me something that will sell!

What will sell this year, if it proves to be male at all, will probably not be able to drink legally. 16-year-old former Star Search winner David Archuleta and 20-year-old Christian jam-bander Jason Castro scored the night's home runs, their earnest, quivering personalities complementing gorgeously bland performances. I will say that Archuleta has that special vocal something-a really creamy, irresistible tone that even the most egregious excesses of melisma can't erase. Castro seems forgettable to me, beyond perfect skin-but the little-girl audience that keeps "Idol" afloat has voted cute many times before.

Add a few to those two Simon-approved cuties and you've got a veritable Jackson 5 of teen dreams: hippie Garrett, "High School Musical" character Colton, and boy-band vet Robbie give girls a chance to range widely, voting for their type. Unless your type is Chris Brown, that is; the only African American male contestant is the singularly-named Chikezie, who's definitely going for the Luther lovers out there. I predict this year's Velvet Teddy Bear won't last the week, and we'll be back to contemplating androgynes.

My favorite androgyne is the slightly older (and already underrated) David Hernandez, who represents for Chicano soul, and has a tone that's almost as lovely as that other David's. But Hernandez is a striver who seems to have been around a couple of blocks, and if innocence is what "Idol" wants to package this year, he may not be long for the stage.

Yet we must also contemplate the opposite of innocence: the Evil That is Michael Johns. Not only is Johns super-seasoned (and, at 29, ancient for "Idol"), Web-circulated rumors say he betrayed his mates in the pretentiously-named band Film to pursue his solo career. But let's face it, people—he's hot. He rocks like someone who's actually had carnal relations, and the vague scent of seediness about him only enhances his charm. Has "American Idol" ever had a real villain—or a real, night-crawling, bohemian rocker? (I like Daughtry, but he's a family man underneath that mascara.) The ascent of Johns could signal something really different for "Idol," rather than just a nice potential date for last year's alpha adolescent, Jordin Sparks. I'm hissing him on.

The Eyeliner Wars

Josh Eells

The streets of Mexico have become a dangerous place
for los emos, where riots have started over boys wearing
makeup and skinny jeans. How did shy, alienated kids
become this country's most hated subculture?

Yahir lives in Mexico City, in a modest apartment he shares with his mom and his sister. A baby-faced 15-year-old with dimpled cheeks and kohl-ringed eyes, he wears his hair in a carefully choreographed ballet of spikes and swirls and paints his fingernails in florid Technicolor—cherry red for the right hand, tulip pink for the left. "Sometimes I like to not match," he says. He enjoys movies and shopping, and his best subject in school is math. Asked to describe himself, he uses the Spanish word sensible—sensitive. In the evenings, after he's finished his homework, his favorite thing to do is to sit in his room and listen to music. And, because he's 15 and sensitive, what he usually listens to is emo.

Two months ago, Yahir was on his way home from school when he was accosted in the subway by a group of older, bigger boys. "There were seven of them," Yahir says and they surrounded him and started calling him names: "Faggot," "queer," "little bitch."

It was 5 o'clock, the height of rush hour, and the station was packed, but no one intervened. Yahir saw two policemen nearby and called to them. They didn't come.

One of the boys grabbed Yahir, pinning him against the concrete wall. He pulled out a pair of scissors. "Your haircut is gay," he said, gripping Yahir's black bangs. "Let me fix it." As the others held Yahir down, the bigger boy started cutting off his bangs, one violent snip at a time. Yahir was terrified. "!Ayudame!" he yelled—"Help me!" The police, he says, just stood there laughing.

In America, being an emo fan—one of those dark, anguished teens who listen to Dashboard Confessional and whose My-Space moods are set permanently to "sad"—might make you the butt of jokes or, worse, totally normal. In Mexico, it makes you a target. In the past few months, waves of anti-emo violence have erupted in cities from the capital to the border. Los emos have been kicked, beaten, spat on, slapped; observers have called it a witch hunt, a crusade and, most frequently, un linchamiento— a lynching.

"I walk around afraid a lot," Yahir says. It's a cloudy afternoon in late March, and he's sitting on the steps of the Glorieta de Insurgentes, a vast red-brick plaza where Mexico City's emos like to congregate. Yahir comes to the Glorieta most weekends, to catch up with friends and talk about bands (AFI is a new favorite). "It's safe here," he says. "We're free to express ourselves."

We've been talking for a few minutes when a fearsome-looking cholo—early 20s, shirtless, with skull tattoos and a shaved head—walks up and, for no apparent reason, thrusts his middle finger in Yahir's face. Yahir ignores him. Sneering, the guy mutters something, flicks his lit cigarette into the boy's face and walks away.

Stunned, we ask Yahir is he's all right. "Sí, sí," he nods, rubbing his cheek. "I'm OK. It only burned me a little."

Why would he do that? We ask in disbelief.

Yahir's voice is sad, but matter-of-fact: "Because he hates us."

Though it probably peaked in the U.S. a couple of years ago, in Mexico, emo is still a growth industry. According to Camilo Lara, the head of EMI Music Mexico, the genre accounts for as much as 25 percent of Mexico's mushrooming rock market. The biggest acts are American bands like Fall Out Boy and My Chemical Romance, but there are also homegrown stars like Panda, a My Chem clone whose 2006 breakthrough, Para Ti Con Desprecio (For You With Contempt), has sold more than 200,000 copies—double-platinum in Mexico, on par with the country's biggest pop groups.

Mexican fans have long embraced the darker side of rock, from mopey '80s groups like Depeche Mode and Morrissey to contemporary gloom magnates like Interpol. "We're a very melodramatic country," says Lara, sitting in his office in Mexico City's chic Zona Rosa district. "Telenovelas, bullfights—we love the spectacle." Add to this Mexico's endless infatuation with mortality—what the poet Octavio Paz once called its "cult of death"—and the fact that 40 percent of Mexicans are under age 18, and emo's popularity is no surprise. Adolescent disaffection, like love, knows no borders.

LosEmos_articleLarge.jpg

But for every heartfelt emo devotee, there's another kid who can't stand it. Mexican Web sites teem with loathing, like the blog Movimiento Ati-Emosexual, or the popular YouTube clip "75 Reasons to Hate Los Emos." (No. 59: "All their clothes are size 14 kids." No. 25: "Everything affects them.") In December, a VJ named

Kristoff delivered an on-air rant slamming emo and the kids who listen to it. "Emo is for 15-year-old girls who are just getting hair you-know-where," he said. "It has not ideas, no musicians. It's . . . a stupid, dumb-ass trend."

In March, the hate turned violent. It started in Queretaro, an industrial hub tw0 hours north of Mexico City. For weeks, word had been circulating via e-mails and message boards that a group of students were plotting to reclaim the city's Plaza de Armas from the emos who congregated there. On Friday, March 7, they struck. Around 7 p.m., what police later described as "a massive concentration of juveniles" (as many as 800) descended on the plaza, pounding their fists and shouting, "Kill the emos!" By the time authorities dispersed the crowd three hours later, 28 people had been arrested and three emos were beaten so badly they had to be hospitalized.

As grainy camera-phone footage of the attacks made its way around the Web, the violence began to ripple outward. Similar clashes occurred in Puebla and Tijuana. Demonstrators took to the streets in the capital. The media weighed in with screaming headlines ("Emo Wars!") and breathless op-eds. Most of the articles condemned the attacks, but others seemed to blame the victims. Several stories included textbookish descriptions of the emos, for the benefit of concerned but clueless parents:

Emos are children between the ages of 15 and 18 whose philosophy is above all emotional . . . Their style is androgynous: tight black pants, pink or purple sweaters two sizes too small, sneakers of the brand Converse or Vans, as many as two belts . . . They listen to bands like My Chemical Romance and Evanescence and have a special appreciation for the films of Tim Burton . . . They wear long bangs covering their forehead and at least one eye . . . They cut themselves with razors and say they're misunderstood.

"It's kind of like watching the adults in Footloose try to figure out why the kids are dancing," says Pete Wentz, the bassist and lyricist for Fall Out Boy. Some of the media's claims seemed patently ridiculous: Emos worship Satan; they're all bisexuals. One prominent psychologist estimated that 40 percent were suicidal. Grandmothers were calling mothers, neighbors were calling friends: Is your daughter an emo? Is she dangerous? Is she evil?

"It's the textbook definition of a moral panic," says Jon Savage, author of Teenage: The Creation of youth culture. "All it takes is one mention in the press and the public goes crazy: 'delinquency of youth,' 'country going to the dogs.' The typical stuff."

The media portrayed the riots as a battle between opposing youth cultures, like L.A.'s Zoot Suit Riots of 1943 or the mod-rocker showdowns in 1960s England. But those were clashes between two distinct groups: drunken sailors vs. Hispanic dandies; bikers vs. fashion plates. The emos were being attacked by everyone—an ad hoc coalition of punks, skaters, gangsters, metalheads and Goths. Viewed from the outside, through blurry YouTube clips and snarky posts on Perezhilton.com, the whole thing seemed bizarre: a cultural civil war being wages by groups that, to American eyes, were essentially indistinguishable. "It's like watching Pakistan fight India," Wentz says. I mean, dudes— you're all 14; you're all miserable; you all think the world doesn't understand you, and it's quite possible that the world doesn't understand you. Shouldn't you be on the same team?"

To Mexican youth, however, the distinctions are clear. Mater Olvera is a sociologist at the Universidad Nacional Autonoma de Mexico and a longtime rock-scene vet who wrote a book, Sonidos Urbanos, about Mexico City's musical subcultures. "In Mexico," she says, "the tribe you belong to is everything." In addition to the emos, Olvera says, there are dozens of other so-called tribus urbanas: los punks, los skaters, los metaleros, los reggaetoneros, los rockabilies, los darketos (literally "the darks," also called los góticos), los fresas (preps, a.k.a. "strawberries," named for their short-sleeve pink Polos), los hippies, los skas.

It's a crowded landscape, and resources are scarce. Mexico has nearly twice the population density of the U.S. but only a fraction of the cultural bandwidth. Tribes have to compete for space both ideological and geographical. "We live in a city of 21 million people," Olvera says. "There are only a few radio stations, only a few newspapers, only a few magazines, only a few playgrounds at which to congregate. It's very difficult to gain a space of one's own."

You can watch this struggle play out every week at a long—running Mexico City flea market called El Chopo. For the past 28 years, the Chopo has been the city's headquarters for all things countercultural, with scores of vendors hawking everything from hand-blown hash pipes to pirated CD-Rs. Yellowing fliers promote upcoming shows, a rickety wooden stage hosts bands and misfit kids flock from all over the city to swap music and gossip. It's MySpace before MySpace existed.

Gogo, 18, comes to El Chopo every weekend. He's loitering in the back in Dr. Martens and frayed black Levis, a red bandanna tied around his neck like a Zapatista. Asked how he'd classify himself—skater, punk, metalero—he shakes his head: "Nada mas busura." Just trash. Gogo claims to have thrown bottles and rocks at emo kids, and he says they deserve it. "They're copycats, plain and simple," he says. "They have no originality. They have nothing of their own. All they do is steal our style."

It's a common sentiment among emo's opponents: The emos are inauthentic, they're posers, they steal from the real punks. (Never mind that most of these real punks were born circa 1990.)

Others say they hate the emos because their music is so terrible, an argument that presents its own problems: "They think reggaeton is terrible, too," says Uriel Waizel, a Mexico City music journalist. "But they don't go around picking fights with reggaeton fans, because reggae-ton fans are big."

In reality, there are deeper issues at work. One of them is class. "The emos are typically from the middle class," Mafer Olvera says. "They have the money to buy the sneakers and nail polish and fashionable haircuts. They have time to spend all night on their computers. They have computers, period. They're simply better off, and a lot of the other tribes resent it." (Reason to hate Los Emos No. 66: "They all have at least one iPod.")

Then there's the matter of homophobia (Reason No. 37: "They've all kissed boys"). "Mexico is a very conservative, right-wing country," says Dr. Hector Castillo Berthier, director of UNAM's Institute of Social Research. "In the areas where the attacks started—Queretaro, Jalisco, Guanajuato—the Catholic church is still very powerful and very intolerant. It's similar to America's Bible Belt. Their basic message is, We don't like you because you're homosexual."

Not that all the emos are gay—in fact, most of the ones we meet say they aren't. But the mere sight of a boy in pink barrettes and eyeliner is an affront both to the church and to Mexico's deeply entrenched code of machismo. Most of the epithets hurled at the emos—puto, joto, maricon—are anti-gay slurs, and several kids recall their dads telling them to "quit crying" and "be a man." For the country's dominant pro-family right, a Mexican boy dressing effeminately and talking about his feelings isn't just subversive—it's a deliberate act of provocation. "Even to others subcultures," says Castillo, "these kids are a threat."

On the last weekend in March, the soundtrack to the emo wars is the noisy drone of a police helicopter. It's a hot, bright Saturday, and hundreds of emos are assembling for a protest march from the Glorieta de insurgents to El Chopo. As kids start to trickle in to the bowl-shaped plaza, they greet one another with hugs and cheek0pecks, and unfurl banners-proclaiming, I'M EMO AND I DEMAND RESPECT! And KRISTOFF, FUCK YOUR MOTHER! Hair product is sprayed; reflections are checked. Makeup is applied, sweated off and reapplied.

Michel, 15, arrives at the Glorieta wearing a silver lip ring and skinny white jeans—"to symbolize peace," he says. An aspiring computer engineer, he'll probably quit the scene by about age 20: "When you grow up, you have to start thinking for yourself. You can't care so much about image." Being an emo has gotten him pushed, spat at and banded gay ("But I'm not," he adds quickly), and he says he hasn't been to El Chopo since a punk stuck bubble-gum in his hair there a few months back. "I don't think they're going to attack us today, thought. Too many cameras."

He's right about that. If there's one thing emo kids—they of the online diaries and bedroom self-portraits—know how to do, it's self-promote. The Glorieta is a zoo—there are twice as many spectators as marchers, and almost as many photographers. Even the police snap camera-phone pics. At one point, a ponytailed radical from a nearby university climbs atop a statue and delivers a fist-pumping speech about free expression and oppressive autocratic regimes. "Keep fighting for your freedom!" he urges the emos. "!Viva libertad!"

At six minutes to 3, a man with a megaphone rallies the troops. "Ready, boys and girls?" he asks. "Remember, try to stay spread out, so it looks like there are more of us. And don't forget to be safe! OK? Entonces, !vamonos!"

With a cheer, the kids begin their hour-long crawl through the streets of Mexico City, a fizzy mass of Pixy Stix legs and fat-ironed hair. Occasionally there is chanting: "Together! United! We'll never be defeated!" or "¡Tolerancia! ¡Tolerancia!" halfway through, two girls break into a pep-squad cheer: "Give me an E! Give me an M! Give me an O! What's that spell?!" On Martinez de la Torre street, a TV news crew materialized, and a girl in leopard ears ducks to hide behind her friends. "That's the channel my mom watches!" she gasps.

Finally the procession arrives at El Chopo. Stretched above the entrance to the marketplace is a hand-painted sign: welcome to the chopo, emos. But the rest of the scene isn't quite so hospitable—200 or so punks chanting, "Emo is shit!" in the middle of the street. Separating them from the emos is a battalion of riot police wielding shields and truncheons; it's meant as a precaution, but it feels more like a provocation. "Assholes! Assholes!" the punks chant at the cops. Someone lobs a half-empty plastic Coke bottle over the barricade, then another, then another. Soon, there are rocks. One punk, in a bandanna and black hoodie that says, BE A PARIOT—KILL AN EMO, rips down the welcome sign and starts stomping on it.

After about 10 minutes, the emos retreat down an empty side street. It's not quite the reception they were hoping for; still, the march is deemed a success. "We had to make our voices heard," says Javier, 18. "We had to show them we're not afraid."

For the emos, being heard is no small victory. "There are many things on the Mexican political agenda right now," Hector Castillo says. "Crime, oil, drug cartels, election scandals, U.S. relations. Young people are not one of them." In a country with more than 40 million young people, the emos aren't just campaigning for tolerance—they're standing up for teenagehood itself.

"A month ago these kids had a fashion," he adds. "Now they have a flag."

A few days later Blender is back at the Glorieta, looking for a club that doesn't exist. We've heard tales of a semi-secret establishment called Los Sillones (The Armchairs), where underage emos can go after school to buy beer and hang out. It even has its own MySpace page. But no one we talk to has ever heard of the place—or at least, no one's admitting it.

Eventually a sympathetic kid named Omar leads us down the street to a skate shop. Upstairs, on the second floor, is a smoky room, maybe 60 feet long, with bare cement walls lit by the glow of blue neon. The armchairs are gone; the owners haled them away six months ago because people kept trying to have sex on them. But Omar says the emos still come to mamazear—a slang term they use to describe no-strings attached makeout sessions with friends or strangers of either sex. "It's just a place to have a drink, listen to music," he says. "And you don't have to worry, because it's OK to be emo."

Omar and his friends call themselves the Scream Senseless Crew—"because we scream and scream, but no one hears us. " They give pro-tolerance talks in the subway and recently organized a weekend street fair. What bothers them more than the abuse and harassment they get from peers are the lies perpetuated about them in the media. "The newspapers say we cut ourselves, or that we're depressed all the time," Omar says. "But it's not true. Sure, sometimes we get sad, just like everyone else. But mostly we lead pretty happy lives."

Los Sillones doesn't close for a few hours, but Omar has to get going. Twice a week the members of Scream Senseless pick up trash around the Glorieta, and today it's his turn. He's also try-

·ing not to spend money: He and the Crew are saving up to print matching T-shirts, which they plan on wearing to the next tolerance march. They found a guy who'll do it pretty cheap, and they already have a design picked out. On the front will be their initials, SSC. And on the back, their motto: Live and let live.

Shit Magnet

*Say what you will about garage-punk phenom
Jay Reatard. He's heard it all before*

J. Bennett

*Never explain. Your friends do not need it, and your
enemies will not believe you anyway.*
—Elbert Hubbard, American philosopher,
illustrator and soap salesman, 1896

There's a rock band on the video screen, three dudes playing fast
and loose in white T-shirts. Camera bulbs flash while people in
the audience bob their heads and point fingers in the air. A guy
in a baseball cap climbs onstage and staggers briefly in the direction of the drum kit. The bandleader grabs the interloper
and attempts to steer him back into the crowd. The interloper's
shirt rips as he's pushed offstage, and the bandleader loses his
grip. The bandleader grabs him again. The shirt rips again. Finally,
the bandleader spins the dude around and decks him—right in
the squash, by the looks of it. The contact sequence is repeated
six times in rapid succession, like a boxing highlight reel edited
for maximum comedic effect. When the footage picks up again,

the band members are packing up their gear. Large factions of the audience are booing. Others are clapping. *Everyone* seems to be yelling. Someone shouts, "You shouldn't get paid then, pussies!" The bandleader is wearing a yellow jacket now. He directs a stream of indecipherable profanities at someone near the front of the stage. Then he walks off.

The next day, the bandleader posts about the incident on his blog: "Last night's show in Toronto got completely fucked up. . . .We don't need people getting so wild that they jump on-stage and smash our gear—but that's exactly what happened. . . . People were throwing beer bottles at us, someone jumped on-stage and smashed my pedals, another guy took a full pitcher of beer and dumped it all over the rest of my pedals and then threw it right at my Flying V, breaking the pickup and the input elec-tronics. After three songs all our gear was smashed and unusable. Even when shit gets that crazy at [a] Circle Jerks show, there's at least some security, but when I asked [the promoter] about it be-fore the show he told me, "I thought you guys were a garage band.""

Another time, in Dallas, the bandleader shows up drunk to his own gig. There's an altercation. OK, *two* altercations: one with the opening band and one with the promoter. The bandleader kicks the opening band off his show because he's just read in an Austin weekly that the group decided not to use the tracks he produced for them. The argument with the promoter is a little more con-voluted. It starts because underage fans are being denied entry— even though it's an all-ages show—and ends with the bandleader leaving the venue (without playing), eating acid and watching *The Shining* in his hotel room. The promoter posts his version of the events on his blog, Parade of Flesh. Brooklyn Vegan reposts his entry. Idolator makes fun of the comments on Brooklyn Vegan. Then Pitchfork contacts the bandleader to write a response. He wisely declines, but the story lives on in teenage-punk-rock-shit-head-Interhole-warrior infamy because the thing about the Interhole is that it never fucking ends.

Welcome to Jay Reatard's Wild America, a place where the bandleader's every move is viewed through the twin microscopes of YouTube and the blogosphere, where everybody has a self-righteous opinion and where everybody wants a piece of the action—whatever the action might be. Type Reatard's name into a YouTube search, and the first clip that comes up is the scene described in this story's first paragraph, otherwise known as "Jay Reatard punching kid at the Silver Dollar." The second clip that comes up is entitles "Jay Reatard—Kicks a dude in the face in Vegas!" Head over to the blogosphere and a torrential shit-storm of misspelled words and grammatically challenged accusations rolls down the screen like virtual punk-rock vomit: tales of hissy fits, walkouts, freakouts, punch-outs, pissing matches, lysergic hysteria, underage MySpace skanks, confrontation, obliteration, elimination. A foul-smelling, never-ending Niagara of he said/she said/Jay said/the promoter said back-and-forth and on and on—allegations, exaggerations and misrepresentations smeared across the digital walls of the punk-rock-blog basement like one gigantic Dirty Sanchez.

"I fell like sometimes I can't do anything anymore without somebody knowing something or going on Brooklyn Vegan and posting some shit," Reatard says. "[That site] is like the TMZ of the blogosphere. If that's a world, they're probably the lamest planet in that universe. They'll run any piece of garbage they can in order to get people to come to their Web site to see adverts for American Apparel."

Not that Reatard claims to be an angel, either: "I take full responsibility for everything I've ever done," he says. "I'm not sorry for any of it. There are exaggerated versions of stories on the Internet, but a wise man once said, 'Don't apologize for anything.' It's just what happens. I don't control the Internet. I've seen days when I wanted to kill it, but I can't control it."

Without venturing down the steep, slippery slope of separating fact from fiction in online forums, it's safe to say that Reatard's biggest problem is that he pays attention to any of this shit to begin with. "I get pissed at myself for feeling like I have to defend myself on any level," he admits. "I've purposely set up a lifestyle where I don't have to answer to anyone for what I do, and the fact that I feel like I waste even one second thinking, 'Wow, man, this dude leaving YouTube comments doesn't like me . . . ' It's like, 'Get a fucking life. I have one. You should try it.'"

On the other hand, Reatard seems to thrive upon negativity. Talk shit, heap scorn, call names—he'll just write another song. At age 28, he has 16 full-length albums under his belt and more 7-inches and compilation tracks than a pirated iTunes playlist. "It's fuel for me, man, fuel for the fire," he explains. "At some point, you get used to people not liking you, and then it just becomes part of life. If you don't like my music, that's fine, but it's like this modern Internet phenomenon that all of a sudden people want to [critique] your personality. Chuck Berry was a horrible human being, but so what? You don't have to get personal. I never listen to a record and go, 'I bet Dee Dee Ramone was a real asshole.' I'm sure he was. Blogs have killed the mystery."

Which begs the question: Why does Reatard have one? "Initially, it was something I started doing when I realized I was going to be in this long process of finding a new label," he says. "I figured I'd put up some new songs for free, just to entertain the few thousand people who might be interested. But the more I think about it, I'm not sure why I did it. It's just another place on the Interweb for people to post hate notes."

RIVER CITY RHIZOME

At the lamplighter lunge in Memphis, Tennessee, longtime bartender Miss Shirley enforces a no-cussing policy. You can order a beer here like they do in the movies—without specifying the brand—because Miss Shirley only serves two kinds: Pabst Blue Ribbon and PBR. Jay Lindsey, aka Jay Reatard, is a regular here. He exalts the virtues of the Lamplighter's grease-caked cheeseburgers, and swears he's seen Miss Shirley throw people out for swearing. She's a regular Memphis institution, it seems, in a city full of institutions such as Graceland, Beale Street, BBQ ribs, Sun Studio and Stax Records.

Reatard has lived in or around Memphis for most of his life, excluding the few months he moved to Atlanta while writing and recording his first solo album, *Blood Visions*. Despite its reputation as a music city, Memphis suits Reatard because few people here seem to know who he is or what he does. "Around Memphis, half the time people don't even know if I'm here or not," he says. "I'll walk into a bar and people will be like, "You're home?" I'll have been home for a month. It's cool, though. I can disappear here."

Moments later, a pitcher of Pabst arrives that neither of us ordered. Miss Shirley points to a man seated at the bar and tells us it's on him. Reatard raises his glass in the man's direction. The man flashes a toothy grin, waves and then leans toward his buddy on the next barstool. "Do you know who that is right there?" the man asks. "He's Memphis's own version of punk fuckin' rock!"

Reatard pours himself a fresh beer. "This whole interview will be a series of contradictions," he says, picking up right where he left off. "I'm always confident when I'm recording here that no one's gonna care what I'm doing. And up until this point—the past year or so—it seemed like I was going to be successful in keeping no one caring. My worst nightmare was that if I signed with a label, I'd have to go to New York or LA to record and have some A&R guy sticking his head in.

As nightmares go, an all-expense-paid trip to New York or LA isn't exactly wake-up-sweating material. But Reatard is used to doing things exactly his own way. He's been recording and producing his own albums since he was 15. When LA's In The Red Records released *Blood Vision* in 2006, the record quickly became the most lauded of his career and subsequently landed him a deal with renowned indie powerhouse Matador Records. It only took a decade-plus of slugging it out in low-rent garage-punk outfits like the Reatards, the Lost Sounds, the Angry Angles, the Bad Times, Terror Visions, Destruction Unit, Nervous Patterns and the Final Solutions for Reatard to realize it was time to go solo.

Even during those early years, Reatard's reputation preceded him. "I was intimidated by him at first," say In The Red founder Larry Hardy. "I had been told he could be a volatile character. The first time I saw the Lost Sounds, they were opening for the Dirtbombs, and I just thought they were amazing. Jay was very confrontational, but in a very funny way in that he was putting down the audience, which I'm a big fan of. But that sort of prevented me from going up and introducing myself. He seemed really unapproachable. So it wound up being funny when I ended up working with him and found out that he's actually super nice."

Reatard's career as a collaborator came to an end in 2005, when the other members of the Lost Sounds—including his then-girl-friend, Alicja Trout, currently or River City Tanlines—wanted to put him on antidepressants. "I guess I was hard to deal with on tour, and after years of putting up with me, as they said, they gave me an ultimatum," Reatard says. "I did it because I didn't wanna lose my band, but halfway through the tour, I started pretending I was taking them when I wasn't anymore. The weird thing is, it was almost like they could tell. So I guess it *was* working."

Unsurprisingly, the medication wasn't exactly conducive to making music. "It was conducive to me giving over control of the band to whoever else wanted it," Reatard points out. "I didn't give a shit anymore. I was taking these pills that took away any ambi-tion I had to fight. And that band was a constant battle for sen-iority, like 'Who's the alpha rocker?'"

"Jay and Alicja broke up while we were working on an album, and I kinda got stuck in the middle of a couple of blowups be-tween them," Hardy offers. "That wasn't much fun, but usually it was just a matter of calming down one party or the other."

Reatard clearly doesn't miss those days. "Music isn't a group sport for me," he says. "The Lost Sounds was a fun band musically, but it was a negative experience overall. It was unfortunate that we started out as friends and ended as mortal enemies, but I'd rather go back and listen to those records than have any of those people as friends. I'm cool with one person from that band, but if I had to sacrifice the rest of them to make music, it was worth it. It's not good to be sitting in a van with a bunch of people you wanna kill."

His current touring band consists of bassist Stephen Pope and drummer Billy Hayes, both of whom were borrowed from fellow Memphis garage denizens the Boston Chinks. "I first started talking to Stephen at—his parents are gonna love this—a drug house that we always used to cross paths at," Reatard says, "I think the initial idea of 'Hey, why don't you come jam with me?' was one of those drug-induced, talking-too-much kind of situations. But then they came over, and we jammed. I didn't tell them I already had a European tour set up."

Pope hadn't played much bass before—he plays guitar in the Chinks—but he already had the essential chemistry with Hayes. "Stephen wasn't so goo at bass at first, but I wanted him in my band because he's probably the raddest person I've ever met," Reatard says. "And that was a lot more important to me than having (bass virtuoso) Jaco Pastorius in my band or whoever."

"I don't know how shocked he was, but I had never even picked up a bass before," Pop admits when we meet him later at his house in Memphis. "I learned the songs really fast, though, and we went to South by Southwest and then to Europe. But I still don't really know how to play bass. I know how to play the songs we do, but I can't improvise at all. Hopefully I'll never have to jam."

Pope, who rocks an impressive Melvins-esque afro (Reatard refers to King Buzzo as Pope's "long lost uncle") and cruises Memphis in a purple Cadillac, has since taken on several additional roles in Reatard's life, including tour manager, babysitter and driver. On their most recent US tour, Pope drove all 13,000 miles. "Yeah, I drive the whole time," he confirms. "I keep Jay's passport at my house. It's fine by me. I know where the money is. And because I have to drive, I can't drink too much, so I don't feel like shit every day. And I get paid extra when we're on tour."

The money isn't just for the driving, though. It's party for playing good cop to Reatard's drunk/angry/bad cop. "Jay's reputation has worked to our advantage sometimes," Pope explains. "When the whole Toronto thing happened, I was trying to figure out everything with the promoter. Jay was obviously already upset, but the promoter of the show really wanted to talk to him. I knew that was a bad idea, so I acted like even I was too scared to talk to Jay, like, 'No, man—he's too crazy. I don't even wanna go near him, so you *definitely* shouldn't.'"

At 22 years old, Hayes and Pope are both younger than Reatard, which is likely a reason why the relationship works so well. "Billy's kind of like me when I was a teenager," Reatard says. "He spends a lot of time alone, and music is all he's interested in. I dig that. A lot of people might say that's lazy, but if you're self-employed, you work when you wanna work and that's always been my goal. My dad never worked for anybody—he always worked for himself. If I don't wanna wake up till noon, so what? That's kind of the allure of it."

From Reatard's perspective, Pope and Hayes constitute the best band he's ever had. "We've played two hundred and fifty shows to-gether in a year and a half, and we've only had one fistfight," Reatard says. "We were in Serbia, and I was all shit-faced at our bed-and-breakfast. They had this wall of empty Coca-Cola crates, and I made up some drunken game to see who could crawl up this fifteen-foot-tall pile of plastic crates. Billy used a chair to climb up and was teasing me, like, 'I won! I won!' And I was so wasted, I ba-sically turned into a toddler and whaled on him over some stupid race at five in the morning. I felt so fucking terrible the next day. I was like, 'Oh, my god, I just jeopardized the best drummer I've ever played with—and a friendship—over a childish game.' Other than that, we get along pretty well, I think. But who knows? My perspective could be pretty fucked up after the Lost Sounds."

PORTRAIT OF THE ARTIST AS A
YOUNG MAN CHEWING ADDERALL

With a back catalog that rivals musicians three times his age, it's understandable that Reatard's name is almost always printed with the word "prolific" in the immediate vicinity. At one point, he was writing a song a day. "I think Memphis has some great musicians, but it's filled with some of the most un-ambitious people I've ever seen," he says. "They just sit around and complain about why things aren't happening for them. I want to be the opposite of that. I don't wanna wake up and not have stability. At some point, it flipped in my head that music was the only way to get that, so I started forcing myself to write a song every day. Even if no one cares, I could say I did it. I still get pissed off if I go to sleep at night and I haven't recorded or written a song."

This self-discipline explains why Reatard's Matador deal launched with six 7-inch singles, pressed throughout the past year. "The way I'm working with Matador, it's kind of slowed down," he explains. "I'm still *working* on a song every day, but I've learned not to put the pressure on myself to be that hyper-creative. I've learned to relax and realize that it's not the end of the world if I can't write a song for a week. Everybody says, "Oh, it must be so much pressure being on a bigger label," but man, I put more pressure on myself when no one was looking than Matador could ever put on me."

All this self-demand is the result of considerably less-than-auspicious circumstances. Reatard moved out of his house at 15 and dropped out of high school. At 16 he lied on an application to land a job at a stained-glass window factory. His parents moved away when he was 17. One day, his employer figured out his real age and fired him on the spot. From that point on, Reatard lived off of music by playing in six to eight bands at a time. "If I played once a month with each of them and made fifty or a hundred bucks each time, I'd get by," he recalls. "I was a 'dollar-menunaire,' man. I as definitely a scumbag, but it worked out."

When we suggest he didn't miss much by ditching high school, Reatard quickly ticks off a list of youthful pleasantries that far too many of us take for granted. "Only the finer things in life—like friends, girlfriends, being able to do fun things on the weekends. This was before the Internet, so there weren't a whole lot of options for meeting people. That was crucial. People are amazed that I wrote all this music when I was so young, but I didn't have anything else to do other than eat fast food and think about killing myself."

He may put slightly less pressure on himself these days, but Reatard is just as regimented as ever. He gets u around 10:30 each morning and lets his dog, Cola—a German shepherd mix—outside. Then he walks to the corner store to get an energy drink. (He's not a coffee-drinker: "It just makes me too nervous, man. But a nice can of Pimp Juice doesn't.") He tries to buy a different brand every day because he thinks he might be developing a tolerance to them. He avoids Red Bull because he associates it with the taste of alcohol, and he doesn't booze in the middle of the day—at least not on a workday. Then he'll talk on the phone for an hour or so, making necessary business calls. By noon he's hunkered down and recording until five or six, at which point he'll grab a bite at his favorite Vietnamese restaurant before returning home to listen obsessively to everything he's recorded that day. "Then I'll try to go to sleep after all the caffeine I've consumed. Wake up. Repeat. It's like that movie *Groundhog Day*. Sometimes I feel like Bill Murray."

Reatard generally doesn't like to take drugs while making music, but this morning he popped some Adderall to enhance his recording mojo. "I went to eat at this restaurant the other day," he says, "and when the waiter brought back my credit card, he'd charged me for, like, half of the stuff we ate and put a bunch of Adderalls in that little leather receipt-holder. I didn't really know the guy, but we have a mutual friend in another city."

Adderall apparently helps Reatard focus. "I just chew 'em up like Flintstones vitamins," he explains. "Snorting it's useless. You just end up with orange boogers."

FAKING IT

The image is one thing, and the human being is another.
It's very hard to live up to an image.
　　　　　　—Elvis Presley, at a June 1972 press conference

As it turns out, *Blood Visions* was a concept record Reatard wrote about stalking and killing his ex-girlfriend. "Only a few people caught onto that," he says, "It's about this stalker guy. I put myself into this exaggerated, sensationalized character where I just took my own personality and multiplied it by ten. Some dude wrote his senior thesis about it and posted it online. It was like sixteen pages, where he breaks down every song. I think he was the only person who got it. It was wicked, man—it's like he was on acid or something. He got everything right" [*Ed. Note: A week after this interview, neither Reatard nor* self-titled *could fine the thesis online.*]

Reatard's forthcoming Matador full-length, which is tentatively set for a mid-'09 release, won't be quite as morbid. "I'm doing what everybody does when they get old and boring," he says with a laugh. "I'm getting introspective. It's more about me than other people. I think I'm getting to that age where I'm not venting o much about things around me. I'm starting to figure out how I fit in. I feel like I'm part of a bigger picture.

That said, his recording regiment remains as stringent as ever. "My idea is to have 16 songs, with multiple versions of each to choose from," he explains. "With any of the op songs I'm writing now, they could be presented infinite amounts of ways, like whether I want them to be punk songs or more like the acoustic stuff I do sometimes.

Given his aversion to collaborations these days, it's perhaps surprising that Reatard's letting Matador help decide what will make the final album. "If this thing doesn't do well, I want them to play a role in it, so I can blame them, too," he says, implying he's only half joking. "So from the demos to the completed versions, there's a list of people. I'll send stuff to—close friends, people at Matador. . . .Occasionally I'll play a tune for my dad because he knows nothing about music and has the honesty of a small child. I mean, he likes Dwight Yoakam, you know? Sometimes people who are the most removed from what you're doing can have the best perspective."

Expectations for Reatard's album are high among label folks who've worked with him in the past. "[*Blood Visions*] was a jaw-dropper," says Hardy. "Since then, everything he's cranked out has been even more accessible and going in directions I didn't expect. I can see big things happening. He's got the talent to back it up: He's a remarkable guitar player, he's got a good voice, he's got a knack for producing, and his songwriting is incredible. He can do it all, and that's rare."

Matadore founder Chris Lombardi recalls seeing Reatard for the first time at New York City's Cake Shop and being blown away. He followed the artist to a Texas music festival. "At that time, Jay was being approached by numerous majors," Lombardi says. "One of the guys he talked to said something like, "Kurt Cobain killed hair metal; you're gonna kill emo.""

But Lombardi prefers pragmatism to hyperbole. "He could write radio singles until he's blue in the face, but I don't think he needs to stop being Jay," Lombardi says. "We're not expecting the next album to be some massive departure, but maybe it will be. There's no pressure from us."

Reatard tells us that the working title of his next full-length is *Faking It*. When we ask the odds of that becoming the actual title, he says he simply doesn't know, then explains its origin in a bring-it-all-back-home kind of way that most journalists live for. "A lot of people think that I'm contrived, that I'm playing a character," he offers. "I've read things where people say they thought I paid that kid in Toronto to punch him so there'd be a media blitz or something."

But that's a little too tidy.

REVENGE, REATARD STYLE

It is therefore a precept of the law of nature, that in revenge we look not backwards, but forward.
—Thomas Hobbes, *De Cive*, 1641

Believe it or not, Fleetwood Mac's *Tusk* is on the turntable at Jay Reatard's house. Above the sofa hangs a framed poster for the 1981 Canadian horror movie *The Pit*. The plot, according to IMDb.com, is as follows: "Twelve-year-old Jamie Benjamin (Sammy Snyder) is a misunderstood lad. His classmates pick on him, his neighbors think he's weird, and his parents ignore him.

But now Jamie has a secret weapon: Deep in the woods he has discovered a deep pit full of man-eating creatures he calls Trogs . . . and it isn't long before he gets an idea for getting revenge and feeding the Trogs in the process!"

The Pit is one of Reatard's favorite movies, which might be one of the most telling details we've uncovered about him so far. *Blood Visions* was, after all, a revenge record. But in hindsight, it was merely a culmination, the apex of a psychological and behavioral pattern that started years ago. When Reatard was 13, for instance, he shot a raccoon with a bow and arrow. "Archery was my big deal," he says. "I was terrible at it, but something was breaking into our pantry and eating all the dry goods. We lived on the outskirts of Memphis at the time, out near this state park. It was a little bit more rural. My dad was like, 'Kid, I'll give you fifty dollars if you can kill whatever it is.' So I stood outside with my bow and arrow all night until I saw the fucking raccoon go in. I had a friend of mine scare it out, and it ran right up a tree. So I aimed and shot it. I kept pumping arrows into it—I think I shot it eight or nine times. It finally fell out of the tree, and I was pissed because when it fell, it broke about fifty dollars worth of arrows. So I cut its fuckin' head off, boiled the skin off and saved it as a trophy."

Do you still have the skull?

No, but that's when I realized I was a weird kid. I was so angry at this raccoon for eating my oatmeal. But I grew up in the country, so life's pretty disposable out there. I grew up in a farming community. Now it seems kind of inhumane, but at the time, where I grew up, animals weren't the most important thing.

Were you into hunting?

I'd go hunting with my dad, but I could never bring myself to shoot a deer, so I missed a few times, on purpose. My dad wasn't so happy, but I'm not gonna kill Bambi, dude. But if my dad kills him, I'll eat him.

Have you ever considered revenge the motivating factor behind the music you make?

I never even thought of that until you mentioned it last night, but it was pretty apparent when you brought it up. Almost every song I've written in the last three years seems pretty spiteful and based in revenge. The constant theme is the underdog creep who prevails in the end. It sounds so petty, I guess, but I'm actually not that kind of person in my daily life.

That's how you express it, though—through your songs?

Yeah, I guess so. The last Matador single ["Trapped here"] has a mantra that repeats the line, "To watch them choke, it makes me breathe." I'm still pretty immature. I've got that teen angst, but it keeps me young somewhat—at least my attitude. You know, there's a saying that if you gave a baby a button that would destroy the world and you could explain to them what the button would do, they'd push it immediately. That was my idea when I started a punk band. I wasn't worried about small goals like putting out a seven-inch. I wanted to destroy everything. Now I just write about that instead of trying to physically do it.

How would you physically do it in the past?

I got really into smashing disco balls for a while. Every time we'd be on tour in Europe, the show would end and a disco ball would drop down and the place would turn into a techno dance club. So I thought, "What would bum these dudes out more than if somebody smashed all their fancy lights?" So I smashed one every night on our European tour. I ended up spending over two thousand dollars on disco balls. The last one I broke was actually in the states, at the Empty Bottle in Chicago, and they made me buy it. It's in my house. I told the guy, "If I'm buying it, I'm taking it." It cost me a hundred and fifty bucks. After that, I refused to play the Empty Bottle. But recently, the guy said if we played there, he'd give me the one-fifty back on top of whatever we made. So sometimes being stubborn works out. But I don't know what the void is in my personality that makes me get satisfaction out of stuff like that.

Is revenge the motivating factor for what you're working on now?

It's probably revenge on myself, for wasting time. I feel like I spent so much time in my youth worrying about trivial bullshit. I wasted so much energy and time on things that didn't matter.

Like what?

Like trying to get back at people.

The Tragedy of Britney Spears

She was a pop princess. Now she's in and out of hospitals,
rehab and court. How Britney lost it all

Vanessa Grigoriadis

A pop star at the mall is an eternal cause for happiness, especially on a Sunday afternoon in the Valley. One moment, shoppers in the Westfield Topanga mall are living in the real world, monotonously selecting a new shade of eye shadow or rubbing perfume on wrists, but upon the rapture of Britney Spears, they are giggling, laughing, orgasmic, already sharing their secret on cell phones. "Her legs are actually really skinny," an adolescent whispers into her Sidekick, as Britney beelines for the Betsey Johnson boutique, pseudo-punk designer of evening dresses and splashy heels worn to suburban high school proms. In person, Britney is shockingly beautiful—clear skin, ruby lips, a perfectly proportioned twenty-six-year-old porcelain doll with a nasty weave. She cuts through the crowd swiftly, the way she used to when 20,000 adoring fans mobbed her outside a concert, with her paparazzi boyfriend, Adnan Ghalib, trailing behind.

Only a few kids are in the store, a young girl with her brother and two blondes checking out fake-gold charm bracelets. Britney rifles the racks as the Cure's "Pictures of You" blasts into the airless pink boutique, grabbing a pink lace dress, a few tight black numbers and a frilly red crop top, the kind of shirt that Britney used to wear all the time at seventeen but isn't really appropriate for anyone over that age. Then she ducks into the dressing room with Ghalib. He emerges with her black Am Ex.

The card won't go through, but they keep trying it.

"Please," begs Ghalib, "get this done quickly."

One of the girls runs to Britney's dressing room, explaining the situation through a pink gauze curtain.

A wail emerges from the cubby—guttural, vile, the kind of base animalistic shriek only heard at a family member's deathbed. "Fuck these bitches," screams Britney, each word ringing out between sobs. "These idiots can't do anything right!"

Ghalib dashes over to console her, but she's already spitting, growling, throwing a big bottle of soda on the floor so that it begins to spill underneath the curtain, and then she's got a box of tissues and is throwing them on top of the wet floor along with piles of discarded merchandise. A new card finally goes through, but by then Britney is out the door, leaving her shirt on the ground and replacing it with the red top. "Fuck you, fuck people, fuck, fuck, fuck," she keeps screaming, her face splotchy and red as she crosses the interminable mall floor, the crowd behind her growing larger and larger. "Leave us alone!" yells Ghalib.

The siblings run after Britney to get a video to put up on YouTube, and some of the shopgirls run after her to hand off the merchandise she left behind, and there's an entire bridal party wearing yellow T-shirts who have pulled out camera phones too. A crush of managers in black shirts and gold name tags try to keep the peace, but the crowd running after Britney gets larger, and now the shopgirls have started to catch up to her, one of them slipping spectacularly in her platform shoes, grazing her elbow. She pulls herself up, mustering the strength to tap Britney's shoulder. "Um, I'm from the South too," she mumbles, "and I was wondering if I could get a picture with you for my little sister."

Britney turns to Ghalib and grabs his arm. "I don't want her talking to me!" she screams. She whirls around and stares the girl deep in the eyes, her lips almost vibrating with anger. "I don't know who you think I am, bitch," she snarls, "but I'm not that person."

If there is one thing that has become clear in the past year of Britney's collapse—the most public downfall of any star in history—it's that she doesn't want anything to do with the person the world thought she was. She is not a good girl. She is not America's sweetheart. She is an inbred swamp thing who chain-smokes, doesn't do her nails, tells reporters to "eat it, snort it, lick it, fuck it" and screams at people who want pictures for their little sisters. She is not someone who can live by the most basic social rules—she is someone who, when she has had her one- and two-year-old sons taken completely out of her care, with zero visitation rights, appeared at Los Angeles' Superior Court to convince the judge to give her kids back, but then decided not to go inside, and she's someone who did this twice. She's the perfect celebrity for America in decline: Like President Bush, she just doesn't give a fuck, but at least we won't have to clean up after her mess for the rest of our lives.

If Britney was really who we believed her to be—a puppet, a grinning blonde without a cool thought in her head, a teasing coquette clueless to her own sexual power—none of this would have happened. She is not book-smart, granted. But she is intelligent enough to understand what the world wanted of her: that she was created as a virgin to be deflowered before us, for our amusement and titillation. She is not ashamed of her new persona—she wants us to know what we did to her. While it may be true that Britney suffers from the adult onset of a genetic mental disease (or a disease created by fame, yet to be named); or that she is a "habitual, frequent and continuous" drug user, as the judge declared; or that she is a cipher with boundless depths, make no mistake—she is enjoying the chaos she is creating. The look on her face when she's goofing around with paparazzi—one of whom, don't forget, she is *dating*— is often one of pure excitement. "For years, everyone manipulated Britney," says a close friend. "There was always a little game. If she didn't want to come out of the trailer, the label would come to me, saying, 'Please talk to Britney, make sure she performs, and we'll take you on a shopping spree.' Now this is her time to play."

More than any other star today, Britney epitomizes the crucible of fame for the famous: loving it, hating it and never quite being able to stop it from destroying you. Over the past year, it's looked several times like she was going to get it together, but then girlfriend messes up again. She started off with a bang—the head-shaving, plus attacking a paparazzi car with an umbrella—followed by rehab, a magazine shoot where she let her dog poop on a $6,700 gown, a hit-and-run (the charge was dropped), an investigation by the Department of Children and Family Services, the sad performance at the VMAs and her hospitalizations on January 3rd and January 31st. Even Michael Jackson never deteriorated to the point where he was strapped to a gurney, his madness chronicled by news choppers' spotlights. Before her first hospitalization, Britney shut herself in the bathroom with her youngest son for three hours, wearing only panties, arguing with cops who tried to give her a sweater. "Don't cover me up," she said. "I'm fucking hot"—meaning warm, although the other interpretation of the word is funnier.

Britney's assistant told police she demanded her "vitamins" (Britney's code for pills), though it's not known what kind she is taking.

Today, Britney is alone: Arrogant, anxiety-ridden and paranoid, she has lost faith in everyone. "She goes through people like she goes through dogs," says a close friend. "There's one instant with everyone where she freaks out and suddenly says, 'I don't trust you, and I don't know what's going on.'" She does not have a manager, agent or publicist (Jive Records no longer speaks to her directly, and the publicist at the label assigned to Britney refused to participate in this article). She has no stylist, image consultant, crisis-control manager or driver. She has pushed away her family: her brother and father ("It is sad that all the men in my life do not know how to accept a real woman's love," she explained); her sister Jamie Lynn, whom she speaks to on the phone and sees rarely; and, most important, her preening, difficult mother, Lynne, whom Britney considers poisonous. Famous for two saccharine books about her fabulous relationship with Britney, Lynne is now desperately trying to help her family, but her attempts have fallen flat: She was the force behind selling Jamie Lynn's pregnancy photos to *OK!* magazine for $1 million and encouraged Dr. Phil's visit with Britney in the psychiatric ward of Cedars-Sinai Medical Center. Ironically, it may be Britney's family who succeeds in retaining control of her now, in collaboration with doctors who are advising that she remain in a hospital setting as long as legally possible.

Britney wasn't allowed to see her kids in January, and it is unclear when she will get them back. Under the terms of their prenup, Kevin Federline was due only $1 million of Britney's estimated $30 million fortune, and his sole route to future riches is custodial support, although his intentions are widely considered to be more honorable. Federline currently receives $20,000 a month, and his hope is to keep at least part-time custody—a goal his lawyer, diminutive powerhouse Mark Vincent Kaplan, is well on his way to achieving in the court of Commissioner Scott Gordon. In her legal case, as otherwise in her life, Britney has alienated those trying to help her—her divorce attorney, Laura Wasser, dropped her a few months ago, and her current legal team of Trope & Trope requested removal at one point. "You can tell Britney all day that she has to follow court orders to get her kids back, and she will lucidly and rationally listen to what you have to say," says an attorney. "But there's a disconnect, and she'll be right back to asking, 'Why does this fucking flea need to take my deposition for me to mother my children?'"

There is one group of people who love Britney unconditionally, and whose love she accepts: Every day in L.A., at least a hundred paparazzi, reporters and celebrity-magazine editors dash after her, this braless chick padding around town on hilariously mundane errands—the gas station, the pet store, Starbucks, Rite Aid. The multibillion-dollar new-media economy rests on her slumped shoulders, with paparazzi agencies estimating that she has comprised up to twenty percent of their coverage for the past year. It's not only bottom feeders running after Britney—a recent memo leaked from the Associated Press, which plans to add twenty-two entertainment reporters to its staff, announces that everything that happens to Britney is news (they have already begun preparing her obit). The paparazzi feed the celebrity magazines, which feed the mainstream press, while sources sell their dirtiest material to British tabloids, and then it trickles back to America. "She is by far the top person I have written about on my Web site, ever," says Perez Hilton. Harvey Levin, founder of TMZ: "We serialize Britney Spears. She's our President Bush."

This mob lurches around town after Britney, descending on her with its notepads and cameras, and passing wild speculation from outlet to outlet. New players enter the gold rush by the minute, with people from around the world getting into the game: The flashiest new player is Sheeraz Hasan, a Pakistani-British immigrant who recently founded Hollywood.tv with backing from investors for His Highness of Dubai. A devout Muslim who can be found at the mosque on Fridays for prayers—and also drives a yellow Lamborghini—he was on the hajj to Mecca when he stopped in a small town on the side of a mountain for a bottle of water, and there he saw a newspaper, and on the cover was Britney. "It seemed to me she was the number-one star in the world, not Tom Cruise, not Will Smith," says Hasan. "Everything Britney does is news—Britney pumps gas, Britney forgets to put milk in her coffee—and there's a war going on, man!" Hasan realized it was his calling to build a paparazzi agency and brand with Britney's soap opera as the centerpiece: "By the blessing of God, my logo is on AP, *Entertainment Tonight* and CNN," he says, looking prayerful. He leans in and confides, "I'm going to take Paris to Dubai—the sheiks said any amount of money she wants is fine—and next I'm going to take Britney," he whispers. "She can have her own island!"

Trying to get an interview with Britney is a whole other level of craziness: A friend of a friend sets me up with a guy she says will introduce me to Britney, but it has to happen right away. The man insists that I have a signed contract from *Rolling Stone*, and he's also going to want money. I tell her to make the meeting. An hour later, a good-looking Danish guy, Claus, pulls up to a Beverly Hills street corner—he was the host of Britney's twenty-sixth birthday party, at his swag event, the Scandinavian Style Mansion (Paris Hilton and Sharon Stone attended). He's the kind of guy who gets the celebrity boutique Kitson to open its doors for Britney at 2 A.M., like he did in January (in yet another shocking image of Britney, she arrived in fishnet tights and without a skirt, her white panties visibly stained with menstrual blood). He gets out of a blue Porsche in a T-shirt that reads FUCK REHAB! It seems to be an unironic shirt. I grab my laptop case.

"Is that the contract?" he asks, pointing at my case. He leans in, "For the interview, are you offering $2 million?"

Of course, I have zero dollars to offer him, but I decide to play along. He tells me to get into his car.

"Britney and I are really, really good friends," says Claus. "That's my contract for her, for a million-dollar deal. But it's all friends. We're going on vacation together soon, on the jet to a supersecret location." He zooms down winding streets. "I'm so sick of everyone in this town thinking that they can get celebrities to come to their events for a free tube of lip gloss. My celebrities get free furs and diamonds. Britney is a queen." He sighs. "You know, the media probably made $12 million off the pictures they took of Britney at my party, and what do I get?" he says. "At least someone could reimburse me for the birthday cake."

These days, Britney may not care much what we think of her, but when she was younger it was all that mattered. Britney was a sort of JonBenét baby, encouraged to enter the pageant circuit early by Lynne, the daughter of a strict Baptist dairyman and a British war bride with dreams of escaping the small-town life of Kentwood, Louisiana. Lynne was raised in the town of 2,200 with Britney's dad, Jamie, a young rogue who popped wheelies on his motorcycle in front of the VFW and divorced his first wife two weeks before he married Lynne. His own mother committed suicide when he was fourteen. An hour inland of New Orleans and the dairy capital of the South until the Seventies, Kentwood was in the death spasms of a faltering economy during Britney's childhood, with few new businesses opening other than a mineral-water bottling plant. Lynne worked as a second-grade teacher, and Jamie as a contractor, with projects in Memphis, a few hours' drive away. He generally came home on weekends and drank too much. "Jamie is clean now, but when Britney was growing up he was a horrible addict," says a former manager. "She is the product of some very, very bad genetics."

Lynne became transfixed on her talented daughter, partially as a way of relieving some of the marriage's pressure. By age three, Britney was enrolled in choir, dance and gymnastic lessons, and by six she'd won Miss Talent Central States. At eight, daughter drove with mom eight hours to an audition for *The Mickey Mouse Club* in Atlanta. She was too young for the show, though Lynne tried to pass her off as nine, but Britney caught the casting director's eye, and he recommended a New York talent agent. The family began to fall into debt as Jamie's construction business took a downturn, but they decided to wager their fortunes by sending Britney to Manhattan. Over the next few years, she and Lynne would split their time between New York and Kentwood as Britney booked commercials, played the lead in a Broadway play, *Ruthless*, and performed on *Star Search*. The family declared bankruptcy before Britney attained her dream: At twelve, she landed a role on *The Mickey Mouse Club*, alongside Christina Aguilera and Justin Timberlake.

After thriving in Disney's world of chaste adolescence, Britney applied her skills to a nearly identical demographic with a rapidly changing sense of what modern teenhood meant. Thanks to the Gen Y boom, teen music began to explode with the Backstreet Boys and the Spice Girls, the perfect music for America's pre-9/11 optimism. Britney was picked up by Larry Rudolph, an entertainment lawyer turned manager who was in the process of packaging 'NSync with Johnny Wright, manager of New Kids on the Block and the Backstreet Boys. They sent Britney to Sweden to record with Swedish pop maestro Max Martin, who had already written her future smash, " . . . Baby One More Time." Then Britney headed back to her Christian day school in Mississippi. She loved it: She had basketball practice and a handsome boyfriend, Reg Jones. She reportedly lost her virginity to him at fourteen. (Britney denies this.)

If true, this was a secret she couldn't share, particularly because Rudolph's plans included marketing her as the teenage Lolita of middle-aged men's dreams. In January 1999, Britney emerged on the national stage with the video for " . . . Baby One More Time," as a Catholic schoolgirl in pink pompom hair barrettes. The genius stroke of her creation was that her next single was a ballad, with a video featuring her dancing in a white outfit on a pier: By emerging as a vixen and then reverting to a child, she allowed the world to breathe a sigh of relief that her temptress act was make-believe. She played along. "All I did was tie up my shirt!" she said to *Rolling Stone*. "I'm wearing a sports bra under it. Sure, I'm wearing thigh-highs, but kids wear those—it's the style. Have you seen MTV—all those girls in thongs?"

On the road, Britney was humble—washing her dishes, doing her laundry, calling older female assistants "ma'am." "We would wake up Britney at 6 A.M., and she'd work on a video for three or four days straight for twenty hours a day," says Abe Sarkisyan, her driver for five years. "She was a kind, generous sweetheart with a big heart and no poor habits." An unedited goofball and girlie girl who wrote flowery notes to friends, burped a lot and liked practical jokes, Britney was almost comically naive—she covered "Satisfaction," but when she found herself in an elevator with Mick Jagger, she had no idea who he was. Lynne retained a minor management role over the years, but she disappeared from Britney's side, enjoying her newfound wealth and laying the star-machine groundwork for Jamie Lynn, a tomboy more interested in her scooter than becoming a star. Jamie was not in the picture. "It was upsetting for Britney to be around her dad," says a friend. "He came backstage one night, and he was wasted. She was devastated." Britney would tell friends that her father was emotionally abusive, and in 2006 she wrote a poem about "sins of the father": "The guilt you fed me/Made me weak/The voodoo you did/I couldn't speak."

The first big blow to Britney's golden-girl image was her breast implants. According to a source, she and Lynne had made the decision for her to get them, on the assumption that the culture demanded it, but the press leapt on her scornfully. (Britney has denied having implants.) "When Britney saw the papers, she was crying in the bathtub uncontrollably, asking, 'Why is everyone being so mean to me?'" says a friend. "It was very hurtful for her to go through something so private so publicly." Britney regretted the implants, particularly because her chest was still growing, and when her natural breasts became larger, she had the implants removed. "When other girls did their boobs, they were like, 'Yeah, I did my boobs, move on,' but Britney was brought up to lie about herself," says Darrin Henson, the choreographer of several videos from Britney's first album and Christina Aguilera's "Genie in a Bottle." Gradually, she began to lose her confidence. "Britney would come offstage after performing in front of 15 to 16,000 people and start crying because she thought she was terrible," says Henson. "The girl doesn't know who she is."

Britney's first two albums sold more than 39 million records, making her part of a teen-pop trifecta, with the Backstreet Boys and

'NSync, that comprised the best-selling acts in Jive's history. Some in her camp argued that Britney was too young to be pushed so hard, and wanted her to return to Kentwood to reconnect with girlfriends. "There were meetings where people would fight about giving Britney a break, but in the end the machine always won," says a friend. "Britney wanted it too, but she wasn't aware of the price tag." Those who advocated too much were shoved aside. Even though she had a squeaky-clean image, things changed backstage. "There were all these slick businessmen for Britney who let seedy people come around, offering her drinks and drugs, and she thought it was fun," she says. "If Britney wanted to party to blow off stress, that's what her team wanted her to do."

Britney's savior was Justin Timberlake, whom she started dating around 1999. "Justin had his head screwed on so straight, and he rescued her from that world," says a friend. "He became the great force in her life, but it started a pattern—she began to look for guys to help her get away from the people who control her." Even though Britney was one of the biggest stars in the world and Timberlake was still just another guy in 'NSync, the power balance in their relationship was solid. "She wasn't competitive about attention," says a close friend. "She just wanted to be in love with him." Once again, her manager gave her instructions: The partnership was to be kept under wraps, and they had to tell everyone they planned to stay abstinent until marriage. "They were always running in between each other's buses, and one night Justin came back to the bus and said to me, 'Dude, smell my fingers,'"says Henson. "Justin slept with her that night." It was another year before they admitted publicly that they were a couple.

Although the world thought Britney was an innocent sexed-up for the cameras, she was always lobbying to appear sluttier, which she thought would make her appear more mature. From the time she was young, Lynne and Jamie let her walk around the house naked. "Every girl in America was wearing crop tops and booty shorts, and Britney felt like she was being held back," says a friend. "She would joke about wanting to do videos topless." Her managers didn't want to scare off her fan base. "These middle-aged guys were so intense about her not being sexual that they pushed her the other way," says the friend. "They'd tell her to put on a bra or that her lip gloss was too dark. They were literally picking out her panties for her."

With her third album, Britney was told that she could change—a little. It was time to enter the "Not a Girl, Not Yet a Woman" phase, but she was ready to leave it behind. All the gay dancers and stylists were always having dirty conversations around her backstage, and one day Britney piped up: "God, I want to have hot sex too! I want to have throw-down, hot sex!" Her primary creative collaborator on her tour, choreographer Wade Robson, agreed that it was her time to blossom, and she owned her new image by draping the proverbial snake around her neck while performing "I'm a Slave 4 U" at the 2001 VMAs. Her sexual curiosity got the better of her, and she reportedly began sleeping with Robson, a friend of Timberlake's who co-wrote 'NSync's "Pop" with him. (Both Britney and Robson have denied the affair.) In February 2002, Timberlake discovered a mash note from Robson in Britney's room. Britney and Timberlake were performing on *Saturday Night Live* that night, and they sat backstage, miserable—he refused to accept her apologies. The breakup was a terrible shock, particularly as it was followed by Britney's parents' divorce two months later. "No one took the time to say to Britney, 'Let's take some time off here, let's get you some counseling,'" says an ex-assistant manager. "They expected her to have the drive, to dust it off."

Britney realized that the machine wasn't going to bring her satisfaction anymore—she needed a man. She began desperately seeking love in nightclubs with inappropriate guys like Colin Farrell and in the studio, most notably with Fred Durst, who violated her trust by boasting about their exploits on *The Howard Stern Show*. Without a strong sense of self, she'd take on the characteristics of whomever was around at the moment, and after her kiss with Madonna at the 2003 VMAs, she decided they were soul mates. "Britney and Madonna became friends after the performance, and she started to think she was Madonna," says an ex-manager. "She said, 'Madonna calls her own shots, I can do that.' But Madonna doesn't need to be told what to do. Britney does." (Britney on Madonna: "Maybe she was my husband in another life.")

Britney returned to Kentwood for Christmas in 2003, staying in a small house on her parents' property with old friends, including childhood crush Jason Alexander, a junior at Southeastern Louisiana University. After fighting with Lynne one morning, she packed her pals on a plane for three days of partying in Las Vegas—cocaine during the evening, Ecstasy in the early morning and Xanax to sleep, according to Alexander. At 3:30 AM on January 3rd, 2004, after watching the Texas Chainsaw Massacre, she and Alexander took a lime-green limo to the Little White Wedding Chapel, where she strapped a white garter over her ripped jeans and held a small bouquet of roses in cardboard for their forty-dollar wedding. Eleven hours later, they called their parents to give them the big news. Lynne flew to Vegas, the couple were separated, and lawyers worked to annul the marriage. Shipped home with a false promise that Britney wanted to stay together, Alexander cracked under the national spotlight and dropped out of school.

This was to have been the new Britney, and she was genuinely disappointed, wearing a wedding ring in defiance. Lynne tried to circle the wagons around her furious daughter, keeping her in Kentwood on the day of the Grammys and taking her to a church service instead, but within a few months, the road called—Britney went back on tour with *In the Zone* a much more mature album with songs about early-morning sex and masturbation. By the time she filmed the video for the ballad "Everytime," she was down the rabbit hole: Her concept was to die in an overflowing bathtub with pills and booze strewn around, and get reincarnated as a baby. There were demons that she was battling, and she wanted everyone to know. Jive insisted on a different method of death, so she ran away from the paparazzi before drowning in the tub. Britney was compliant on the first day of the shoot, but on the second, she refused to leave her hotel room. "Finally, Britney agreed to do it, but first she said, 'I need three Red Bulls, and call my doctor,'" says a friend.

She found her soul mate a few weeks later, on the dance floor: Kevin Federline, a twenty-five-year-old cornrowed white boy who had been a dancer for Timberlake, a high school dropout and son of a Fresno, California, auto mechanic with one baby by his girlfriend, Shar Jackson, and another on the way. Nicknamed "Meat Pole," he was a fixture on the L.A. club scene, and one broke-ass dude: Before he met Britney, Federline's Chevy had been repossessed. Britney got stuck on him—"part of it was that she wanted to pimp Justin's dude, get his spot and throw it in Justin's face," says a friend—and invited him on her tour, where they got matching tattoos of dice on their wrists and filmed each other obsessively with video cameras, movies that would become the basis for their reality show, *Chaotic*. With little else on her mind, Britney was relieved when her knee gave out in the middle of the tour, and Jive announced that doctors had prescribed four months of rest. But the next week, she asked Federline to marry her (he refused, mock-horrified, and proposed a few minutes later), and they got hitched immediately, with Juicy tracksuits for the bridesmaids (in pink) and groomsmen (in white) embroidered with MAIDS and PIMPS.

Two weeks after the wedding, Britney fired her managers, Rudolph and Lynne. "Kevin convinced Britney that he was going to get the users out of her life, and they were going to run her business together," says a friend. Their life became the main business: They sold their wedding photos to *People* magazine for $1 million, and Britney began to blog on her fan site, charging a twenty-five-dollar club-membership fee. She popped out two kids quickly—Sean Preston, a year after she and Federline were married (the baby pictures were also sold for $1 million to *People*), and Jayden, one year later (she kept him under wraps for months, in hopes of a big payday, but a paparazzi caught her carrying him on a beach in Maui, Hawaii). Her interest in her recording career was minimal. She recorded three songs in three years.

Federline gave Britney license to fully embrace her white-trash side—walking into gas-station restrooms barefoot, dumping ashtrays out hotel windows, wearing novelty tees like I'M A VIRGIN, BUT THIS IS AN OLD SHIRT and, most notably, not strapping the kids into car seats. But he liked the high life, buying a $250,000 silver Ferrari with monogrammed rims and getting stoned in their home recording studio while cutting his rap album. "Kevin didn't step up to the plate and be a man to Britney in their relationship," says a close friend. "He was a boy to her, turning his back on her for his bros and that fame." He made her feel a lot of her old insecurities—loneliness, fear of abandonment—and she started partying and spiraling downward again, attributing her crying jags to postpartum depression. "When Britney had children, that should've been the end of her wild ways, and it wasn't," says a friend of Federline. "She turned into someone who only wanted to hear 'yes,' and if you're not going to say it, get the hell out of her way."

Meat Pole wasn't the one for Britney, and she asked him for a divorce by text message in November 2006. (His response: scrawling on the wall of the nightclub bathroom, "Today I'm a free man—Fuck a wife, give me my kids, bitch!") She rehired Rudolph immediately, and he took her ice-skating at Rockefeller Center in Manhattan for a photo op. But she wasn't ready to be a little girl again. Night after night, she hit the L.A. scene lost, vomiting in public, exchanging clothes with a strip-club cocktail waitress, and, perhaps most dangerously, hanging out with Paris Hilton—the two of them even splitting a pair of fishnet stockings, each wearing one leg, and she copied Paris' cootchie-flashing stunts three times before Rudolph quashed their friendship (Paris' nickname for Britney: "The Animal," because she doesn't think before she acts).

The Animal had to go to rehab: Eric Clapton's Crossroads, in Antigua, but she stormed out one day later, flying to Miami and then coach-class to Los Angeles to see her family. She arrived at Federline's house for her babies, but he had joined forces with Lynne and Rudolph, and wouldn't talk to her until she registered at the Malibu rehab center Promises. She circled his house three times, furious at having to concede to their demands, before pulling into a random hair salon in the Valley and taking her hair off in big clumps, less as a penance than a liberation. Then she stayed up for forty-eight hours straight, driving around, sucking down dozens of Red Bulls, afraid that she was being followed by demons, or that a cell-phone charger was taping her thoughts, and obsessively listening to the radio for news about Anna Nicole Smith's death earlier that month. That was her fate, she declared—she was next.

After rehab, Britney was deeply angry and cut out every person in her life who had argued for it—her parents, Federline, Rudolph, even old best friends. She claimed not to have a drug problem, and stopped returning calls to her disloyal subjects, changing her phone numbers. "She was queen of the ghost moves," says singer Keri Hilson, who did backup vocals and co-wrote "Gimme More." "She'd be in the booth one second and then security would come get her, and we wouldn't know she was gone." Britney's former bodyguard claimed in an interview with a British tabloid that she suffered a near-overdose with singer-songwriter Howie Day, whom she met at Promises, in a Los Angeles hotel room—the room was trashed, a glass pipe alongside a white substance that the bodyguard claimed was cocaine or meth.

Jive was cautious about booking Britney on the 2007 MTV Video Music Awards, but it was too good a promotional opportunity to pass up. Britney signed a new management contract with the Firm and started working out a few times a week. The day of the show, she arrived early to the arena. Timberlake was rehearsing. Suddenly, her face fell, and she started getting panicked, nervous, afraid—what was he going to think of her performance? What about the rest of her peers? She headed backstage and was pacing in her dressing room when Timberlake knocked on the door. She refused to come out. She didn't want to see him yet.

Soon, she was going to put on her hair, and maybe she would feel better. There was a wig waiting for her by master coiffeur Ken Pavés, who created Jessica Simpson's cascading fake tresses—it had been seven months since Britney shaved her head, and her real hair was less than six inches long. All she had to do was sit for the afternoon so the wig could be glued to her head, piece by piece, then remain very still for an hour so it could set, and she would be the old Britney again.

Suddenly, Britney declared that she didn't want Pavés to touch her. She asked for his assistant, but the assistant didn't want to betray Pavés. The hair divas turned on their heels, leaving the Firm to try coaxing them back while insisting to Britney that she must change her mind. When she finally granted Pavés entree an hour before the show began, it was too late to apply the wig, so someone grabbed Nelly Furtado's stylist, who glued on some straight blond hairpieces. Britney sat for those in her glittery black bikini and then stepped into the rest of her outfit, a Posh Spice–style corset-dress. Then she took it off, refusing to wear it. She wanted to go onstage without artifice, as naked as possible, and for us to love her just the way she was.

The edge of Mulholland Drive is the lip of a pit, a vertiginous fall into destruction. Britney's house sits at the top, jutting over the glittering city. It's a rainy weekday a couple of months after the VMAs. She knows she messed up her performance—"Afterward, she kept asking, 'Was I terrible? Was it terrible?'" says a friend. "This is just the way it is with her: It's circular, manic thinking"—and because she's not doing any promotion for *Blackout*, other than a seven-minute radio interview with KISS-FM, there's not much else going on. The Firm stepped down from managing her, without making a cent, because they were no longer able to speak with her directly: Her phone is now answered by Osamah Lutfi, also known as Sam, a jovial thirty-three-year-old who a friend of Britney's describes as her "life coach." They met at a party in 2007, and he called her then-assistant, Kalie Machado, to meet at a Santa Monica Starbucks. According to Machado, Lutfi told her that he worked for Federline as a private eye, and he knew that there was a tap on Britney's phone and a warrant to search her Malibu home for drugs. (Federline's rep has denied any connection.) Lutfi has had two temporary restraining orders issued against him for harassment.

It's Lutfi who has kept Britney together through the months, filling in as her assistant and trying to be a manager, talking to her record label, and driving her around town. There are constant breakdowns about all the people who have sold Britney out to celebrity magazines—the assistant she forgot to pay, the bodyguard who claims he's seen her do cocaine and regularly walk around the house nude, the twenty-one-year-old college kid she made out with topless in a hot tub on the roof of a hotel in downtown L.A. A new rumor crops up every day: She feeds soda in baby bottles to her toddlers (whose teeth she also asked a dentist to whiten), her choice of poison is the Southern rap scene's "Purple Monster" (vodka, Red Bull and NyQuil) and she has a sex dungeon in her Beverly Hills villa with spanking paddles displayed in a glass jar (and a large covered candy dish of lotions and toys she calls her "pleasure chest"). In this embattled state, Britney has become a recluse, in a way— she's never out to dinner or at a nightclub, spending most of her nights at the Four Seasons in Beverly Hills.

For weeks, she slept there almost every night, and Lutfi is often downstairs at the hotel, like everyone else who is working this story—the red-carpeted lobby bar has become the de facto center of Britney operations, with reporters, paparazzi and lawyers from the child-custody case holding meetings with hope that the object of everyone's desire might come wandering by. It's like the United Nations in this bar, with folks from myriad ethnicities, and everyone acting deadly serious. I have coffee on separate occasions with two men from Federline's attorney's team: Aaron Cohen, a former Israeli operative, who served the subpoenas to some of Britney's friends, including Lutfi—along with his regular job, which is training SWAT teams in Israeli anti-terrorism techniques. "With Britney, I penetrated the inner circles of Hollywood," he tells me. "It was not unlike counterterrorism, in that I worked with both enemies and friends." I also meet with Michael Sands, the media liaison for Kaplan, who gives me a key-chain light stamped with a picture of the Pentagon, an FBI lapel pin and another from the CIA, and a commemorative Navy coin—one might think he works for one or all of the agencies. The rumor flies around the lobby that the government is looking into Lutfi, curious about his connection to the Saudis.

Britney's Danish pal Claus makes an appearance at the Four Seasons as well, with two business associates. They'd like to talk about the $2 million, which now, for some reason, everyone is talking about as $1 million. This is how it will go, they explain: I will give them the money, and the cash will be held in escrow. Britney will know that she won't get any money until she completes the interview and photo shoot (they will take a ten percent finder's fee, payable whether or not she shows up). They will be at the shoot, making sure Britney is happy—I will have to bring five photographers, five stylists and five makeup artists in case she is not. They do this all the time: They just took Paris to Moscow, and did the deal for Britney's New Year's Eve 2007 appearance at the Vegas nightclub Pure, the one where she passed out. "My guy was behind her, holding her up that night," boasts one guy.

Ryan Seacrest stops by the table. "Hey, guys, what's up?" he asks.

"We made Ryan $3 million last year," they say after Seacrest leaves. "It's all friends, so friendly."

The next night, Claus, again in his FUCK REHAB! shirt, has a new plan: He will tell Britney that he's going to give her $1 million. I'll give him the $1 million, and then he'll give it to her. "This way, no one will ever know that *Rolling Stone* bent over to pay Queen Britney," he says. He is very pleased. He calls Lutfi to tell him. "Sam says that *OK!* magazine was going to pay $2 million for an interview with Britney," he says.

Claus takes off for Citizen Smith, a rock bar in Hollywood, to meet Lutfi and Britney's twenty-six-year-old cousin, Alli Sims— a naive climber with hopes of releasing her own album. It's a birthday party for Jason Kennedy, an E! reporter who may or may not be dating Sims.

"We really just want someone to tell the truth," says Sims. "Britney's such a good girl." She screws up her face, thinking about nice things to say. "Britney never talks bad about anyone behind their backs, ever, seriously," she says.

"That is one of her best characteristics," agrees Lutfi. He turns to me. "Just to let you understand something as far as her psyche goes, she really doesn't need to do another thing in her life. Her big thing with me is that she doesn't want me defending her against anything fake in the magazines. But she understands that's the way they make their money, because it's the way she made hers too. She really doesn't care anymore."

"We're going to need pre-approval over the article," says Claus.

"Also, Britney has a friend who is a photographer whom we would want to shoot the photos," says Lutfi. He thinks for a moment. "You know, this is so much more than a magazine article— we've been doing dictation, she's been telling me her story, and I've been writing it all down. It would make a great book!"

It's 1:30 A.M., and the bar is closing. The lights flick on, and we hug goodbye.

After explaining to Claus that there is no money, I write to Lutfi many times, explaining that we are still very interested in interviewing Britney and telling her side of the story.

No response.

As 2007 comes to a close, Britney starts to really enjoy her paparazzi chases. She races around the city for two or three hours a day, aimlessly leading paps to various locations where she could interact with them just a little bit and then jump back into her car. A Britney chase is more fun than a roller coaster, but with the chance that the experience could cause lasting harm. "Britney is the most dangerous detail in Hollywood," says Levin of TMZ.

There are twenty paps in the core Britney detail, a bunch of hilarious, slightly scary thugs who use expert drag-racing skills to block off new guys who try to get in the mix. It's like a game of Frogger, with everyone jostling to be the first car behind Britney, the better to shoot all over her when she stops (and then watch their feet, because several have found themselves on crutches after she speeds away). "She's nuts," says Craig Williams, a photographer for Hollywood.tv. Williams, a former beatmaker for Death Row Records with a long braid slithering down his back and multiple silver rings on his fingers, gets in front most of the time, riding her Mercedes SL65 hard. Almost all the paps drive rental SUVs, most with dents and scrapes on the sides, because no one wants to get their real cars messed up. A plastic bag swings from the door to the trunk of the SUV in front of us—the pap had been using it for trash all day and forgot to dump it.

Britney pulls into her driveway, and Williams waits down the street. He puts Blackout on his CD player. "Let's summon Britney," he says. "She's gonna come back out after she does her drugs or changes her clothes, whichever comes first," he jokes, lighting a cigarette. "She didn't get enough chase today."

An hour later, the white Mercedes whizzes by, and it's on: up and down Coldwater Canyon and across Mulholland Drive for one hour, with paps jostling behind. Then she flips a bitch and heads right back where she came from. The other cars get lost as she circles a Ralphs supermarket twice, dumps her assistant at the Starbucks and zooms down the street to a red light. Williams pulls out his video camera.

She waves hi. "Hey, Brit, I listened to that new album," says Williams. "It's awesome! Good album. Good job. Vocals were tight, girl."

"I know," Britney yells. "I'm the shit."

Williams laughs. "You the shit!"

"I know it, baby," she yells, with a coy smile. "It's hard to be this hot."

"Tell me about it," says Williams, laughing. "It's Britney, bitch!"

This kind of flirtation is a daily occurrence, and she starts to prowl the pool for a dude—of all the guys, Adnan Ghalib is the hottest one, and she knows it. He's a British Afghani who has claimed he fought for the Mujahdeen and has the shrapnel scars to prove it, a smoldering thirty-five-year-old in Gucci sunglasses (far more appealing in person than he is on the news). Once Britney asked him into the bathroom of a Quiznos; his wife has filed for legal separation, and he has said that he plans to marry Britney and get her pregnant. The unimaginable happens one night right before Christmas, when Britney decides that she's had enough of being lonely—she pulls over on the Pacific Coast Highway, jumps into Ghalib's car, pops on her pink wig and takes him to the Peninsula hotel for a late "lunch," as he called it.

For the past few years, Britney has begged friends to help her run away, to leave everything behind and become a stylist or schoolteacher, or move to an island where she can work as a bartender. Ghalib helps her achieve her goal, evading the paparazzi for weeks on violent, terrifying chases. The relationship is just starting to build when Britney is taken to the hospital for the first time, and as soon as she comes out, Ghalib absconds with her to crisscross the West

Coast, listening to their favorite music in the car (her: Dixie Chicks and Janet Jackson; him: System of a Down), making stops in Palm Springs and Mexico with his buddy, a paparazzi who would shoot the two of them for exclusive sale by Ghalib's then-agency. The other agencies are having nervous breakdowns. Ghalib gets on the phone with *Rolling Stone* because he's a fan of the magazine. "You must understand something about Britney," he says, in arguing her side of the story. "People turned on her. They were only there when the getting was good. She has become very Columbo-esque— she acts a certain way so that people don't think she's intelligent, and then people volunteer information, and she is able to put together what is going on. It's not the blogs or magazines or the people on the street she cares about. She knows that the people who had a responsibility to support her bailed out and is very hurt by their actions."

A tug of war begins between Ghalib and Lutfi for control of Britney, and on January 20th, when Ghalib goes to a funeral in Northern California, Lutfi invites a few paparazzi from a friendly agency, X17, over to Britney's house, and shows them what he claimed was a restraining order against Ghalib. "He folded it over so they couldn't see what he was showing," says Ghalib, chuckling. "I'll give it to you, he's good, he's very good at what he does." Lutfi has spread rumors that Ghalib sleeps on the couch when he's at Britney's house. A pap catches a text message: Lutfi writes, "You're a manic trigger. If you continue to have any contact with her, you'll kill her. It's your decision."

Britney finds herself right where she used to be: Again, there's control, pressure, fighting. She argues with Lutfi, and Ghalib rushes in to save her, but Lutfi calls security to keep him off her property. Lynne arrives, dragging her daughter around town, and

Britney begins to spin out, staying up for sixty hours straight. On January 30th, she arrives back home after a day at the Beverly Hills Hotel, and meets with a psychiatrist, according to X17. They put out the news at 11 P.M.: She's attempted suicide.

Seventy-five paps gather around the entrances to Britney's gated community, stamping their feet in the chilly winter night, as a police helicopter circles overhead. "You don't want an ambulance to roll out with a body bag and miss that," says a French photographer, checking his battery. These guys are jaded after all that's happened. "Man, Britney can't die, because then I don't get my money!" says a guy in a Famous Stars and Straps baseball hat. Someone starts running down the block, and everyone runs after him; they hide in a driveway and laugh when everyone catches up. Although she doesn't seem to have tried to commit suicide, the doctors are on their way again: Police and paramedics descend as the LAPD blocks off all exit paths from her house, stations twenty cops in her driveway and takes her out (her code name: "The Package") without a single picture. The next day, her parents file a restraining order against Lutfi.

A world without Britney, where she is set aside in rehab or a psychiatric center, is hard to contemplate: She's the canary in the coal mine of our culture, the most vivid representation of the excess of the past decade. She didn't think there was a tomorrow worth saving for, and neither did we. After blaming everyone else for her problems, Britney's finally starting to realize the degree to which she's messed up, but her sense of entitlement keeps her from admitting it to herself, or to anyone who is trying to help her. We want her to survive and thrive, to evolve into someone who can make us proud again. Or maybe, we just don't want the show to end. "Look

at George Foreman: He's the oldest heavyweight champion ever,"
says Ghalib. "That's what Britney's going to be. She said it best to
me: She refuses to live her life anymore reflected in the eyes of others." Then he gets very quiet. "Be gentle to her," he says. "That's
a personal request."

Theoretically Unpublished Piece About Girl Talk, For a Theoretical New York Magazine Kind of Audience, Give or Take an Ox on Suicide Watch

W. David Marx and Nick Sylvester

GIRL TALK, THE MASH-UP DETONATOR

Gregg Gillis, a 26-year-old college graduate who likes pop music and owns a laptop, became Girl Talk in the first year of the 21st century. Taking cues from Britney Spears' self-positioning circa 2001—when she was famously "Not a Girl, Not Yet A Woman"—Gillis is not a DJ, but not a traditional musician either. With the aid of computer editing software, he creates danceable sound collages that often incorporate over 15–20 audio sources: namely, popular and less popular rock, rap, dance, and electronic songs, no era or genre excluded. The sources are mostly recognizable, and his songs—Gillis calls them "songs"—carry the force of nostalgia but are reconfigured and "mashed up" enough so as to sound fresh and new and free of the groan that collects when somebody insists on playing all four minutes and seventeen sec-

142

onds of MC Hammer's "U Can't Touch This" at the holiday party. With Girl Talk, we get that blissful moment of recognition without having to suffer through the next three minutes and thirty seconds remembering exactly why it hasn't been Hammertime for more than a decade now.

Like many others before and after him, Gillis found his success after the indie music website Pitchfork Media bestowed positive reviews upon his third album, 2006's *Night Ripper*. "Pittsburgh native Greg Gillis (Girl Talk) absolutely detonates the notions of mash-up," wrote reviewer Sean Fennessey. "As an illegal art form, it's surprising no one came along with an idea like this sooner." The review came out on July 17—so maybe the summer heat kept the typically spot-on Fennessey from remembering John Oswald's Plunderphonics, the all-stolen-sample recording from 1985.

Either way, for Pitchfork and many others, Girl Talk raised the bastard-pop bar. He was not just playing two songs on top of each other like 2ManyDJs or Freelance Hellraiser, nor was he playing two songs next to each other in an anything-goes free-for-all DJ set a la Optimo or Erol Alkan. Instead Gillis is something of a surgeon, scalpeling out drum breaks from one song, vocal melodies from another, a guitar riff from another, and stitching them into some danceable semblance of a new song. These Frankensteins were emblematic of the indie-rockcentric Pitchfork's growing appreciation for Southern rap, modern pop, and dance music too, so it was no surprise when the site took the opportunity to award Gillis's album Best New Music, its highest honor—to celebrate Girl Talk was, in a way, to celebrate the site itself.

Around that time, Gillis hooked up with the Chicago-based Pitchfork buds Windish Agency. He quickly began touring the world with his sweaty dance parties. He had a well-blogged reputation for inviting people on stage to dance with him as he huddled over his computer, triggering his samples live, and soon he became a festival headliner. A career in music firmly established, soon Gillis quit his Pittsburgh day-job as a biomedical engineer. And now Gillis is at the point fame-wise where MTV News is more than happy to run a story about his last show, to take place on December 21, 2012. That date counts for the end of the Mayan calendar—believed by some to be the day the world will end. For a guy who plays others people's music, more or less, Gillis is not doing so bad for himself.

I'LL BE YOUR WHATEVER YOU WANT

Girl Talk, to his immense credit, is an avatar of the most important musical-technological developments and music-industrial complications from the last decade: (illegal) music hyper-consumption in the face of record industry meltdown; the blurring of distinctions in major and indie labels; the plumbing of indie cool; an indie-rock about-face towards "selling out"; an unprecedented participatory music culture, a next-next-level fan club. (i.e.: It's not enough just to go to the shows, or buy the t-shirts, or track down the seven-inches.) The mega-fans are remixing their favorite songs, lacing them with dance beats and synthesizer presets, posting their remixes on their blogs, commenting on those of others. Even if there were precedents for these complications, the 21st century form of mashups is a very palpable convergence: an internet-mediated, meta-pop moment.

There was a time of openly loathing but secretly loving 2ManyDJ's blend of Skee-Lo's "I Wish" over "Cannonball" by the

Breeders. But it wasn't clear at the time (late 2002) that this would be a New Musical Movement with artist heroes and collectives. The mashup was at best the democratization of once elite techie show-off skills. Pro Tools Free or Fruity Loops or Live (cracked or otherwise) were now widely available, and so anybody with an ounce of computer know-how was able to twist and contort their favorite songs into a seamless mixtape. Soon, an army of sixteen year-olds would surely adopt the mashup as a standard protocol in their early musical careers. Soon they'll figure out a way to impress girls by putting Indigo Girls tracks over "Tootsie Roll."

HE WISHES HE WAS A BALLER

A month after *Night Ripper* received Best New Music, Gillis told critic Ryan Dombal, "I'm trying to separate myself from other people by having songs that would be considered—technically— original things. I don't seek out mashups. I'm associated with the whole mashup movement, and it's too bad because I'm not a huge fan of them." Two years later, Gillis told Robert Levine of the New York *Times*, straight up, "I want to be a musician and not just a party D.J.. . . .and like any musician I want to put out a classic album." Then again, Gillis doesn't need to say anything of this sort, with the militia of sycophants he has lined up to defend his work. Our favorite is Chris Bodenner, a guest blogger at Andrew Sullivan's Daily Dish blog. Bodenner not only insists Girl Talk is an artist, but believes him to be "the artist for the Age of Obama":

> [Obama]'s campaign—buoyed by young fans and volun-
> teers—embodies that generation in so many ways, as does

Girl Talk. Obama is a young, diverse, and unique politician running an innovative, grassroots campaign that thrives offs the Internet. Similarly, Girl Talk is a young, innovative, Internet-based artist whose level of sampling is unique and incredibly diverse—racially and stylistically. And both Obama and Gillis draw from the same demographics: African-Americans and young liberal whites. Plus, they both put on killer live shows.

Suffice it to say, we did not expect the glorification of mashers-up to the point of being artists—as if "talented DJ" just couldn't suffice. Even Belgian duo 2 Many DJs kept their dark arts in the realm of the "DJ mix." The Skee-Lo/Breeders track, for example, boasted no pretensions of song title other than a listing of its ingredients. But for some reason this *Night Ripper* set was an "album" rather than a "mix," made of "songs" and not of "mashups."

Perhaps this posing is required, however, because *Night Ripper* doesn't particularly work as a straight DJ mix. There is no build; it doesn't breathe. The genius of 2 Many DJs and some of the other first wave mashup artists was the naturalness of their blends. Without tinkering too much, the harmonic and melodic elements would align to make a sonically pleasing moment. Christina Aguilera sounded plausible singing over The Strokes in "A Stroke of Genius." No DJ superhero could be heard pulling the strings. In the pre-Girl Talk days, the standard of judgment was the seamlessness, the beauty of a ridiculously paired, yet ironically similar set of songs.

But this is Girl Talk. *Night Ripper* is a "postmodern musical creation." This posits itself as Art—challenging all prior definitions of what it means to make music.

A NITPICKY DIGRESSION B/W BEFORE THEY WERE GIRL TALKS

Technology obscures the fact, a simple one to me, that "mashing up" is the fundamental process for music making: i.e. combining and recombining different sounds into pleasing and/or at the very least hopefully-not-boring configurations. Lynyrd Skynyrd were known to mash up guitar and bass and drums into the configuration of "Sweet Home Alabama." Weezer had a pretty good mashup called "Say It Ain't So." Some people/bands make terrible mashups. Other people/bands make pretty good mashups!

All's to say, there is a context for Girl Talk's cut-and-paste aesthetic. Technically he is working in the tradition of musique concrete, which when Pierre Schaeffer and Pierre Henry and Stockhausen and friends did it, comprised cutting up physical vinyl records and tape reels and re-pasting them together—using prerecorded sounds and reconfiguring them and then playing them as pastiche.

These were compositions but not traditional songs. And most of these compositions, to be frank, are more fun to think about than listen to. But since then, the concrete nature of recording has been exploited tremendously as part of the modern recording studio setup. Most radio pop songs are cut-and-pastes of previous takes actually, looped and warped and seamlessly woven together. And so musique concrete, one could reasonably argue, has significantly altered the path of recorded music, not necessarily with its content but as a process.

ROMAN CANDLE IN THE WIND

What's tricky is that Gillis wants the Art-ness of musique concrete and the Popularity of Pop Music. Unlike musique concrete artists, even more popular ones like Matmos, Gillis wants, needs even, his samples to be fully recognizable. He is using well-known songs too, not field recordings of, say, a squeaky door hinge—so there is an element of junior-high level trainspotting to the album's appeal, right down to the title: *Night Ripper* clearly plays on the Beatles song title "Day Tripper." The tracklisting of the *Night Ripper* song "Smash Your Head" counts (at least) 17 samples, from Fall Out Boy to X-Ray-Spex to the Pharcyde, whose "Passing Me By" itself samples at least two songs. The effect is an advanced version of that game on the iPod, which challenges you to figure out what the song is from a four second random clip. It's a game, and because Gillis keeps a steady beat, it's technically danceable too.

It's rarely listenable though—at least in any traditional, "I am taking pleasure in the configuration of these simultaneously occurring sounds and words" sense of pop music listening. Although Girl Talk has a few choice moments like the "Where Is My Mind" vs. "Hate Me Now" blend, he relies on pitch-shifting and time-distorting everything to fit within the same BPM—cramming all his various found elements into the same one-size-fits-all bed a la Greek villain Procrustes. He is obedient more to his process than the finished product. His most beloved blend of Biggie Smalls and Elton John pitches up "Tiny Dancer" to a ludicrous degree, and to add insult to injury, Gillis lets John's artificially-chipmunked lyrics step all over Biggie's rhymes. (This would surely prompt a severe drubbing if done in real life.) Gillis' labored matching of "Ain't to Proud to Beg" over "Friends of P" just sounds like "I Love the '90s" projectile vomiting.

There are also sloppy segments on *Night Ripper* where the songs' keys don't match up—like Ciara's "Oh" over Elastica's

"Connection"—which I doubt was an intentional experiment in audience-polarizing post-modernism. Maybe we shouldn't say that the errors are "unmusical" but they have the groove of a elementary school violin recital.

The ultimate glory of Girl Talk is supposed to reside in a brand new expression of "pop obsession" for a radically-different generation. But as it stands, Girl Talk just seems to love pop music as a sadistic steward, morphing all the hooks and cherished moments of the last forty years into devalued fodder for a long stream of time-stretched mid-range EQ mush with no peaks or dynamics.

Notice we don't find Girl Talk offensive to copyright, "the ontology of art," or pop music in general. We just think the relatively innovative gimmick of his style has exempted him from critical thought put towards the actual result. Are we a pop culture generation easily placated to hear our "references" bounced back to us, no matter the context or skill? Recall the Weezer video for "Pork and Beans." Is the whole game now: "Hey, I know what that is!!"?

I'M GONNA ADD SOME BENEFIT OF THE DOUBT

Late this summer, Girl Talk released his *Night Ripper* follow-up called *Feed the Animals*. (This is possibly a subtle reference to Belly's "Feed the Trees," but I doubt it.) Since *Night Ripper*, Gillis's technical abilities improved, and there are fewer "unmusical" moments when keys don't line up or samples seem sloppy. With fewer mistakes to distract us, the Girl Talk Thesis Statement seems more apparent, i.e. there is a Girl Talk Thesis Statement after all. Like a good crate-digging producer, Gillis aims to salvage what the past has discarded and wishes to figure out how to make worn-out songs sound good again.

A pretty clean example of that: He updates the build of "Dance To the Music" by Sly and the Family Stone, the part when Sly sings "I'm gonna add a little organ" and then the organ comes in, repeat with guitar, repeat with bass—except Girl Talk makes very simple substitutions for the original responses to Sly's calls. If anything, it's clever, a good party trick. Later Girl Talk rescues the one great chorus from an otherwise terrible Southern rap track (cf. Shawty Lo's "They Know" or Cassidy's "Drink N My 2 Step") and finds it a better backbeat. Gillis sometimes just goes for broke and it works, combining awesome with awesome and giving us awesomer: For an all-too-brief time, Blackstreet's "No Diggity" chorus glides over Kanye's "Flashing Lights" instrumental. Getting paid is a forte; this is something else entirely.

Girl Talk is definitely Gillis's Ongoing Project—and these records, as long as he keeps making them (four more years, dude!), could very well approach an Aesthetic if not a Point. From a technical standpoint, this is also a project that requires a certain degree of time and effort and patience (and an endless supply of a cappellas). He could just be combining any old songs, but he isn't.

Obviously sometimes his combinations and sequences don't taste good. But with music at least, the best moments are more value-indicative to me than the plethora of shitty ones. Shittiness is an inevitability. As pointed out, digital music manipulation tools have become cheaper and more available and the d-word, shudder, democratized. The ignobile vulgus doesn't have the best track record when it comes to artmaking. Remember what happened when synthesizers became readily available in late disco, giving birth to house music: We first got Frankie Knuck-les' "Your Love," but then we got, you know, everything else af-ter that. Some of it was awesome. Most was terrible.

We're not saying Girl Talk is the Frankie Knuckles of mash-ups. But compare him with the rest of what the internet has put out there for us—all the ridiculous song title puns—and you realize the extent to which he does care how he puts things together. His records have rough patches sonically, and he doesn't have a handle on pacing, knowing only one speed (fast) and one density (brick) and one EQ setting (lots of mids). But he's not exactly taking the piss, or the same kind of piss, as the rest of these people.

DJ HERO

That being said, Girl Talk's insistence on not being a pure DJ is a key to why the music sounds like it does, why it has only one speed, one timbre, and one density: if he lets a sample or phrase or loop breath on its own without some kind of additional per-cussion or secondary element, he is violating his own semantic scruples. Rule Number One of Girl Talk Club: Everything must be mashed at all times or otherwise the whole musique concrete / "art compounded from other art" rationale falls away, and Gillis is "just a DJ."

This is a bar of poetic, Babel-like heights—an exciting concept, one to which Girl Talk's execution rarely lives up. But in doing so, Girl Talk has deftly avoided the mashup label, and the musique concrete label, in favor of a brand-new artform whose result, crit-ics be damned, has no point of comparison.

If not an outright lie, most times uniqueness is a bad excuse for Not Art. Many artists recoil at the mere suggestion that someone is doing something else just like them. To that end, these artists create new rules so that no one is on the same court. They get away with it, in no small part because most snobby music fans hate the idea of music having a "playing field" anyway, where music becomes like sports—scratch DJs or guitar soloists who have to practice, practice, practice, who try to outdo their rivals through sheer technical skill, who play at Madison Square Garden for screaming fans, who wipe the sweat with actual towels. (Except when it's a video game, then we suddenly love it.)

Girl Talk doesn't want to go to the Wimbledon of mash-ups, so he created his own sport. Let's call it Speed Mashball. I don't think he's the best Speed Mashball player he could be (he's definitely gotten better since the Night Ripper Tournament), but with no competition stepping to the plate to kick a "goober-ball" (we will discuss the rules and jargon of this complicated athletic metaphor later), Girl Talk is the undisputed gold medalist. And by using every sample known to man (and every a cappella downloaded from Jam Glue), he basically outmoded the entire circa 2003 mash-up sport.

We can put Girl Talk under the umbrellas of musique concrete or loop-based pop music itself, but these titles further confuse Gillis, making him out to be some kind of outsider or misunderstood auteur. Truth is, however, Girl Talk is first and foremost a campus favorite, a party rocker, that serious DJ flown in for the Kappa Alpha party who you go and ask if he has any De La Soul; he screams at you indignantly "I just played some!" and then you go back to looking for where Carrie Ann went off to. Unlike Matmos or Pierre Schaeffer or anything musique concrete, Girl Talk needs "the critics" as much as Tay "Chocolate Rain" Zonday does—which is to say, not at all. Dude's likely got every weekend for the next year booked without all the ink spilled from the pens of eggheads.

As a second cousin, Girl Talk has that guy who sped-up all the Beatles albums to fit in a single ten minute file. But that particular music auteur gets no love from Pitchfork, no respect as "an artist." Must be his subpar Street Team.

THE LEGOMANIAC

Can a process truly be called "repurposing" or "recontextualizing" when Repurpose and Recontext is built into the content's genetic code? When it's all part of the master plan? Disco and funk producers didn't intend for their drum breaks to become the stuff of rap samples—yet with Girl Talk compositions, one wonders how much of Gillis's ease is a testament to his technical prowess, and how much is just an articulation of the fact that pop music has become increasingly standardized, its parts more or less interchangeable. All major rap singles, for instance, come with an instrumental and a vocal a cappella; the verses are mostly all the same length, about 16 bars; the choruses are all more of less the same length of time too. It is understood within the architecture of pop and hip-hop music these days that the song is waiting, begging even, to be mashed up.

A modern audience likely won't find anything remotely violent or controversial or confrontational to Girl Talk presenting this information either. Rock has coexisted with hip-hop has coexisted with noise. Our ears are better-than-ever equipped to handle these kinds of recombinations. Girl Talk has a moment on *Feed The Animals* when he puts a rap over the French disco-house track "Music Sounds Better With You," and another one when we hear Lil Mama over Metallica's "One." It's telling how little these tracks sound out of the ordinary, because ten years ago I suspect they would have. Just last year, Kanye took Daft Punk's electro track "Harder Better Faster Stronger" and put rapping over it, called it "Stronger," and it went to #1 on the Billboard Pop 100. Discounting the precedent of the Beastie Boys, Jay-Z's best-selling *Black Album* in 2003 was filled with Lil Mama/Metallica-type moments. In the public imagination, these artistic decisions are no longer scandalous.

We're seeing this in other situations, as the idea of user-generated content delights our commerce so—that the line between Ultimate Fan and Actual Artist is rendered the same in terms of exchange value. In 2008, Girl Talk is pop music's Ultimate Fan. But the extent to which the music he's working with is so portable, so building-block ready, makes it seem like he's not making art so much as merely following industry directions: Step by step, like he's putting together a Lego spaceship. There is no violence in this process, in other words; he's hardly repurposing much of anything. Instead it's like a video game in which Gillis has found the warp level—yet keep in mind, somebody somewhere had to program that warp level precisely so that it would be discovered.

THE 21ST NIGHT OF SEPTEMBER

And as the Ultimate Fan, Girl Talk exists as a mover not of music but nostalgia. He is the guy at the party who says, "Remember slap bracelets?" Dude: How about devil sticks?

Although there are things to hate about the whole "mass nostalgia" angle, who can gainsay the fact that the first major role of our new internet-based culture is to dig back in the near past and scream, "Yo, you remember this shit?"—whether it's 1970s toy commercials on YouTube or Super Mario Bros. mycology sets on BoingBoing or funny Russian Speed Racer overdubs on Some Awful Thing. There is no way VH1 could have a "nostalgia for this week" show unless they felt the pressure to one-up the Internet where it's all nostalgia all the time. Girl Talk fits into our national cultural mood extremely well. Gillis is the musical equivalent of "Best Week Ever." And I am sure that even that show could be legitimized as "a perfect manifestation of what McLuhan and Warhol augured" rather than Lowest Common Denominator TV.

(A personal note from David: As someone living in the far Orient and generally ignoring recent American "popular" music to listen to David Brooks and Mark Shields battle it out on podcasts, I am either the least or most qualified person to make a judgment on Girl Talk. I had no idea Kayne West made music; I just thought he was that whiny Fauntleroy in shutter sunglasses always hanging out at colette in Paris. Forget art. The question is, without a public hungry for the references, is *Feed the Animals* anything at all? Does Girl Talk hold up as "music" without all the extratextual information? If you had no idea about mash-ups or hip-hop or "No Diggity" or "Epic" by Faith No More would you really be all that impressed? It would just be a long stream of unstructured pop drone. Imaginary straw-men that have lived in a underground bunker for fifty years would totally hate Girl Talk!)

To extend the earlier Lego metaphor: Just as bloggers have two basic options—write original content or become a central link warehouse—musicians now can either mold the musical blocks for other "secondary" artists or build the "spaceship" from the publicly available kit. But these are not equal options. I doubt that anyone will ever sample Kayne's "Stronger." It's a dead-end, a cultural vasectomy.

A REALLY EASY WAY TO CONNECT TO PEOPLE

"The whole basis of the music is that people have these emotional attachments to these songs," Gillis told Pitchfork. "Being able to manipulate that is a really easy way to connect with people."

If Girl Talk has done anything, his dead-end project is a reminder of how fiercely dominant Western pop music has become. This is a capitulation, an audio essay even, of the last 25 years of American pop music: loop-based, interchangeable parts that, turns out, are more similar than maybe we'd like to admit. The "isn't it funny how 'Smells Like Teen Spirit' sounds like that Boston song" moment is taken to its darkest, veil-lifted extreme. That we're back in the Tin Pan Alley, and all pop music might actually be the same after all. That the difference is truly manufactured, that the concerns of each song are not interesting. Taking cues from the Grand Wizard Theodor: pop music is not art, but sound design.

Therein lies the insidiousness. Adorno pulled no punches. But Girl Talk poses as a pop optimist. He loves pop music—all pop music. It's all so unique. It's all just so great to him. Implicit in his project is that: It's all so similar to him too. That it all sounds the same in the end. That listening to a bunch of songs we used to care about in his refracted, rejiggered form is, at its heart, the same exact thing, compositionally and otherwise, as listening to a brand new song by a brand new musician. Why bother, right? This project, worse than any covert corporate sponsorship, he calls a celebration of pop music. What he himself doesn't know is we already had a name for it: la danse macabre.

A month or so ago, n+1 published an article by Jace Clayton called "Confessions of a DJ." First time through, my first thought was "holy shit, it's 2008 and dj/rupture just made a joke about laptop DJs checking their email during sets." My second time through, what stood out was Clayton's humility. "I was inspired to become a DJ by nights spent in an after-hours club in Boston where you couldn't see the DJ performing. The DJ wasn't an icon of cool there, he or she was a faceless person surfing the restless slipstream of musical pleasure," he writes towards the end. Clayton is one of the best DJs out there, from every possible angle. He digs deep and wide, he has style and technique, he knows the theory and could egg heads forever, but more than anything, you get the sense he'd rather you just dance. If any straight-up DJ wanted to claim he's an Artist, it's Clayton.

And yet he doesn't, and in fact you could say the piece is about Clayton refusing the title of artist. The distinction for him is a somewhat counterintuitive economical one: Artists make products, and at the moment, it's neither financially nor legally possible for the theoretical DJ-artist Clayton to make the DJ-Art-Product that he would theoretically art-sell. Instead he seems to think of himself as a technician, and his performances as careful recitals of other people's music. He's a gifted performer, in the same way that (I don't know) Luciano Pavarotti is (was?) a gifted singer or Glenn Gould a gifted pianist or Freddie Hubbard a gifted trumpet player.

At some point, I don't know when—I remember Wyatt in *The Recognitions* going on about this at one point—it became cooler (not sure that's the word) to be an "original artist" than a "gifted performer." I'm sure the economy has something to do with this. (Maybe the word is money-savvy.) The line in The Recognitions is

> That romantic disease, originality, all around we see originality of incompetent idiots, they could draw nothing, paint nothing, just so the mess they make is original . . . Even 200 years ago who wanted to be original, to be original was to admit that you could not do a thing the right way, so you could only do it your own way.

I bring all this up not to shit on Freddie Hubbard's original compositions, but to make room for the totally fine and great possibility that Girl Talk is a technically proficient user of audio software. Let's poke out his eyes and call him the laptop Bocelli. Seriously. I mean do whatever you want here. But please let him be what he is. Do not do this:

> I decided in the end to choose the records that I enjoyed the most, period—pleasure principle over agonizingly weighted critical judgment. Which is how I arrived at Girl Talk, aka Pittsburgh DJ Gregg Gillis, and his exuberant collages of classic rock, raunchy hip-hop, power ballads, and '80s bubblegum. (Typical segue: Unk into Twisted Sister into Huey Lewis and the News.) Some would have you believe that Gillis' songs say something serious about musical genre or the carnal and the spiritual. And they do say something—just not something serious. Girl Talk is a comedian, really. Beat-matching and pitch-shifting software has taken the technical wizardry out of mashup art,

and what's left to Gillis are in-jokes, funny contrasts, a cheeky higher form of fanboyism. In "Let Me See You," he sets up a battle of the sexes showdown between 2 Live Crew's "I Wanna Rock" and MIA's "Boyz": The Miami rappers command "Pop that pussy!"; M.I.A. answers with a schoolyard taunt: "Na na na na na na na na!"

Gillis' signature trick is juxtaposing melodramatic rock instrumentals with filthy hip-hop to underscore the pathos and the silliness and the plain fun that lurks in both gangsta rap and bombastic rock—an equal-opportunity celebration of pop's depths and pop's shallows. The irony is that while Girl Talk's mashups epitomize musical ADD in the iPod era, Feed the Animals is an expertly paced and sequenced song suite. Many tracks begin with snippets of the song that ended the previous one, and the whole megillah is framed by the UGK/Outkast song "International Player's Anthem," with the album coming full circle, Finnegans Wake style, to end where it began. In other words, Feed the Animals hangs together like a traditional album better than most anything else I heard this year. Which may be Gillis' best joke of all.

So instead of an "agonizingly weighted critical judgment" that *Slate* expects Rosen to deliver, he gives us this agonizingly apologetic bullshit for why Girl Talk is really guys an Artist. The first sentence of the second paragraph . . . Look, I can forgive him for going on about things that "epitomize musical ADD in the iPod era." I mean, it's Slate. You pretty much have to drop one of these gems in every other sentence. But Jesus, the first tune is the same as the last tune and he calls it "Finnegans Wake style." His shirt matches his pants and suddenly it's a "battle of the sexes showdown." You're seeing dead people, Jody! You're like the guy from fucking *Pi*!

One reason you don't see music writers talking about technique is because many of them review music they don't know how to make or play, so how would they even begin. Let alone the recording process. Lord knows I am not saying you need to know how to play banjo or else your Sufjan Stevens review is just worthless. We've been through this. You know I don't feel this way. Sufjan might actually feel this way if I remember correctly, but I don't. Granted I don't have some willfully naive approach either, but anyway so:

There is this really helpful distinction that music writers could make when they talk about Gillis—the performer vs artist one—and part of me thinks had we made that distinction from the beginning, he wouldn't be going around talking these huge lines about being an Original Artist. And more importantly, lest you think we've spent thousands of words quibbling over a semantic distinction, maybe Gillis would have realized the wildly insulting comment his Girl Talk project is making about pop music in the process.

Etc., etc.—NBS

Confessions of a DJ

Jace Clayton

I've DJed in more than two dozen countries. What I do isn't remotely popular in any of them.

It's hard to reach North Cyprus—the Turkish portion of the island that seceded after a war with Greece in 1974—not least because only one country, Turkey, officially recognizes it. Yet there we were, whizzing through arid country past pastel bunker-mansions, the architectural embodiment of militarized paranoia and extreme wealth, en route to an empty four-star hotel. We were going to rest for a day and then play music in the ruins of a crusader castle. It was the year 2000. I was the turntablist for an acid jazz group from New York City. The band didn't really need a DJ, but it did need someone to signify "hip-hop," and that was me. There were six of us—our saxophonist leader, Ilhan Irsahim; a singer, Norah Jones, before she was known for anything besides being Ravi Shankal's daughter; a bassist, a drummer, and a Haitian sampler-player. There were four attendants in the hotel casino, bored behind the gaming tables, and only two other paying guests—British pensioners, holdovers from remembered pre-1974 days when Cyprus was undivided.

I sat beside the pool talking to our host, trying to figure out why we were there. Down the coast, thirty miles away in the haze, a tall cluster of glass-and-steel buildings hugged the shore. "What's that city?" I asked. It looked like Miami. "Varosha," she said. Completely evacuated in the 1974 conflict. A ghost town on the dividing line between North and South Cyprus. The only people there were UN patrol units and kids from either side who entered the prohibited zone to live out a J.G. Ballard fantasy of decadent parties in abandoned seaside resorts.

If North Cyprus represented the forgotten side of a fault line of global conflict, how were we getting paid? Who owned those scattered mansions that we saw on the way from the airport? Was our trip bankrolled with narco-dollars, to please the criminals hiding out in an empty landscape, or with Turkish state funding, to win tourists back? I never found out. I bough a laptop with my earning, quit the band, and moved from New York to Barcelona.

DJed music develops in the great centers: London, New York, Paris. But the artists made much of their living in forays to the periphery. To state culture bureaus, our music sounds like art and the "avant-garde," a means of prestige. To kids coming of age in a world of technology and unhinged capitalism, our music seems to sound the way global capital is—liquid, international, porous, and sped-up.

Yet our sounds are also a vocabulary for those who detest the walled-off concentrations of wealth, and steal property back: the collective that build their own sound systems, state free parties, and invite DJs to perform. The international DJ becomes emblematic of global capitalism's complicated cultural dimension. On flights and at the free Continental breakfasts in hotels, often the same soul-destroying hotel chains in each city, we get stuck chatting with our fellow Americans and Western Europeans, the executives eager to find compatriots. We make small talk with these consultants and deal-makers in the descending elevators in the evening—then go out to the city's dead-end and unowned spaces or its luxury venues to soundtrack the night of the region's youth, hungry for something new. DJ music is now the common art form of squatters and the nouveau riche; it is the soundtrack both for capital and for its opposition.

As a process, DJing is inevitable and necessary for our times, an elegant way to deal with data overload. As a performance, it's what the kids are grooving to the world over. As a product, it's largely illegal.

In 2001 I recorded a three-turntable, sixty-minute mix called *Gold Teeth Thief*. I put it on the internet so my friends could listen. Who else would? One magazine reviewed it, then another, and soon a lot of magazines, leading to hundreds of thousands of downloads. Meanwhile, I was in Madrid without regular internet access. I didn't know what was up. A few months after it went online, I got a phone call from a large European independent label. I'd used one of their songs on the mix. They loved it! It was the best DJ session they'd heard in ages! They wanted to license the mix, assuming they could pay the various labels a few of $1,000 per track. (There were eighteen tracks on the run list.) "That'd be fantastic," I said, "but pretty expensive. I use forty-four different songs on it. Some of those are major pop tunes, and a bunch are unlicensable bootlegs. It'd be a nightmare to do legally." They insisted that I send a complete track list so that their legal department could decide. Result: "Impossible. Our lawyers laughed at us."

If I were a band, and *Gold Teeth Thief* an album, not a mix, that would have been my big break. A powerful label, big advance fees, well-connected publicists, a coordinated tour. But it's more common for even a popular DJ to receive a cease-and-desist order than to get a mix-album deal with a large label.

It's hard to care. Viral culture doesn't play well with intellectual property laws. I knew *Gold Tooth Thief* couldn't enter the commercial world when I did it. I didn't need it to. Word-of-mouth buzz and bootleg mixes are the DJ's symbolic currency; gigs provide the cash. I've toured well in countries where my music wasn't available for purchase—people had heard it. On his first visit to Moscow, a rapper friend named Sole found his own music bootlegged in a black-market mall. In fact, the place is called the Black Market Mall. He was thrilled, and with good reason—that night's audience sang along word for word. He was able to tout. Metaphors of the "underground" and codifications of the "commercial" mean less and less with MySpace.

Economics favor the DJ. A club can make an event out of one big-name DJ plus local support, and pay just the headliner. (And DJing can make for a long night of drinks-buying: in a rare example, eight hours' nonstop entertainment from a particularly famous Chilean-German drugged-up minimal techno superstar.) A popular indie band would have to be paid vastly more for each member to walk away with similar earning. Plus it's only one plane ticket for the DJ; the band needs to drive, needs roadies, et cetera. Even in cheapskate America—a country notoriously apathetic toward DJ culture (which it created!)—upper-echelon techno DJs have received, say, $18,000 for a three-hour club performance in Manhattan. That's $100 a minute. But only a few dozen DJs worldwide can command those fees. The much more common scenario is that of the DJ who plays for free drinks and cab fare, never earning more than he spends on records.

At the other end of the spectrum from the official luxury clubs lie the squatted venues, the microcommunities. These anarchic spaces are best understood as alternative social centers, especially in Western Europe where property laws offer squatters a modicum of legal protection. A thousand people came to the last party that my friend Filastine and I threw in La Makabra. La Makabra sprawled across *media manzana* (half a city block) in the Barcelona district called *Poble Now*—"new city," in Catalan.

The squat had a gymnasium, library, nursery, skate part, two concert halls, and space for at least thirty people to live. They had a lawyer. We met Swiss gallerists and homeless kids, all dancing. Six months later the cops evicted the residents (illegally) and bulldozed the place within hours. But Makabras exist all over Europe: in Milan, Paris, Ljubljana.

Between the rich and spiritually vacant venues and the poor and illegally occupied ones are all manner of places to perform, from crazy artist-run clubs like Hamburg's infamous Golden Pudel to countryside festivals with temporary populations the size of a small town (including the teknivals staged by "travelers," a European hybrid of ravers, anarcho-punks, and off-the-grid nomads). Not to mention middle-range loopholes where economic rules are suspended. Government money for cutting-edge parties? It happens. Impossible things become possible. Dead of winter, somewhere in Austria: we're playing outside—well, technically we're playing *inside* a subzero meat locker in a parking lot near a cleaned-up industrial canal. We, the performers, are in one meat locker, and the speakers are in two adjacent meat lockers for the audience, where the thermostats are set as low as they can go.

I can't remember if the hot cider was free or not. I can't imagine why it wouldn't have been: everything else was funded by Austrian taxpayers. Arts funding in Europe is like magic dust.

When you're back home, a different kind of magic accompanies the DJ's aura: the easy money or remixes, corporate events, advertising. Twice I've been scheduled to play a gig with a really well-known DJ. Twice he's canceled to do a corporate event. Global brands fly him around the world to entertain their private parties. Since these events pay so well and are so fundamentally uncool, there are DJs whose corporate earnings far exceed that from their public gigs—but they'll never admit it. A couple of years ago a magazine even flew me across an ocean to play for forty-five minutes. Naked girls on pedestals got their bodies painted and everybody else shouted at each other over mouthfuls of free sushi.

I do receive plenty of remix offers, courtesy of everyone from an Algerian rai singer to a Spanish girl group asking me to "improve" their number one hit. You can't improve a number one hit by making it better—not in these people's world. When people request remixes, what they really want is to attach a DJ's name to theirs. Aura is contagious, aura rubs off. The music tends to be secondary. And so the more money a label offers me to remix, the less time I spend on it. For remix offers of $1,000 and up, my time limit is eight hours of work, start to finish. If I spend any longer, the track will inevitably get more personal and the label people will be less likely to accept it. Besides, eight hours is a lot of time to spend on something that you won't necessarily get paid for. If a label rejects your remix, you can't release it elsewhere, since the label owns the music.

On tour, life becomes simplified. Travel, wait, play, sleep, repeat. Countries blur. Languages splinter; all you need is English.

Few musicians bother to learn about the countries they perform in. We're the opposite of tourists. All cities look the same when you arrive at night, get driven to the venue and leave the next morning. But DJ's understand rooms as few others do. You can walk into an empty venue and instantly envision how that night's crowd will react to the architecture of that space.

Both DJing and electronic music production are learned in an artisanal way. One is generally either self-taught or apprenticed. The mechanics of DJing are simple to demonstrate. All you need to do it right are years of practice and the sensitivity of real listening. For the DJ, the actual performance is never just about the musical selection and mixing, something you can work out in advance. There's the dynamics of the sound system to contend with, and how the bodies are reacting to what comes out of it, and what you then have to do about it. When I DJ, I almost never pick out individuals in the dancing crowd. At a good party, the temperature will noticeably heat up when you put on a song that makes people move. You can feel it on your skin even if you don't look up from your decks.

You have to be watchful for the pieces of musical culture that don't translate, even when they come from the places you're playing in. A few months ago I performed in Dubai, part of the United Arab Emirates. I'd mix in a big Arabic tune, but blend it with other rhythms, so that people would hear my mix style cutting up and overlaying the Middle Eastern source records. I'd do a dancehall reggae riddim underneath Egyptian cabdriver chaabi. A stuttering breakbeat pulse bulwarking Rachid Taha's remake of Dahmane el-Harrachi's exile song "Ya Rayah." The Lebanese contingent went wild. But a concerned Arab came up to the booth. "Could you play less Arabic music?" He pointed to two blond

Western Girls he was getting down with. Arabic language alienated them, whereas the "niggas" and "bitches" of my rap a cappellas made then want to party. I changed course. Later in the evening the Scottish club manager came over with the same request. "Too much Arabic music. Do you mind ending with something in English?" "It's not Arabic," I said, "it's Berber. From North Africa—Morocco." He shrugged. He later told me that nobody had ever played Middle Eastern music on his night. He'd be able to spin the whole thing into a noble example of his ecumenical curatorial slant.

Near the beginning of my career, I wound up doing a DJ set at the Montreux Jazz Festival. Up in the mountains of Switzerland. For me it was crazy. I was DJing in front of a thousand people for the first time, and it was working, they were following me. I was doing what I would do at home, no holds barred. It's a predominantly white, European crowd, and I'm a black DJ. (The festival program said I was a woman of Egyptian-Italian descent, but we all make mistakes.) There's lots of security up front, and I see this one other black guy, trying to reach me.

"Hey!" he's yelling. "Hey DJ!"

I didn't look up. Ten minutes later he's still there, still gesturing.

I asked the security to let him get close so I could hear. "'Back That Azz Up'!" he shouted. "Play 'Back That Azz Up'!"

Ten years alter, it's no longer a Juvenile song, but a song by a kid from Juvenile's crew—Lil Wayne—that somebody will still shout for, every night, anywhere in the world.

Bands perform songs, DJs perform records. With the old techniques, scratching, cutting, beat-matching, and blending. DJs synchronize two records around a common tempo, using a mixer to blend the songs together. The how-to developed in the hip-hop scene of the South Bronx in the 1970s and has changed little since. The workhorse turntable, standard in clubs the world over, is still the Technics 1200. The design of this twenty-six-pound behemoth hasn't changed since its 1978 debut. I purchased my 1200s, secondhand, over ten years ago. They work as good as they did the day I bought 'em.

I use three turntables, which makes things more delicate. One slip will send the pattern from harmony into "Trainwreck," so-called because the arrhythmic clatter of beats will derail the dance floor. But if you mix right, you can get a single "new" totality, whose individual elements can still be heard clearly if you know what you're listening for. A fan who's been watching comes over and says, "I really like that song. What is it?" I can only ask, "Which one?" The DJ's job is to make disparate records sound like a whole, and the more successful you are at it, the less likely the novice onlooker is to know it. DJs have to work to avoid silence and make things appear seamless. You build things up. One of the paradoxes central to the DJ's art is that some of the most demanding, virtuoso work is the hardest to recognize.

Live electronics performers, streaming their own recorded music from laptops, work differently. They follow the basic template given to us by dub reggae. Take a preexisting song, add effects, momentarily remove ("dub out") parts. Live electronica performers basically mess up their own music, which is pre-built and then disassembled. The more "active" they appear, the more the original piece is being interrupted.

Just as there's a limited number of computer programs that let you make beat-based electronic music, only a few let you perform it. In the past half dozen years, nearly all have been supplanted by a popular upstart—Ableton Live. The majority of "live" dance music acts now use Ableton, won over by its performance-opti-mized stability. I grind my teeth when I recognize Ableton's built-in FX. *That ping-pong filter delay algorithm is so obvious! It's like pouring ketchup on everything!* My friends tell me to relax.

Which program you use can affect the product and sometimes nearly determine your genre. With Ableton, it's as if the software's Berlin-based programmers wanted everyone to play techno. Max/MSP tends to produce tone-clouds of granulated noise. FruityLoops favors the stiff drum programming found in reg-gaeton. The most popular music software in the favelas of Rio de Janiero and their villa counterparts across Latin America is Acid (what I started on, and my favorite program to date, truth be told), a simple application for making sample-based music—perfect for folks without much musical training.

Nearly all of us DJs try our hands at making original electronic music at some point. It's a tricky proposition. Good DJs must have great taste, but great live DJ mixes are exciting in precisely the way that great original albums aren't—they're heterogeneous, unanticipatible, improvisatory.

In 2005, I made an original album, *Special Gunpowder*. I'm not sure Ill ever make another. Why? I'm lazy. I was trying to push too many different kinds of sounds instead of one marketable line. The album-as-major-statement seems less viable nowadays, any-way. (Watch out, novel!) Between the "shuffle" function on portable MP3 players and the single-song downloads of iTunes and audioblogs, the album's heyday as a sequentially ordered object of contemplation is ending.

It'd be easier to dispense with the notion of albums (and album sales) if Americans were more hip to DJ culture. Unless you're playing weddings, this is a bad country in which to be a DJ. The fees tend to be lower than in Europe, and the treatment by venues is almost always worse, not to mention the ubiquity of rock sound systems ill-equipped for dance music. It's not uncommon for DJs and electronic musicians who can draw a substantial crowd in middle-size European towns to face half-empty rooms in US cities.

Why hasn't DJ culture taken off here like elsewhere? I'm not sure. Americans do love a spectacle. One of the most talked about electronica groups of recent years, Justice, perform their Parisian electro-disco with a stock of iconic Marshall amplifiers, unplugged, onstage. Without the rock façade (and Daft Punk's manager steering their career) they'd be another faceless techno act.

American audiences like to see the artist expressing inner joy or channeling demons (or at least dressing up and dancing). The connection between a guitar and its player is physical: each action corresponds to a sound. The same thing is true of a DJ using vinyl, but the correspondences are more difficult to see. As for musicians and DJs using laptops, for all you know they could be onstage checking their email.

I recently moved to New York City after seven years in Spain. My "quality of life" ratcheted down several notches; my living expenses doubled. I no longer live next door to an active bullfighting ring with views of the Mediterranean, Gaudi's Sagrada Familia, and the mountains. (At the start of my time in New York, I lived in a room in a shared loft. Rent on that Brooklyn room cost approximately as much as that of a family-size apartment in Barcelona.) Staring at my bank account, a strange fact hits home: as an International DJ, the scale of my income is completely uncoupled from the costs of wherever I happen to live.

It's inadvisable to live in one of the world's most expensive cities when your workplace is global. Money burns faster here.

DJs are improvisers, however. We adapt. As for me, I take a lot more transatlantic flights than I'd like. I do more concentrated touring now.

Media attention cycles continue to shorten. Trends in dance music accelerate, with each new flavor yielding a clutch of DJs and producers offering free material online, their sheer numbers slowly pulling entry-level booking fees downward. Hot DJs spend less and less time in demand, especially ones coupled to a particular style. Dubstep, a genre splintered from UK garage, is only two or three years old, yet it has become codified, arthritic. The genre's pioneers distance themselves from the name as satellite scenes outside of Britain trudge on in disbelief—"How can this be dying down if it hasn't really started here?" MP3 revenue doesn't compensate for plummeting CD sales, which prompts record labels to make highly conservative decisions when signing artists. And let's face it: even if you can survive all this to scrape out a living, do you really want to be playing raves when you're 40?

I'm not saddened by the state of things. I was inspired to become a DJ by nights spent in an after-hours club in Boston where you couldn't see the DJ performing. The DJ wasn't an icon of cool there, he or she was a faceless person surfing the restless slipstream of musical pleasure. Now is the best time ever to be a music fan. The overall movement is toward more ways to share music (and ideas) with like-minded individuals, whether online or face-to-face, body-to-body. What DJ is not first and foremost a music fan?

Between tours I've been tapping into the enormous amount of unreleased music I receive. In addition to releasing other people's music on my homemade label, Soot, I've gotten involved in another start-up—Dutty Artz. We're producing an album by Jahdan Blakkamoore, a Guyanese reggae vocalist who sneaked into America, alone, when he was 8 years old. Our business model would be incomprehensible to an old-time record exec. We're releasing music commercially, giving away more pieces for free, pumping internet TV episodes into YouTube (interviews, street fashion, cooking shows, party footage), and, on rare occasions, deliberately inserting our official releases into the bootleg CD gray market economy. (One man's piracy is another's distribution network.) A trio of Africans runs the NYC bootleg market. If you hand them your original, they give you a flat fee of $250, and then make as many copies as they like, selling them for $5 apiece. Of course the $250 is really a courtesy since they bootleg whatever they want anyway and usually don't pay a dime.

When you tally up the work we put into them, the records we release don't make money—they push sound into the world. Business model be damned. In 2008 you need to believe in music or money, not both. And what I do with all the artists is try to tell them the truth about what's happening. Since the official music industry is a kind of pathetic vivid nightmare, run by greed people, dilettantes, and folks who don't like music, it's surprising how helpful honesty can be.

Everybody Loves Difficult Music

Machine Project, Los Angeles, 2008

Michael Pisaro

Inside the museums,
Infinity goes up on trial.
Voices echo
this is what salvation
must be like,
after awhile.

—Bob Dylan, from *Visions of Johanna*

Is thought difficult?

Is listening thought?

Is it easier to think when plowing through thickets of tones or is thinking easier when nothing appears to be going on?

Do you find it hard to sit for ten minutes without doing anything, or is that your idea of a trip to Jupiter?

Is performance more difficult when the fingers move faster?

Does the mind move faster when the fingers do?

Is it more difficult to write music or to play it?

Is it more difficult to write difficult music or is it more difficult to write easy music?

Is there such a thing as easy music? And where?

Is it more difficult to abstract from a process or to pin it down in all its particulars?

Was the "new math" more difficult than the old?

Does your mind fog over when you see the names Weierstrass, Cantor, Dedekind, Zermelo, Fraenkel and Gödel?

Or Schoenberg, Xenakis and Ferneyhough?

Are certain languages more difficult than others?

Is speaking the language of the tribe (as Mallarmé would have it) easier than subtracting your language from the language of the tribe?

How difficult would it be not to make art at all?

The term needs definition in order to be useful. One "difficulty" is a vestige of the modernist revolutions of the 20th Century. What is often being described as difficult is an art that resists easy assimilation because it does not fit within the common language of the time. That art, be it Non-Figurative painting, Abstract Expressionism, Avant-garde music, Conceptual art, Experimental Theater, Music or Film, created new worlds: worlds that would not have been possible without the vision of those artists, but to which for many, there was no easy entrée. It was as if a blockage had to be cleared away before the art could be seen or heard. To the extent that an artist takes on the task of exploring new worlds, her art risks *difficulty*: it may resist categorization in the old laws, may not be easily visible or audible to most who encounter it, and may not be entirely clear to the person making it.

"True," you might say, "but we also have Duke Ellington and Howard Hawks"; i.e., artists who create new worlds but whose work is not difficult in this way. [In these cases we might say that if there is difficulty, it has more to do with the "how" than the "what."]

Perhaps difficulty of *reception* is just a side effect, and not really a preoccupation of the artist (like the nausea that comes along with medication). Maybe it's like the question of accessibility: diagonal to the act of creation, based on the assumption that the artist has something to say, is trying to communicate something. (Things are difficult when you have the feeling that someone is trying to tell you something that you can't understand, no matter how hard you try.)

Perhaps, as Gilles Deleuze says about philosophy, Art is not communication. It's always trying to subtract its relation to communication in the service of a remainder: something we hear or see or experience that "says" nothing so that it can "do" something (or nothing).

Orion is.
Music of Changes is.
Au hasard Balthazar is.
Poor little rich girl is.

They are artistic facts that work on us, almost without our knowing it. Nobody knows what they do: but they do something. The question of "understanding" hardly enters into it: there is nothing, really, to understand.

"Difficult" poet Oswald Egger says that his poetry works *around* understanding.

Try this:

*Early—not for me—umber and unending their night
    shadow days.*
*Mallows, tapping up the mirror-orach to nut-
    cloudflakes mountain narde.*
*Melisse greet you, catnip, nepeta are mouth-
    watering early in the year.*
*I drink birch-wine in the new marshfield of muscatel
    under medlars.*
*A composition swam in the wine barrel, glowing-
    morels, leaf bulbs.*
*Promise of differences—heaven between waste lands,
    the snow lines.*
*Nib-twirls mostly in the graining of urgent stick-
    mesh of green twigs.*
*Medlarks, tricked through ivy marshwort, Nivose
    and maple elders.*
*The lightbirch blooms, tangled confusions in
    unsleeping clouds, and fog.*
*Like paws, and frost nuts numb-bramble flames
    nipping these—the nittles.*
*And in almond colors stacked cordwood without
    gaps, morel winterashes.*
*Threading through slumber its marrowbeam lace-
    strands in the resin-garland.*

Does it make it easier to know that is not one poem, but twelve one-line poems?

My first response in trying to read and then translate this text from Oswald Egger's *Hänggärten* was to give up. A good decision, because "giving up" is really a kind of "giving in": a way of saying that you'll agree not to "understand" anything, to give yourself credit for not understanding, when there is nothing to understand. You stop understanding in order to start thinking.

Maybe this has always been the message of music: don't understand, but listen—listen as thinking.

Here's something I can think of doing with the idea of "thinking" (in sound): It is a piece that was easy to write, but which I find extremely difficult to perform:

Imagine a world full of sound.

Subtract, one by one, each particular sound you hear, without loosing the sounds that are already there.

A composer could make this easy for you by making a realization. What's difficult about the piece in this form, is keeping it all in your head, keeping it going. It's on strain on the powers of memory and imagination.

And yet, the experience of music sometimes (for me) leaves precisely this kind of residue: an impossibly rich but incredibly fleeting set of sensations that cohere after the fact into a kind of mental configuration, an idea of some kind: striking, abstract, intangible. A composite world: an egg, a nut, a bullet. The residue of an *event*.

At its most radical, art is caught up in an event—something the artist has not created, but to which she is accountable. The difficulties come from maintaining the inchoate vision opened by the event, keeping the possibilities open even as the path seems to narrow, or to split, or to disappear altogether.

One model for the courageous pursuit of a set of artistic consequences would be Samuel Beckett, whose motto (as Alain Badiou points out) is: "I can't go on, I'll go on." Onward into the fog; from one fog to the next, driven nonetheless, with no confidence, but with a kind of blind determination:

. . . perhaps it's a dream, all a dream, that would surprise me, I'll wake, in the silence, and never sleep again, it will be I, or dream, dream again, dream of a silence, a dream silence, full of murmurs, I don't know, that's all words, never wake, all words, there's nothing else, you must go on, that's all I know, they're going to stop, I know that well, I can feel it, they're going to abandon me, it will be the silence, for a moment, a good few moments, or it will be mine, the lasting one, that didn't last, that still lasts, it will be I, you must go on, I can't go on, you must go on, I'll go on, you must say the words, as long as there are any, until they find me, until they say me, strange pain, strange sin, you must go on, perhaps it's done already, perhaps they have said me already, perhaps they have carried me to the threshold of my story, before the door that opens on my story, that would surprise me, if it opens, it will be I, it will be the silence, where I am, I don't know, I'll never know, in the silence you don't know, you must go on, I can't go on, I'll go on.

(quoted from the last passage from *The Unnamable*)
An event is (even when it is not).
But it has consequences.
Consequences are never easy.
If you are patient, determined, lucky; these consequences might lead you somewhere you didn't know existed.
What would be difficult is a world *without* this possibility: the possibility of a new world, of new worlds, of *other* words. That would be a world without salvation.

Your Trusted Source for Music Reviews
Carrie Brownstein

The Black Crowes are lashing out at Maxim magazine
for reviewing the band's new album—apparently without
actually hearing it first. The review, published in
Maxim's March issue, gives the Crowes' 'Warpaint' a
rating of two-and-a-half stars out of five. The writer . . .
has not heard the album.

—Black Crowes Say Maxim Review a Fraud,
Associated Press, Feb. 23, 2008

BEAR IN HEAVEN—*RED BLOOM OF THE BOOM*

The latest effort by BIH, RBOTB, is a swirling, dizzying, daring, vertiginous ride. "Bag of Bags" blends angelic harmonies with toast. And "Fraternal Noon" left me wanting a warm sweater that I could then layer over a T-shirt only to be too warm and have to wear just the T-shirt.

Rating: Double Tall Sugar Free Vanilla Latte. Or, Go Bears!

THESE UNITED STATES—*A PICTURE OF THE THREE OF US AT THE GATE TO THE GARDEN OF EDEN.*

By the time I finished reading the title the album was already over.
Rating: 2 F**ks and 1.5 Yeahs.

KAKI KING—*DREAMING OF REVENGE*

I've been waiting for this CD for 11 years and it finally arrived.
"Life Being What It Is" is King at his best, while "Open Mouth"
is King even better than he usually is. "Air and Kilometers" is a
beautiful song about traveling in a plane in a country that uses the
metric system and "Montreal" is about a city in Canada.
Rating: Happy Milkshake

WYE OAK—*IF CHILDREN*

This album is one, long beautiful poem beginning with the line
"If Children. . . ..." I don't even need to tell you the rest. It's Whitney Houston's "The Greatest Love Of All" except angrier and totally against mid-wives.
Rating: 7 divided by 3 times 10 plus your sun sign.

THE SHINS—*HONEY POKE SHIMMY LANTERN*

James Mercer and crew can do no wrong. They've added the De-
cemberists, the Thermals, and Spoon to their lineup. Recorded
inside a deer carcass, the sounds on Honey Poke are haunting and
cervid. These songs will change your life back to the way it was

before The Shins changed it the first time. Remember that song "Red Rubber Ball?" It's on this album!

Rating: $800

THE WHITE STRIPES—*PALE PAIL*

This album was recorded on an abacus.

Rating: Seborrhea

TIFT MERRIT—*ANOTHER COUNTRY*

Tift Merrit sings the book by James Baldwin.

Rating: Really, really fun.

"The Fly In The Ointment"

Preface to 100 greatest singers

Jonathan Lethem

Look, contrary to anything you've heard, the ability to actually carry a tune is in no regard an absolute and forbidding disability in becoming a rock-and-roll singer, only a mild disadvantage, like coming to the plate with a strike or two against you. As proponents of such dismayingly adept vocalists as Aretha Franklin, Van ("The Greater") Morrison, Jeff Buckley, and P.J. Harvey will attest, virtuosity can be gotten around. Conversely, nothing in the limitations in the vocal instrument of a Lou Reed guarantees a "Pale Blue Eyes" result every time out—as a sample of any one the several million forgettable spoken-whined-mumbled-intoned flat "indie-style" vocals now in the banks (a few committed by Lou Reed himself) will quickly testify. Yet there's a certain functional, time-tested sturdiness to the least-likely-to-hit-the-notes approach forged by Reed and his cohort—including touchstone figures like Bob Dylan and Jim ("The Lesser") Morrison and Jonathan Richman, and which defines a tremendous amount of rock and roll singing, both for those wishing to extol it and those still looking, at this late date, to denounce it, in the Frank

Sinatra-on-Elvis manner. ("His kind of music is deplorable, a rancid smelling aphrodisiac . . . " God, how happy that quote always makes me—it tells me I have a culture!) Because expressivity is the only standard, the low-chops approach helps define rock and roll singing, which is both egalitarian ("Anyone can do this!") and Dionysian ("But only if you're crazy with passion!") in its premises. Nor are technical limitations solely a male province. I'm looking at you, Patti Smith, Chan Marshall, and—oh, hey!—Nancy Sinatra. And the excellent thing about an incompetent singer is that, unlike an incompetent band, which is always threatening to learn how to play their instruments to the detriment of their greatness, the incompetent singer is pretty firmly mired. You can swap the cancer sticks for nicotine patches, you can seek coaching (or pitch-control software) but there's something about a voice that's personal, that its issuer remains profoundly stuck inside, like the particular odor or shape of their body. After all, that's pretty much what it is: summoned through belly, hammered into form by the throat, given propulsion by bellows of lungs, teased into final form by tongue and lips, voice is a kind of audible kiss, a blurted confession, a soul-burp you really can't keep from issuing as you make your way through the material world. How helplessly candid! How appalling!

You'll think I'm being slightly disingenuous. I suppose I am, to the extent that I've implied that I think Bob Dylan, for instance, or Patti Smith, are anything less than superb singers by any measure I could ever care about—expressivity, surprise, soul, grain, interpretive wit, angle-of-vision (I'm succumbing here to all those dubious abstractions that makes this subject so confounded to describe in the first place). Those two folks, a handful of others: their soul-burps are, for me, *the soul-burps of the Gods*. But my exaggeration is in the cause of driving a wedge into the embarrassing question of what we're feeling when we make such declarations as those I've made in the sentences above. The beauty of the singer's voice touches us in a place that's personal as the place from which that voice has issued—a nifty syllogism that's not going to get me out of my task here. If one of the weird things about singers is the ecstasy of surrender they tend to inspire in us when the connection is made—which forms the "Madness of Crowds" mass insanity associated with voices as diverse as Elvis, Om Kalsoum, Teddy Pendergrass, etc., but is also present in intimately exclusive situations, such as when a listener first communes with Jeff Buckley's "Lilac Wine" or Joni Mitchell's "Amelia" alone on headphones in the dark—another weird thing is the defensive debunking response a singer can arouse in us just the moment after we've recovered our senses. It's as if they've fooled us into loving them, played with our hardwiring, located an innocence and vulnerability we thought we'd long-ago armored over. Falling in love with a singer is like being a teenager every time it happens.

Singers *are* tricksters. Sometimes we'll wonder if they're more like movie actors than musicians *per se*—we'll decide that the "real" R.E.M. is embodied by Buck, Berry and Mills, not that kooky frontman Stipe, or the "real" Rolling Stones is Richards-Wood-Watts-Wyman, rather than that irritating capitalist Jagger. But beware—go down this route and soon you'll find yourself wondering how The Doors sound sans "Mr. Mojo Risin," or imagining someone can better put across Dylan's gnarled syllables than Dylan himself. Firm evidence is on the table against both those lines of inquiry. In truth, so often what makes a band like the Stones or R.E.M. (or the band Dylan transformed from The

Hawks into The Band) so truly unique and powerful is in how the instrumentalists rise to the challenge of creating a home for the vocalists' less-than-purely-musical approach to a song: the braggadoccio or mumbling, the spoken asides or too-many-syllables crowded into a line that destroys traditional rhythm or measure, those movie-star flourishes that compel us to adore and resent the singer at once.

The funny thing about this kind of imposter-anxiety is that it infects singers themselves, to the extent that certain well-known vocalists have been known to decorate themselves onstage with a carefully-unplugged guitar (I know of a couple, but I'm not telling). And it certainly explains the "rockist" bias in favor of singers who are also the writers of the songs they sing. If a vocal performance that tenderizes our hearts is a kind of high-wire walk, an act breathtaking and preposterous at once, we can reassure ourselves that Neil Young or Gillian Welch or Joe Strummer have at least dug the foundations for the poles and strung the wire themselves. Singers reliant on existing or made-to-fit material like Janis Joplin, Rod Stewart, Whitney Houston—or, for that matter, a band's pure vocal instrument, like Roger Daltrey—might just be birds alighting on someone else's wire. Listening to singers who are like magnificent animals wandering through a karaoke machine, we may derive a certain thrill from wondering if they find the same meaning in the lyrics they're putting across that the lyric's writer intended, or any meaning at all—as opposed to dwelling in a realm of pure sound-as-emotion.

Well, for my own purposes here I'd like to throw that distinction completely aside, and assert that what defines great singing in the rock and soul era is some underlying tension in the space between singer and song. A bridge is being built across a void, and it's a bridge we're never sure the singer's going to manage to cross. The gulf may reside between vocal texture and the actual meaning of the words, or between the singer and the band, the musical genre, the style of production, or the audience's expectations, what have you. In other words, there's something beautifully uncomfortable at the root of the vocal style that defines the pop era, though we may have grown so comfortable with the discomfort that we're left stranded—bored, disappointed, put to sleep—if we don't detect it. The simplest example comes at the moment of the style's inception, i.e., Elvis Presley: first listeners *thought that the white guy was a black guy*. It's not too much of an exaggeration to say that when Ed Sullivan's television show tossed this disjunction into everyone's living rooms, American culture was thrilled by it, but also a little deranged, in ways we haven't gotten over yet. If few vocal styles since have had the same revolutionary potential, it wasn't for want of trying. When The Doors experimented with how rock 'n' roll sounded fronted by sulky bombast, or The Ramones or Modern Lovers offered the sound of infantile twitching, a listener's first response may be to regard their approaches as a joke. Yet that joke is the sound of something changing in the way a song can make us feel.

I'll make an ever wilder assertion: the nature of the vocals in post-Elvis, post-Sam Cooke, post-Ray Charles popular music *is the same as the role of the instrumental soloist in jazz*. That's to say, if it isn't pushing against the boundaries of its form, at least slightly, it isn't doing anything at all. Whether putting across lines that happen to be written by the singer, or are instead concocted in a Brill-Building or Motown-type laboratory, or covering a song pulled in from another genre, from the blues, or bluegrass, or a showtune, the singer in rock, soul, and pop has to be doing something ineffable that pulls against its given context. Etta James, Ray Davies, Mama Cass, Mark Kozelek, Levi Stubbs Jr.: these singers might not all seem like protest singers, but they are always singing "against" something; whether in themselves, in the band that's backing them, in the world they've been given to live in or the material they've been given to sing, or all at once. We judge pre-rock singing by how perfectly the lyric is served. That's the standard Frank Sinatra exemplifies (but which, paradoxically, can also be met by someone handicapped in the manner of Fred Astaire). We judge popular vocals since 1956 by what the singer unearths that the song itself could never quite. It explains why voices such as Joan Baez or Emmylou Harris or Billy Joel never really seem to be singing in the contemporary idiom, no matter how much they roughen up their material or accompaniment, and why Elvis–or Dylan–is always rock, even singing "Blue Moon." It also explains precisely why such virtuosic pipes as Aretha Franklin's or, yes, Karen Carpenter's, function in the new tradition. No lyric written by themselves or anyone else could ever express what their voices needed to, and they weren't going to wait for the instrumental solo, or for the flourish of strings, to put it across for them. They got it into their voice, and their voices got it out into the air, and from there it passed into our bodies. How can we possibly thank them enough?

Funk's Death Trip

Yuval Taylor

It was 1971, and death was changing shape. For centuries it had been feared, reviled, or simply swept under the rug. But now it was being celebrated.

Lieutenant William Calley was on trial for murdering 102 Vietnamese civilians in cold blood at My Lai, and the fan letters were pouring in—ten thousand of them by February. Legislators from Jimmy Carter to George Wallace condemned Calley's conviction, and more than 200,000 copies of "The Battle Hymn of William Calley" were sold. At the same time, Charles Manson's trial made public the adoring testimony of his lovers and acolytes; "Charlie was a father who knew that it is good to make love, and makes love with love, but not with evil and guilt," gushed Squeaky Fromme. Meanwhile, in Detroit, a jury acquitted James Johnson, who had methodically shot and killed three men in a Chrysler plant with an M-1 carbine, finding his acts were justified by his ill-treatment at the factory.

Death was not just OK, it was cool. In a study of near-death experiences in *Omega* magazine, Dr. Russell Noyes Jr. reported that they were a lot like the mystical states of consciousness brought on by LSD and recommended that scientists should

189

study people on drugs if they wanted to know more about what it was like to die.

Detroit, which boasted the country's highest murder rate, also boasted no fewer than four extremely loud bands with screaming guitars and wild stage shows, and at least one of these was taking plenty of LSD, immersed in thoughts of death. When Funkadelic released its third album in July, it captured the mood of the era perfectly—not just druggy, but toxic.

The cover. Her head is poking out of the dirt, but she's not dirty. She's screaming—or is she laughing?—mouth wide open, eyes shut tight, afro glistening, teeth gleaming and perfect. The dirt looks good too—some straw, some pebbles, but nothing crawling. The rest of her body is invisible—buried. The word above her, in day-glo orange: FUNKADELIC, a psychedelic funk, a stink so strong it's hallucinatory. The words below her: MAGGOT BRAIN.

Inside the album's gatefold, under an 11-inch image of a maggot, is a long screed about fear attributed to the Process Church of the Final Judgment, which ends as follows:

> As long as human beings fail to see THEIR fear reflected in these and a hundred other manifestations of Fear, then they will fail to see their part in the relentless tide of hatred and violence, destruction and devastation, that sweeps the earth. And the tide will not ebb until all is destroyed.

On the right is a blurry, faded photograph of the band, black men mostly in their early twenties, posed casually in front of a crumbling brick wall. Lead guitarist Eddie Hazel appears to have just woken up; Billy "Bass" Nelson's cap almost shields his eyes, as if he's asking, "Who the fuck are you?"; keyboardist Bernie Worrell stares off into space; drummer Ramon "Tiki" Fulwood is dressed like an outlaw in black hat and cowboy boots; rhythm guitarist Tawl Ross looks like he's wearing a holster under his red, white, and blue leather jacket and pitch-black sunglasses. As for lyricist, producer, and conceptual mastermind George Clinton, he's not in the picture.

On the back cover, the dirt looks lighter now, vapor rising in the heat. And in place of the beautiful black woman's screaming head is a shining clean skull with its eye sockets aglow.

The music. First up is an emotionally draining guitar solo called "Maggot Brain." According to some accounts, the title was a phrase Clinton came up with after his brother died and nobody knew; maggots were crawling out of his skull when he was finally found. Before the song's recording, Clinton told Hazel to imagine his mother had just died. It only took one take. Clinton then erased Nelson's and Worrell's playing completely and put Fulwood way back in the mix, leaving only the two guitars, Ross playing a series of four six-note arpeggios and Hazel playing, in Chuck Eddy's words, "ten weaving and swelling minutes of . . . disorder that may well express the saddest emotion I've ever heard wrenched from a mere musical instrument."

The album ends with another ten-minute guitar excursion, a burning hot prefiguring of what Miles Davis would do on *Agharta*, called "Wars of Armageddon," with Hazel's apocalyptic fervor accompanied by at least three percussionists, and the music overlaid by a barrage of sound effects—gunshots, cuckoo clocks, flatulence, crying babies, heartbeats, bombs.

In between it asks if you can "get to" the fact that you're really dead—"I once had a life, or rather it had me"—in "Can You Get to That." "You and Your Folks, Me and My Folks" begs for togetherness, but turns sour with Nelson's screamed lyrics like "You know that hate is gonna keep on multiplying and you know that man is gonna keep right on dying"; behind "there won't be no peace!" and "there never was folks!" the incessant background "yeah yeah yeah"s begin to sound like the "no no no"s on Neil Young's "Last Dance." And in the fiercest song on the record, "Super Stupid," Hazel hollers out the story of someone who mistook heroin for cocaine and kicked the bucket (the song was based on his own drug misadventure).

Maggot Brain is one of the loudest, darkest, most intense records ever made. The funk is undeniable—"Hit It and Quit It" is the apotheosis of everything funk was about, and "Super Stupid" takes it to the point of no return—but so is the madness and anger, the wailing and gnashing of teeth that Eddie Hazel's guitar seems to personify. Ronald "Stozo" Edwards, who would later provide cover art for P-Funk albums, testifies, "Niggas have always been scared of Funkadelic. . . . That *Maggot Brain* album was the scariest shit I had ever heard."

Yet underlying it all is a madcap sort of humor, exemplified by the end of "Wars of Armageddon," where over piercing shrieks a voice intones, "More power to the people, more pussy to the power, more pussy to the people, more power to the pussy." As George Clinton says, "I didn't never want to be pretentious about shit, so I would always make sure I was being funny."

Maggot Brain is no concept album; it's simply a collection of seven songs, some short, some very long. But as a whole, it opens up a vision of the world completely unlike that suggested by any previous record—a world of darkness, death, and destruction that actually seems like a terrific place to be.

Black Sabbath's second album, *Paranoid,* a loud, slow, record which had gone to number one on the UK charts and number 12 in the U.S. in late 1970, had also centered around death. But as the title suggested, Sabbath *feared* death as intrinsically evil; their view of the universe was Manichaean; good and evil were not mixed.

But for Funkadelic, death was to be celebrated. With its biting, defiant, overwhelmingly funky music, Funkadelic welcomed death as one of its motley crew. The band's previous record, *Free Your Mind . . . And Your Ass Will Follow,* featured a track called "Eulogy and Light," whose music consists of the song "Open Your Eyes" played backwards; over it, Clinton yells a twisted version of the Lord's Prayer and 23rd Psalm, culminating in a dramatic reversal of the usual illumination. He runs *away* from the light at the end, his voice rising as the tape unspools too fast—"I run, I back away, to hide, from what? From fear? The truth? The light?"

On *Maggot Brain,* fear has been conquered, and there is no light left.

Perhaps this was because of George Clinton's immersion in the literature of the Process Church. Founded in 1964 by a British Scientologist named Robert de Grimston, the Process Church of the Final Judgment worshipped God while loving Satan—on one wall of their churches was a Christian cross and on the opposite was a goat's head in a pentagram. It urged followers to choose between Jehovah (the ascetic life), Lucifer (the sensual life), Satan (the violent life), and Christ (who unified all three), and then to follow one's chosen path to its extreme. The unification would take place in an apocalypse, which was coming soon.

The cult's magazine, *The Process*—from which Funkadelic quoted at length not just on Maggot Brain but on its next record, *America Eats Its Young*—was heavily into Hitler, Satan, blood, and doom. It devoted an issue to freedom of expression, featuring Mick Jagger on the cover; another to fear, filled with disturbing images and printed in purple, red, and silver ink; and another to death, including an article by Charles Manson celebrating death as "peace from this world's madness and paradise in my own self." Another Process pamphlet, Grimston's *Satan on War,* is perhaps the most explicit celebration of death and war ever published: "So rise, Man, and be joyful! For WAR you shall have in abundance. . . . Revel in the multiple delights of WAR. . . . Release the Fiend within you! . . . Stand proud in the monstrous presence of violent death! . . . Invoke the cataclysm!"

The Process Church was not very active in Detroit, and neither Clinton nor anyone in his band underwent its arduous initiation procedure. Clinton would soon develop an elaborate and dauntingly original cosmology of his own, borrowing from sci-fi movies and comic strips. Clinton's P-Funk empire would become a kind of radical organization sporting its very own eschatology, aesthetics, and pantheon of minor gods. Funkadelic albums would become vehicles for a peculiar kind of evangelism, with mystical pronouncements sharing grooves with bathroom humor. But the Process Church proved an important source for him, for it gave Clinton moral permission to embrace and celebrate the dark side of human nature.

Tied to all this was Black Power. Funkadelic wasn't as explicit about this as, say, the Last Poets, but the racial harmony of Sly and the Family Stone was clearly not in its vocabulary. Funkadelic was always a purely *black* thang.

To embrace and celebrate blackness was one of the central goals of the Black Power and Black Arts movements; this meant rejecting the association of blackness with evil that had been more or less built into the English language. Langston Hughes had written about this identification back in the 1940s, in "That Word *Black*." In this story, Hughes's protagonist wonders why every word or phrase containing "black" is negative—black cats, blacklist, black-balled, blackmail, the eight-ball, the Black Hand Society, black sheep, black magic, black mark, black as hell, black heart. "Wait till my day comes!" he exclaims. "In my language, bad will be *white*. Blackmail will be *white* mail. Black cats will be good luck, and *white* cats will be bad."

The phrase "Black is beautiful" has become such a cliché that it's easy to forget its revolutionary import, which was, as Rickey Vincent puts it in his history of funk, that "the demeaning language of European culture was finally, ultimately, being dissolved. Inverting the meanings of the term *black* was a monumental task."

Larry Neal, in his 1968 manifesto, "The Black Arts Movement," wrote about "the need to develop a Black aesthetic," and posited that "the Western aesthetic has run its course: it is impossible to construct anything meaningful within its decaying structure."

In this he was echoing Don L. Lee, Etheridge Knight, and LeRoi Jones, who had written, in his "State/meant" of 1965,

> The Black Artist's role in America is to aid in the destruction of America as he knows it. . . .
>
> > *The fair are*
> > *fair, and death*
> > *ly white.*
> > *The day will not save them*
> > *and we own*
> > *the night.*

Inspired by Jones and Malcolm X, the Black Power and Black Arts movements went so far as to call for violence, associating that violence directly with blackness. In "Black Art," from his 1969 book *Black Magic*, Jones wrote,

> *We want "poems that kill."*
> *Assassin poems, Poems that shoot*
> *guns. Poems that wrestle cops into alleys*
> *and take their weapons leaving them dead*

Funkadelic played a variation on this theme: everything dark was beautiful, whether it be blackness, dirt, or death. Clinton started redefining blackness as early as the first Funkadelic album, a record of deep-fried blues. In the song "What Is Soul?," after a cry of "All that is good is nasty," he compares soul to a ham hock in your corn flakes, the ring around your bathtub, a joint rolled in toilet paper, and chitlins foo yung—in other words, a mix of the nasty with the good. Clinton wasn't simply reversing the English language, as Hughes and the "black is beautiful" people did. He was taking blackness's negative associations and making them positive. In the new slang of the era, bad meant good.

And things got progressively funkier from there. The word *funk* originally meant body odor; the music was therefore dirty and sexy, intimate and hot. It involved people playing closely together, figuratively rubbing up against one another. Funk embraced heavily distorted electric guitars, bent notes and pulled strings, basses that popped rather than hummed, irregular drumming that split the difference between swing and straight time. Funk vocalists grunted and moaned, shrieked and sobbed, slurred their words and stretched them out.

Under George Clinton, funk embraced not just stink and dirt but went far beyond that, embracing death, war, and even the apocalypse. Yes, other funk artists shared this tendency—one funk band called themselves War, and James Brown released albums entitled *Superbad* and *Hell.* But War espoused peace and love, Brown self-reliance. Funkadelic, especially on *Maggot Brain,* reveled in decay.

For Clinton, funk was the answer to Hughes's conundrum of how one could celebrate blackness while rejecting its meaning in the white world. Funk was a celebration of both blackness and its meaning in the white world—darkness, death, destruction. The process of reclaiming blackness had just been taken one step farther—and as far as it could possibly go.

Funkadelic had initially come together as the backing band for the Parliaments, a vocal quintet led by George Clinton since 1955.

The name Funkadelic was suggested by Billy Nelson, who was all of 17 years old. It was Nelson who recruited the other four instrumentalists in the band, and who, with Hazel, was largely responsible for their sound and image. "Cream, Blue Cheer, *Sgt. Pepper's*, Sly, Vanilla Fudge: that's what we were listening to constantly," Nelson remembers. "And once Eddie started listening to Jimi Hendrix, he found his niche. Immediately, he was like, 'Damn, Bill, I can do that! Can you play that bass shit, muthafucka?' I was like, 'Hey, man, I guess I'm gonna have to.'"

The band was formed in Detroit in 1967, the time and place of the country's most destructive urban riot, soon to be labeled "The Great Rebellion." Forty-one people died, 347 were injured, 3,800 arrested, 5,000 rendered homeless. More than a thousand buildings were destroyed, 2,700 businesses were looted, and damage estimates reached half a billion dollars. Clinton, Nelson, Clarence Haskins, and the rest of the Parliaments were holed up in the Twenty Grand Motel, where, as Haskins explains, "people [were] getting their fingers, arms, wrists cut off for their jewelry. National Guard had us all pinned up against the wall. Took our uniforms out of the car, stomping on them, lookin' for weapons. We were just afraid of being shot."

In the early 1970s, Detroit was the fifth-largest American city (now it is 11th), and it was, by almost any measure, the worst. Even the chairman of the Greater Detroit Chamber of Commerce admitted that "Detroit is *the* city of problems. If they exist, we've probably got them." Because of horrifying labor conditions, unrest was at its peak: In 1970, one quarter of Ford's assembly-line workers quit, and on any given day, a full five percent of General Motors' workers would be missing without an excuse, a figure that would rise to 10 percent on Mondays and Fridays. Public transit was practically nonexistent, the school system was on the verge of bankruptcy, thousands of homes were deserted because of corruption in lending institutions, the police department resisted segregation and created secret elite units, racism pervaded all aspects of life, and Motor City became Murder City.

But at the same time, Detroit was the site of one of the nation's most revolutionary black liberation movements. In response to the riots, a group of black workers combined Black Power with the more radical elements of the labor movement to formulate a new vision and a new social movement, one that directly confronted the establishment. At the vanguard were three revolutionary organizations: the Dodge Revolutionary Union Movement, which organized wildcat strikes and published widely read newspapers; the Black United Front, which encompassed sixty organizations ranging from black churches to a black policemen's group to DRUM itself; and the League of Revolutionary Black Workers, whose name speaks for itself.

Funkadelic quickly established itself as a fixture on the Detroit rock scene, sharing management and performance venues with three white bands: the Stooges, the MC5, and the Amboy Dukes, led by Ted Nugent, with whom Clinton would often go hunting. Their publicist once staged an onstage marriage between Clinton and Stooges leader Iggy Pop, both of whom would regularly display their penises during their shows. And Detroit was also home to Alice Cooper at the time.

Along with rock bands, of course, were the Motown bands, of which the Temptations came closest to the Funkadelic style. (Clinton actually wrote some of the Temptations' songs, and called Funkadelic "the loudest black band in the world, Temptations on acid.") What all these bands had in common was a balls-to-the-walls aesthetic—loud guitars; fierce and steady rhythms; shouted-out lyrics about sex, drugs, and rebellion; songs that could go on for half an hour; flamboyant and violent onstage gestures; and an implicit menace, an unstated—or occasionally baldly stated—threat.

By the time Funkadelic recorded *Maggot Brain*, Hazel and Nelson had been playing together for nine years, with Tiki Fulwood joining them in 1967. The trio had developed a solid rapport and, together with newer members Tawl Ross and Bernie Worrell, recorded two albums which reached the R&B top 20 (as would *Maggot Brain*). Although Fulwood's drumming was steady and forceful, there was an layer underneath of complex, mercurial rhythms that seemed to coexist uneasily with the central beat. Nelson's playing was propulsive, inventive, and stylish; Ross's guitar was solid; classically trained Worrell's keyboard solos were both blues-and outer-space based. But what really made the band stand out was Eddie Hazel's axe.

Jimi Hendrix had died on September 18, 1970, shortly before the recording of *Maggot Brain* began, and it's possible that "Maggot Brain" was meant as a sort of requiem. To the white community, Hendrix's death hardly mattered at the time: *Time* magazine's contemptuous obituary read, in its entirety, "Died. Jimi Hendrix, 27, Seattle-born rock superstar whose grating, bluesy voice, screechy, pulsating guitar solos and pelvis-pumping stage antics conveyed both a turned-on, fetid sense of eroticism and, at best, a reverberated musical equivalent of the urban black's anguished spirit; apparently of an overdose of drugs; in London."

To Funkadelic, though, Hendrix mattered. Hazel was widely considered his successor. It's easy to compare the two guitarists—

both were blues-based and heavily electric, both embraced the psychedelic aesthetic while keeping it grounded in rhythm-and-blues, both displayed amazing proficiency with jaw-dropping ease. But while Hendrix was eager to experiment and grandstand, Hazel was no show-off. Moreover, he was an indissoluble member of the P-Funk family—he needed them as much as they needed him.

On its previous two albums, Funkadelic had been loose, sloppy, and ragged—in fact, *Free Your Mind* had been recorded in its entirety in one LSD-fueled day. But on *Maggot Brain,* the musicians focused their energies so that every note counted. Clinton now says that he produced the record while on acid: "I just got in there and turned the knobs. It was such a vibe. I didn't know any better—you can only do that stuff when you don't know any better." But he's being disingenuous. Rather than in one day, *Maggot Brain* was recorded over a period of several months. It featured a number of guest musicians, including Gary Shider from the band United Soul, some female vocalists from Isaac Hayes' backing group, and McKinley Jackson, trombonist for the Politicians.

Funkadelic was essentially a riven band at this point. The five instrumentalists were functioning as a sold unit creating the music; George Clinton was functioning not only as their producer but as their saboteur. Nelson still resents being mixed out of "Maggot Brain," and has called the cover and liner notes "bullshit, satanical to say the least. . . . That's George sabotaging us again.

"It's OK to be the bad guys of rock and roll, but look at how much class the Stones had with it. Then there's the other point of, Wait, don't go too far with it; we're not white. There are things we cannot get away with because we're black. But George didn't care about none of that, at our expense. . . . Funkadelic was straight-up X-rated. He wanted to keep Funkadelic *dirty*." Clearly, Clinton, taking his cues from Detroit, wanted *Maggot Brain* to be as extreme as he could make it.

After the release of *Maggot Brain*, Funkadelic essentially disbanded. Within a year, Worrell would be the only original member left. Clinton fired Fulwood for his heroin addiction, though he would later rejoin the band. Hazel, who was also addicted to heroin, spent a year in jail, convicted of smoking angel dust and assaulting a stewardess; he rejoined the band for a few later records, but his career then went into rapid decline, and he died in 1992. Nelson quit over financial matters (he claimed Clinton was keeping all the money and getting rid of the band made doing so easier), and went on to play with the Commodores, Chairmen of the Board, Lionel Richie, Smokey Robinson, Fishbone, and the Temptations. Tawl Ross barely survived an overdose of LSD and speed, and suffered irreversible brain damage.

Clinton soon replaced the rhythm section with players who had defected from James Brown's JBs. Funkadelic's next two records, *America Eats Its Young* and *Cosmic Slop,* were unfocused, ineffective, and in parts unlistenable. The heavy blues-based funk sound was almost completely abandoned in favor of a string section and a variety of off-the-wall parodic approaches, none of which had sticking power. By the time the band found its groove again—on 1974's *Standing on the Verge of Getting It On,* essentially a George Clinton–Eddie Hazel record that attempted to do for sex what *Maggot Brain* had done for death—they were no longer as focused or ambitious.

As for funk itself, it soldiered on, producing many indelible hits and delectable obscurities. Even if it never got as heavy as *Maggot Brain* again, it remained a tremendously creative force, and it supplied the soundtrack for black America for the remainder of the decade. Eddie Hazel and *Maggot Brain* were essentially forgotten; Clinton's P-Funk empire grew so huge that between his various bands and spin-offs they were releasing as many as eight records a year, all but burying *Maggot Brain* under subsequent product.

But for a brief moment in the early seventies, a band captured the odor of the age, the stench of death and corruption, the weary exhalation of America at its lowest. And it smelled very, very funky.

Hey Ludwig, Grab Yourself a Pigfoot

Barry Gifford

Monk's "Functional" (1956)
    kicks me in the same place
    as Beethoven's 3rd movement
("Adagio ma non troppo—Fuga.
    Allegro, ma non troppo")
of his "Sonata No. 31 in A flat major,
    Opus 110")
Monk made Beethoven over
    strolling on 63rd Street
    just whistling
    on the way home
    from the liquor store—
Or is that
    too simple?

Unauthorized!

Axl Rose, Albert Goldman, and the renegade art of rock biography

James Parker

I think it may have been sometime in the 1970s—and I'm being as half-assed as I possibly can here, in keeping with my theme— that the term "unauthorized" became sort of cool. The authorized version: that was what *the Man* gave you. You didn't want that. You wanted the illicit, illegitimate, sniggering-behind-your-hand version. Not the truth exactly, but something that smelled a bit like it.

A market emerged, and books, here and there, began to advertise their unauthorizedness. Soon books about rock music, which was the sound of the kids, etc., absolutely *had* to be unauthorized, otherwise what was the point? Give us the action! And so he was born, our hero—a dreamer of dreams, a peddler of scurrilities, the worst researcher in the world: the unauthorized rock biographer.

As unauthorized rock biographers go, Mick Wall—whose *W.A.R.: The Unauthorized Biography of William Axl Rose* (St. Martins Press, 352 pages, $26.95) debuted this past week—is impeccably credentialed. In 1991, having displeased the band with some tactless journalism, he was called out, by name, in Guns N'

205

Roses' bloated blooz-rant "Get in the Ring." "You punks in the press," burps Axl Rose in a spoken word section, while the guitars get surly, "that wanna start shit by printing lies instead of the things we said . . . That means you, Mick Wall! . . . Fuck you! Suck my fucking dick!" Fixed immortally in the zodiac of Axl's paranoia—not bad for a writer from *Kerrang!* magazine. "Suck my fucking dick!" You don't get much more unauthorized than that.

Then again, when Johnny Rogan was researching his Smiths history *Morrissey and Marr: The Severed Alliance*, he trespassed so deeply into the Moz-zone that the vengeful singer wished aloud to a passing newspaperman that Rogan would be killed in a highway pile-up. Asked about this comment a few weeks later, Morrissey seemed to have had a change of heart: now, he said, he wanted Rogan to die in a hotel fire. The relationship between the unauthorized rock biographer and his subject has ever been strained.

FATHER OF LIES

"Is he really dead?", Phil Spector is said to have asked upon learning of the passing of Albert Goldman. "Is he *really* dead? Make sure he's really dead." A mordant epitaph for the man who had produced, in 1981's *Elvis* and 1988's *The Lives of John Lennon*, two works of persistent, near-magical malignancy. Drive a stake through his fat heart. Nail him to the grave. Let there be no possibility of illusion or (worse) revival. Tonight, at last, the village can sleep.

Because Goldman, who died in 1994 with his biography of Jim Morrison unfinished (hallelujah!), really was a kind of nightmare. *Ladies and Gentlemen—Lenny Bruce!*, his 1971 breakthrough book, gave no hint of the dizzying animus he was preparing to unleash on rock-and-roll. His literary lineage could be traced back a hundred years, to a time when the binges and brothel-crawls of New York–society types were gleefully recorded in scandal sheets like *Town Topics* and *The Weekly Rake*. His aesthetic forebear was Kenneth Anger, whose pioneering Hollywood Babylon had ministered candidly to an atavistic public need for sexual/chemical slander and crime-scene photos. His rival in notoriety and bestsellerdom was Kitty Kelley, perfumed author of 1986's *His Way: The Unauthorized Biography of Frank Sinatra* (Mob ties, suicide attempts, scrambled eggs inhaled off a hooker's breasts). Still, Goldman was one of a kind: a professor of English at Columbia—10-dollar words, quotes from Chaucer and all—whose mind was in the gutter.

The books were huge and tireless. The prose style was multi-valved, gusting from rock-crit hyperbole through debauched Mailerese to straight porno ("a group of girls would strip down to their panties and wrestle while Elvis stared out his eyes with a rocklike hard-on pressing up against his underwear"); the dominant tone, however, was a poncey, parodistic voice that seemed to be his own. "Diurnal acid dropping," he wrote in *The Lives of John Lennon*, "produces an effect rather like XTC, the 'love drug.' Hence, instead of mental pinwheels, the tripper feels himself bound in an affectionate communion with everything he sees, like Titania embracing an ass."

And how he *loathed* his subjects. Goldman's Lennon, in addition to being a textbook case of Multiple Personality Disorder, suffered from "poor coordination; jerky spastic movements" and "inability to perform simple acts like driving or operating domestic appliances." Surprisingly for a world-famous musician, he couldn't even play the *guitar*, hacking out chords with "an iron-fingered rigidity that summons visions of Parkinson's disease." Goldman's

Elvis, meanwhile, was a pharmacist's pincushion, incapacitated and nearly insensate, "propped up like a big fat woman in recovery from some operation on her reproductive organs." Both men were galvanic sociopaths, perverts, and despots, while simultaneously being as helpless as babes-in-arms. Bit of a paradox, that. Scarcely a fact underwrote these claims, and no one had authorized Goldman to make them: in this new science of character extermination, he had the devil's own authority.

GOLDMAN, THOU SHOULDST BE LIVING AT THIS HOUR

There is, of course, a contrarian case to be made (and it has been) for Albert Goldman—as iconoclast, as hustler. He was creative, or at least inventive.

In a disgusting way, he was even rather punk rock. And reading the unauthorized literature on, say, Madonna, or Sting, or Mick Jagger, we are startled to find that we miss him. So there are "sexual marathons" in these books, and "ruthless ambition." So Jagger once lay back on Moroccan cushions and "drew deep breaths of pure Thai opium," and Sean Penn tied Madonna to a chair—big deal. Mere pieties of the genre. We miss the dirty fabulist flavor of Goldman: the stink of his obsessions; his quack diagnostics; the prose that goes beyond purple and into bruise-like shades of morbid excess. We miss (as Champ Kind says to Ron Burgundy in *Anchorman*) his *musk*.

True, he had freedoms that are denied to many an unauthorized biographer.

His victims were already dead, number one, which made them unlikely litigants. And they were both of them, Elvis and Lennon, vast repositories of mass-cultural psychic energy, such that almost anything could be said about them and be, at some level, true. (Ish.) Still, no one in the field of rock biography has even tried to pick up his torch. It lies there, Goldman's toxic torch, fuming with neglect. In fact, let me suggest that the only document produced since his death that might be deemed worthy of him is not a book but an album: Nirvana's *In Utero*, to be precise, which every child knows is a Goldmanoid shitstorm of drugs and regression and whining and superstar sexual neurosis. Throw down your umbilical noose, indeed.

What might Goldman have done, what sport might he have had, with a biography of Axl Rose? Mick Wall, as described above, has a special warrant to write this book. And *W.A.R.* also boasts two further hallmarks of classic unauthorizedness: no index (too cheap) and no lyrics (couldn't get permission). Nonetheless, despite these emblems, and despite his robust style and knack for characterization (Rose is described as having "definitely something of the mistreated dog about him, avoiding eye contact, glancing at you warily when he thought you weren't looking"), Wall fails to close in, so to speak, for the bloody unauthorized kill.

LIMBO DANCING

We can be sure that Goldman would have made more, for example, of Axl's epic decline from saucy rock-and-rollerdom into New Age hypochondria—his decay, as it were, into health. Here's Wall on why GNR were always two hours late for their frigging concerts: "Preparations would begin in the late afternoon, when he'd spend an hour on mainly cardiovascular exercises—running, stepping, bicycling. . . . He would follow this with an extensive massage from tour masseuse Sabrina Okamoto. After taking a shower and grabbing a light meal—often a specially prepared

salad of fresh vegetables, fruit, nuts, grains, white meat or fish—
he would begin his daily vocal exercises either alone or with his
vocal coach, Ron Anderson." And then the long-distance call to
the past-life regression therapist Suzzy London; and then the
binding of the ankles "to help prevent him twisting them onstage"; and then another 45-minute session with Okamoto, fo-
cusing this time on the lower back. And so on. While the rest of
the band do drugs and idly peruse the wank mags "fanned out for
them backstage like in a dentist's waiting room." Would Goldman
have been going nuts, or what?

Neither, one feels, would he have been able to resist the philo-
sophical implications of GNR's always-in-the-making, eternally de-
ferred, millions-down-the-drain album *Chinese Democracy*. What
a title. What a concept. A white whale, a black box, a thing into
which everything goes, every motive and idea and association,
and nothing comes out. It should enter the language immediately:
"Ah, Helga. (Sigh) She was my Chinese Democracy."

Axl has been working on this bastard since 1996, hiring and firing like a schizoid plutocrat; by 1999 he claimed to have demo'd
nearly 70 new songs, some of which were rather "advanced" in their
approach. The year 2000 found him ordering a wood-and-wire
chicken coop to be built in the studio for his post-Slash guitarist
Buckethead, who wears a KFC bucket on his head and had told Axl
that he would be "more comfortable working inside a chicken
coop." In 2002, a song called "Rhiad and the Bedouins" was pre-
miered at the Belgian Pukkelpop festival, although no one could
really hear it. By this time, Axl was saying that he had the *follow-
up* to *Chinese Democracy* already written . . . Buckethead quit in
2004, and shortly thereafter GNR's label, Interscope—in a fit of
wishful thinking—announced that *ChineseDemocracy* would be in
stores by the end of the year. Never happened.

Is there a way out of this Eco-esque labyrinth? Will the album ever be complete, or releasable? Not until the people of China have a democratically elected government. And perhaps not even then.

WHIMS OF DESIRE

Another contemporary figure crying out for the Goldman touch is soul man/lubricant R. Kelly, whose unauthorized biography *Your Body's Calling Me: The Life and Times of "Robert" R. Kelly— Music, Love, Sex & Money,* by Jake Brown, was published in 2004. Brown has some interesting, unauthorized-style touches— one of Kelly's non-sexual friendships is described as "plutonic"— but nothing can obscure the divine comedy at the heart of the book: the struggle in R.'s soul between God and sex, or at least the kind of sex that R. likes. He believes he can fly, he starts every day with a prayer, but in 2002 he was charged with 14 counts of child pornography. The trial is scheduled for May of this year.

"Despite how small his star may fade," concludes Brown, on a note of consolation, "he does shine bright and divine on millions of lives that otherwise would have had no one to inspire or remind them that, at heart, we are all God's children." On second thought, the proper redactor of the R. Kelly story might not be Goldman but rather Nick Tosches, whose 1982 *Hellfire: The Jerry Lee Lewis Story* reads like a bulletin from the brink of damnation: "The booze and the pills stirred the hell within him and made him to utter hideous peals. At times he withdrew into his own shadow, brooding upon all manner of things—abominable, unutterable, and worse. At times he stalked and ranted in foul omnipotence, commanding those about him as Belial his minions." Remember: bring God into your unauthorized bio, and you'll be bringing in His old buddy the Devil, too.

THE WITCH IN THE DITCH

But let's stop going on about Albert Goldman. On the tangled field of unauthorized rock biography, have there been no triumphs outside his? There have, of course. Scott Robinson's *Yes Tales: An Unauthorized Biography of Rock's Most Cosmic Band, in Limerick Form* performs exactly as advertised. Thus a paragraph describing the entry into the band of guitarist Steve Howe, "a fierce performer with an almost feral energy," is succinctly recapped as follows:

> *Late of Bodast, Tomorrow, In-Crowd,_*
> *Axe-man Howe arrived, entered, and bowed_*
> *He could solo for days_*
> *And avoid all clichés*
> *And in spite of this, wasn't as loud.*

Craig Bromberg's *The Wicked Ways of Malcolm McLaren* (1989) is a success of a different order—a forensic, undeceived account of a master bullshitter. McLaren—libertine, impresario, red-herring merchant, and one-man culture virus—masterminded the Sex Pistols, Bow Wow Wow, and the late-stage New York Dolls. He gave Adam Ant the Apache stripe across his nose. He's a trickster, and would doubtless love his biography to be full of obnoxious fictions. But Bromberg brings down his quarry with the snares of truth, tapping nearly 200 sources to get things straight; he even does a bit of shoe-leather reporting, very rare for the genre, tracking down McLaren's estranged mother in a London suburb and attempting to give her a bunch of flowers. "Go away," she says. "Just *go* away. I have nothing to say about him."

We'll end, though, with an image from Fred Vermorel's *The Se-cret History of Kate Bush (And the Strange Art of Pop)*, from 1983: a work of mystical genealogy in which the spoor of Kate's inspiration is hunted back through time, through the mist, into her witchy pre-Christian origins. ("Kate Bush is our goddess Frig," he writes. "And like the Saxons we both revere and fear her. Shroud her in the mystery of her power and the power of her mystery.") Ver-morel, an art-school pal and occasional co-conspirator of McLaren, conducted no interviews at all for this book. Instead, he went clam-bering up the trunk of the Bush family tree, to wobble in specula-tion among its most etiolated boughs: Aluric Busch (11th century), Henry del Busk (13th century), Roland atte Bush (14th century), and John Bush, "Kate's first certain ancestor," born in 1769. John be-gat Henry, a boozy laborer in a bowler hat who staggered homeward on the night of December 2, 1872, missed his path, and drowned in a ditch. "I found that ditch," declares Vermorel. "And one Decem-ber evening in 1981 I recreated the incident."

Vermorel stresses that he was not drunk ("I never mix alcohol with work"), but something emboldened him, warmed his spirit, some wild unauthorized urge. He threw himself headfirst through the antagonistic brambles, and he "felt Henry's panic 109 years be-fore flooding my body and I clawed in the black winter ditch and sucked for air to feel the shock of cold water in my mouth."

Can you dig it, rock biographers? The commitment, the risk, the immersion? The dark ditch beckons. Leave your facts behind in the daylight, and take the plunge.

Bass is Loaded
Babe Ruth's hip-hop homerun

Jesse Serwer

"The Mexican" might be the unlikeliest of all b-boy anthems. Recorded in 1972 by Babe Ruth, a British progressive rock band whose second-greatest claim to fame may have been opening the West Coast leg of the *Frampton Comes Alive* tour, it certainly doesn't seem to have the same inherent connection to New York Afro-Latin culture as, say, the Jimmy Castor Bunch's "It's Just Begun." But after speaking with Babe Ruth founder and "The Mexican" songwriter Alan Shacklock, I learn his inadvertent role in the early development of hip-hop culture seems oddly fitting.

Over the course of our interview, Shacklock cites Albert King's "Cold Feet"—a proto-rap track if there ever was one, and the basis for Wu-Tang's "Protect Ya Neck" and Diamond D's "Check One, Two"—as his greatest inspiration as a young guitarists. He explains that he wrote the lyrics to "The Mexican" as a response to John Wayne's one-sided 1960 film *The Alamo*, which didn't bother to humanize the Mexican troops, who lost the infamous 1836 battle to Sam Houstons's army. The fifty-eight-year-old classically trained guitarist names J Dilla, the Roots, and A Tribe

214

Called Quest among his favorite contemporary artists, and quotes from Jeff Chang's 2005 hip-hop tome, *Can't Stop Won't Stop*.

"The Mexican" wasn't just a Babe Ruth song, it was *the* Babe Ruth song. The first tune every recorded by the band (they ultimately released five albums), it was the *only* track on the original demo used to seek out the record contract that led to 1972's *First Base*. With its funky bass line, driving drumbeat, and climactic interpolation of Ennio Morricone's *For a Few Dollars More* theme, it was also the culmination of a life's worth of influences on Shacklock, who grew up enamored with African American music and Wild West shoot-'em-ups.

Born thirty minutes north of London in the town of Hatfield, Shacklock picked up the guitar while still in his single digits. By age twelve, he'd formed a band called the Juniors with future Rolling Stones guitarist Mick Taylor, who was just fourteen at the time, and eventual Jethro Tull bassist John Glasscock, then eleven.

"I was fascinated with the blues, and the soul music coming out of the South like James Brown and Derek Martin," recalls Shacklock, who now lives in Nashville, Tennessee, where he works as a record producer. "We'd study who the players were on these records and try to imitate them. We were fanatics. I remember getting a 45 with 'That Driving Beat' by Willie Mitchell, and it was just awesome. I still listen to that and 'The Midnight Hour' by Wilson Pickett, and it's matchless to me."

The Juniors released their lone single, "There's a Pretty Girl" b/w "Pocket Size," for Parlaphone in 1964. Soon afterward, Shacklock found himself in blue-eyed soul singer Chris Farlowe's band, the Thunderbirds, an act whose lineup would briefly include a pre-Zeppelin John Bonham. In the late '60s, however, he put his rock career aside and enrolled in London's prestigious Royal Academy of Music, mastering classical Spanish guitar. "That's where the Spanish influence you hear on 'The Mexican' came from," Shacklock says.

After graduating in 1971, Shacklock decided to apply his command of classical song structure to a combination of hard rock and the driving soul music he grew up on, recruiting bassist Dave Powell. The foursome took the name Shacklock and began developing material that its eponymous founder had composed while at the Royal Academy.

FIRST BASE

"I was fascinated with Motown and [with] what arrangers like David Van DePitte and Paul Riser were doing. I wanted us to be very simple, and very much based on a constant groove," Shacklock says. "My philosophy was, if they didn't like the music, they might like the beat, and if they liked the beat, they might come around to liking the music."

"The Mexican," he says, was not constructed democratically but rather dictated to the members: "I told the drummer, 'Don't do any fills, just keep the groove constant like in the soul days, and we're gonna lay this crazy stuff over the top.' Our bassist came from a blues background, so he got it, [but] it was difficult for me to tell our drummer not to play fills, because that's what he got off on. I loved the massive orchestral arrangements in the spaghetti, Clint Eastwood westerns. I thought Morricone's orchestration was pure genius. So I got this crazy idea to put "[For] a Few Dollars More" over the same drumbeat. Really, they were two different pieces—we segued it in and tagged that on at the end. I thought it was a nice instrumental break. As they say in [*This Is*] *Spinal Tap*, it was something between stupid and clever."

Shacklock, who was also the band's lead singer in its earliest stages, also wrote the song's lyrics, "I'm someone who's always been in favor of the underdog," he says, "I wanted to [reflect] what it would be like on the other side, in Santa Anna's army. Chico Fernandez was a fictional character that I made up. I figured there had to be one of those in the army.

After A&R man Nick Mobbs caught a performance at London's Marquee club, EMI/Harvest agreed to sign the band, under the condition they find a permanent lead singer, and a new name. "EMI wasn't disrespectful to Alan's singing," recalls bassist Dave Hewitt. "They were saying, 'You're doing all these harmonic runs and intricate guitar playing, why sing lead too? It's too much.'" During a round of tryouts, Janita "Jenny" Haan, an attractive, eighteen-year-old jolt of energy, instantly stood out. "Jenny was totally different: one, because she was female, but [also] because she was so athletic," Hewitt recalls. "She was doing cartwheels and splits. We never thought of a female until she appeared, but when she did, it seemed really exciting."

Though she was British, Haan had spent her adolescent years just outside of San Francisco, and, despite her youth, her powerful voice already evoked hippie heroes Janis Joplin and Grace Slick. "I was a free-spirited, San Franciscan type, so I'd put every ounce of energy and emotion into the songs and interpret them the way I felt," Haan recalls. "I'd listen carefully to how the music was structured and match the intensities of the sounds with my voice."

The quintet cut *First Base* at Abbey Road Studios with Beatles engineer Tony Clark in early 1972. In addition to "The Mexican," it included covers of Frank Zappa's "King Kong" and Jesse Winchester's "Black Dog," along with originals "Joker," "The Runaways," and "Wells Fargo," which reprised the Western theme of "The Mexican."

The name Babe Ruth was proposed by the band's first manager. "We didn't even know who Babe Ruth was, except for Janita," Shacklock recalls. "She'd been a cheerleader in the U.S., so it just kind of fit. People used to think she was Ruth."

Coincidentally, Shacklock's friend Roger Dan, whose iconic album covers for Yes would define the prog-rock aesthetic, had just created a space-age baseball scene, which would become the cover art of *First Base* and, eventually, the band's logo.

While *First Base* fared only modestly in the U>K>, the band found that in certain North American markets, particularly Quebec and the Midwest, they were instant superstars. "When we saw our first sales-figure statement, we immediately got in touch with promoters there," Shacklock says. "ZZ Top opened for *us* in Milwaukee. It was bizarre."

OUT AT SECOND

When it came to follow up *First Base*, Shacklock found that EMI was willing to give him unbelievable latitude. "It was the progressive-rock era," Shacklock says. "Risks were being taken by the record companies—they had almost unlimited budgets in those days. Being classically trained, I was a kid in a candy store. I said, 'Oh, we'll have eight cellos on this, book a horn section for this.' We had guys from the London Symphony Orchestra come and play."

However, for various reasons, their sophomore LP, *Amar Caballero*, would not be *Second Base*. "My publisher had said, 'Hey, you're a good writer. Can you get a song to Diana Ross? The Temptations?" Shacklock recalls, proudly. "I was trying really hard, 'cause these were my legends. It didn't happen, so I adapted these songs for the band, and it turned into a mishmash."

Meanwhile, the group replaced drummer Dick Powell with Ed Spevock and experienced an unfortunate series of events that drove keyboardist Dave Punshon from the band. Following a gig in Liverpool, their van flipped over, seriously injuring several members; at a show in Sunderland, they were severely beaten by bouncers. "Dave was following the Maharishi at that time, and experimenting with drugs, and he just freaked out," Haan says. "It was a devastating blow, because we kind of lost the signature sound, the harmonic runs that Al and Dave did together."

To a degree, their third album, 1975's *Babe Ruth*, was closer in spirit to *First Base*, with interpretations of Morricone's " Fistful of Dollars," William Bell and Judy Clay's "Private Number," and Curtis Mayfield's "We the People Who Are Darker Than Blue" scattered among more straightforward rock numbers. "There was a consciousness within the band about race, which we always tried to address, lyrically, in a passive way," says Haan, who by this time, was taking on a greater role when it came to songwriting.

However, the edge the band sought to bring to the album was dulled somewhat by decisions beyond their control. "EMI didn't trust me anymore," Shacklock says, "Because I went off the rails on the second one. So they gave us a producer who wasn't really right for us. We lost the plot a little through the powers that be coming on too heavy." As Babe Ruth headed to the studio to record its fourth LP, *Stealin' Home*, an increasingly frustrated Shacklock left the band. "It was like somebody cut off my right arm," Hewitt says, "because Alan's writing was what the band was all about. From then on, it was just the dregs of fulfilling the contract. The soul was gone."

Stealin' Home would produce one vital song in "Elusive." The up-tempo track ironically found the band influenced by disco, a style whose development the band may have influenced. Released as a single in 1976, it became a minor hit in New York and a northern-soul favorite. By this time, though, Haan and Hewitt had left to start the short-lived Jenny Haan's Lion. The Babe Ruth that recorded 1976's dismal *Kid's Stuff* included no original members.

Hewitt blames the group's management for its disintegration. "It was unfortunate, because somebody that was more aware could have kept us together." Hewitt says. "We had all these things going on with us, but we didn't have a clue."

NIGHT GAME

The "shadow history" of "The Mexican" goes something like this: New York jock Steve D'Acquisto was in Montreal, according to Bill Brewster and Frank Broughton's book, *Last Night a DJ Saved My Life*, when *First Base* first hit there. Recognizing the inherent danceability of "The Mexican," he took a copy to David Mancuso, who began playing it at his legendary underground New York City venue, the Loft. Sometime within the next two years, it came to the attention of DJ Kool Herc, who made "The Mexican," with its extensive instrumental break, a staple of his eclectic Bronx DJ sets. With its thunderous dun-a-dun-a-dun-dun-dun bass line and Latin flavor, it became a favorite of early uprockers and, eventually, a b-boy staple.

"It was made famous first by motorcycle gangs that used to have uprockers in their groups as well," says Rock Steady Crew president Richard "Crazy legs" Colon. In the b-boy era, "Once you heard that Spanish guitar, you'd start lacing up your sneakers or get your little two-step on right before going into some crazy styles. You knew once that song came on, there was gonna be some strait-up battling. It could be good, bad, and ugly." By the 1990s, there was even an organized break-dancing competition named for a key lyric in the song, "Chico got to have his share." It's one of the songs passed down by whoever came before us, and we accept it as tradition and pass it on to the next," Crazy Legs adds. "What we do, for us, is folk-dance. And this is one of the songs that go along with those dances."

"The only awareness I ever had that anything was going on was on tour in Montreal, in 1975, I think," Hewitt says. "A girl invited me to this nightclub, where they were playing "The Mexican.' It was mind-boggling, because we saw ourselves as this progressive rock band, and they're playing the heck out of 'The Mexican' at this really plush nightclub like we're disco stars."

Shacklock got his first visit from the ghost of "The Mexican" in 1982. He was producing *Like Gangbusters*, the debut album by British new wavers JoBoxers, when their U.S.-born lead singer, Dig Wayne, returned from a trip home with a white-label copy of "Planet Rock" by Afrika Banbaataa and the Soulsonic Force. "I'm listening, and I hear what sounds exactly like the drumbeat from 'The Mexican,' but instead of 'For a Few Dollars More' over it, it's the theme from *The Good, the Bad and the Ugly*," Shacklock recalls.

Two years later, he was at Abbey Road with Welsh rockers the Alarm when a DJ and aspiring producer, calling himself Jellybean Benitez, phoned him. "He told the lady who answered that he was the best DJ in New York and [that] he was Madonna's boyfriend," Shacklock says. "Of course, it all turned out to be true. We finally spoke, and he told me 'The Mexican' was his favorite song; he'd like to remix it. I said, "That's great, if they'll let you have the tapes." He called me back and said either they can't find the tapes or wouldn't let him have them, and asked if he could rerecord it, and [if I had] contact information for the singer. He'd like to fly Jenny to New York."

That call led to Benitez's 84 version of "The Mexican," a progenitor of the emerging New York freestyle sound and a huge dance hit in its own right. But it wouldn't be until 2002, when the circa '73 lineup of the band reunited for an appearance at the U.K. B-Boy Championships in London, that the legacy of "The Mexican" would be fully illuminated for them.

[Competition organizer] DJ Hooch was saying, 'You just don't realize, you're pretty much the anthem of b-boys internationally," Shacklock says. "[When we performed], the breakers were dying to come on with us—security was holding them back. Eventually, Crazy legs just broke loose. It was amazing." Encouraged by the experience, the band returned to the studio to make an album, embracing the culture that embraced them all these years. Released in 2007, the digital-only LP *Que Pasa* features an updated version of "The Mexican," a cover of "Apache," scratches by Shacklock's son Jesse (aka DJ Kidsmeal), and a return to the Spanish flavor and Western themes that colored *First Base*.

Who's Biting J Dilla's Beats?

Hip-hop producer's legend ascends posthumously;
estate struggles to maintain control

Jeff Weiss

No art form lionized its fallen quite like hip-hop. Forget Biggie and 2Pac. Their reputations were sealed the moment the doctors zipped the body bags—though, to be fair, few can argue against their posthumous crowning in the pantheon. More telling is the postmortem red carpet rolled out for Big L and Big Pun, two prodigiously talented artists who released a mere single great album each, dying before they had a chance to ruin their reputations with the inevitable 2005 Houston bounce track. No, in hip-hop, molehills are turned into mountains, with even lesser talents like Dipset flunky Stacks Bundles earning a spate of po-faced eulogies and a prominent "R.I.P. Stack B, Ima keep you alive, kid" shout-out from Lupe Fiasco on last year's *The Cool.*

J Dilla is a different case. Unlike the aforementioned names, when the 32-year-old beat-maker/rapper, born James Yancey, passed away at L.A.'s Cedars-Sinai Medical Center in the winter of 2006 (due to a cardiac arrest stemming from complications related to Thrombotic thrombocytopenic purpura, a rare and incurable blood disease), he was neither savior nor super-nova. Instead, he was an *underground legend* in those pre-Internet days, when the term actually meant something. Racking up a string of left-field hits capable of stacking up against any producer of the late '90s/early '00s, Dilla quietly dropped bombs working with the Pharcyde ("Runnin'"), De La Soul ("Stakes is High," "Itsoweezee"), A Tribe Called Quest ("1nce Again," "Find a Way"), Erykah Badu ("Didn't Cha' Know,"), and Common ("The Light"). Meanwhile, with Janet Jackson, Dilla had his only brush with mainstream success, caring Joni Mitchell's "Big Yellow Taxi" into the lean proto-chipmunk soul of "Got Til It's Gone," his only single to ever reach the Top 40. In what would become a pattern, Dilla never saw full credit, with Jimmy Jam and Terry Lewis "mistakenly" getting credit in the liner notes. Nonetheless, the track's sonics directly influenced the next generation of crate-diggers, with Just Blaze, 9th Wonder and a certain college dropout all taking notes.

Like most producers, Dilla's mike skills couldn't match his otherworldly ear, but he still managed to amass a respectable discography as one-third of Slum Village (whose *Fantastic, Volume 2* is often regarded as a subterranean classic); a Jaylib collaboration with Madlib; and *Welcome 2 Detroit*, and uneven solo effort. Cumulatively, it wasn't as eye-popping as it was a portent, a start to what would inevitably have made for a first-ballot Hall of Fame career, considering Dilla's notoriously rigorous work ethic.

He died the same week that L.A.-based Stones Throw released *Donuts*, an impossibly soulful trip of head-nodding, hip-hop instrumentals that served as a gorgeous, plaintive requiem. It was also Dilla's finest work, earning him the 2007 Plug Inde-

ʾpendent Music Awards for Artist of the Year and Producer of the Year. *Donuts'* greatness and the sentiment engendered by Dilla's passing helped to kick-start construction of the Church of James Yancey.

In the short span since, Dilla's stature has increased exponentially, both critically and commercially. His higher-profile collaborators have ceaselessly kept his name alive, with Badu, the Roots and Common dedicating songs and/or entire albums to his memory and constantly praising him in lyrics and interviews. In turn, a new generation of producers and rappers has started taking cues from Dilla's sound, chief among them two of hip-hops brightest stars: Back Milk, a fellow Motown native who got his start working with Slum Village; and Jay Electronica, a Badu-affiliated New Orleans native who has gotten the Internet crazy by kicking fierce rhymes over long-lost Dilla beats. To say nothing of the hordes of MySpace MDs aping Dilla's style and in the process discovering what Kanye West found out on *Finding Forever*: how inherently difficult it is to mimic Dilla's twisted alchemy of tweaked-out soul samples, black mountain drums and twinkling keys.

But as successful as the deification has been, the budding Dilla empire has foundered, thanks to astronomical health bills, which forced Dilla to go into hock with the government and die with high six-figure IRS debt and few tangible assets—save for a few hard drives of beats and a publishing deal with Universal Music. Ironically, as Dilla's stock is at an all-time high, the executors of his estate have been bedeviled by a one-two punch: scrambling to pay his tab while fighting rampant Internet piracy of his material, both aimed at the ultimate goal of providing an inheritance for his two young daughters. "It's frustrating," says Arthur Erk, the estate's executor and Dilla's former business manager. "People have been cropping up left and right, trying to make money off Dilla's name and likeness. There was something called the Dilla Foundation, which doesn't even exist legally, yet it was trying to host charity events, claiming authorization from the estate. If there weren't young children involved, we'd give up. No one needs this type of aggravation."

Enforcing copyright in the Internet age is a Sisyphean task, and trying to protect one of the first big names to die young in the RapidShare world, Dilla's estate has been beset with a dilemma that figures to plague families of all prematurely deceased musicians henceforth.

Explains Erk: "The problem is that Dilla was friendly with a lot of people—many of whom I know, many of whom I don't—and there have been dozens of bootleg situations we've had to expend estate cash on to shut stuff down. If we don't it cheapens the value of his brand. We're trying to protect his legacy and his heirs."

Keeping track of the wealth of Dilla beats floating around the Web is practically impossible. Most notably, Busta Rhymes released a free *Dillagence* mixtape last year, featuring an introduction from Dilla's mother, a matter that Erk claims is currently in mediation. This April, the recording masters of *Pay Jay*, Dilla's never-released MCA record, were illicitly leaked to the Internet, sabotaging an estate plan to rerelease them at a yet-to-be-determined date. In a last-ditch effort to assert control over the heavily pirated material, the estate recently took out a full-page ad in *Billboard*, informing the industry that the only person, including friends and family, legally authorized to execute transactions or make *any* decisions regarding the commercial use of

Dilla's name, music, merchandise, photographs, video appearances, artwork, etc., is Erk.

"We're not sure how many Dilla beats are floating around," says Micheline Levine, Dilla's former lawyer. "It's been an absolute nightmare. [Erk] and I have been working without fees, and neither of us dreamed that copyright infringement would be so extensive and harmful to the estate. We're trying to get the message out to third parties, who may in some convoluted way think they're helping out the heirs but are really depriving them of income."

A Dilla tribute is tentatively planned, as are several lawsuits against copyright infringers; both actions are meant to deliver at least a modicum of income beyond the modest royalties. With the gospel of Dilla secure and reasonably certain to grow, his legacy and brand certainly have the potential to provide for his children. Whether or not they do lies in his empire's efficacy in striking back.

Interview with J Dilla's Mother,
Ms. Maureen Yancey
Jeff Weiss

A few weeks ago, I wrote a piece discussing the difficulties J Dilla's estate has had in enforcing copyright law and paying off the six-figure IRS debt left behind. In the aftermath of the story's publication, I had the chance to speak with his mother, Ms. Maureen Yancey about Dilla's legacy and her current estrangement with the executors of his estate.

Q: *In the original article, some comments from Dilla's estate's executors made you take pause. What were they and what sort of problems have you had with the estate?*

A: I understand the side [estate executor] Arty Erk's coming from and what he's trying to do. However, there has been no communication between them and the family in a year. The only time I hear a peep is if there are some propositions between attorney's going to court. That's the only time I'm made aware of things.

It's ridiculous. I still have contacts with all of Dilla's friends and people in the hip-hop community. We still talk, we still keep in touch, we've became friends. They check in on me and I've had the opportunity to direct them to the estate thinking they'd be able to help do projects. But most of the time, none of their inquiries have been addressed. There's no one that has made it accessible to them to contribute and get work done. I've stopped sending people there. They haven't been forthright, I was told they didn't appreciate the help, that we weren't supposed to use Dilla's name or license. By the time, I understood what was happening and learned about the legal ramifications, I took down the website for the Foundation that we'd created as to be in compliance with state laws. I figured in the coming year, they'd reevaluate their decision, but it never happened.

One of the things Dilla wanted me to do with his legacy was to use it to help others, people with illness, kids who were musically gifted but had little hope due to poverty. I wanted to use my contacts to help people and out and it was squashed because we weren't in compliance with the state and there was nothing we could do about it. I'm Dilla's mother and I can't use Dilla's name or likeness, but I know that I still can honor him by doing his work.

What were your intended goals for the Foundation?

I wanted to set it up to help others but also to be a nucleus for the fans who wanted to do tributes and honor Dilla. It would be a place for artists to be able to show their support. When the estate chose not to communicate with us, they sold themselves short. The A-list artists stay in contact with me directly and they're basically cutting off the quality talents that made themselves closest to Dilla. Anyone with a knowledge about his work would know this, but those in charge haven't a clue to Dilla's worth. They haven't a clue as to who he was as a man or what his relationship was with his fans and his peers. It's a community, those artists coming out of the underground. You can see this when you travel around the world and see how large his fan base really was. People are still discovering the extent of Dilla's influence.

He has a young audience just coming into the community who he's had a major influence on. Then there's the issue of the jazz community. Dilla grew up with jazz. That was his lullaby and the connection is far greater than the estate realizes. It's more than just notes. There's so much that can be done and the estate hasn't got a clue. It's such a waste of time. But I'm not closing the door on them yet. Dilla worked alongside with me and I was a big part of my son's past. I moved to LA to take care of him, I worked for him from day one, that's why the communication with his peers and me has been so great.

What do you hope happens with the estate?

At the end of the day, we want our voices to be heard. We want the community to work with me and the estate. We want everyone to work together. It's been the estate's choice to not communicate with us and it jeopardizes the future quality of his projects. They make the decisions for him without the proper musical knowledge. Their depth of musical knowledge just isn't enough.

How did this entire mess come about? Why did Dilla pick these people if they didn't know anything about music?

He definitely wouldn't have chosen any of them if he knew better. The thing is, Dilla got along with mostly everyone, but if he knew about certain people who have collaborated with the estate he'd been spinning in his grave. They might as well have gotten someone off the street to oversee things. They know the words but they don't know what they mean.

Arty Erk was never his business manager as he portrays himself. During Dilla's lifetime, he was strictly an accountant. Now they constantly threaten to sue at the drop of a dime, I don't want to risk my health so I try not to worry about these things too much but it's upsetting.

It all happened because of our lack of knowledge. Dilla was the first person in our family to even have a will, he was the first to even have anything to designate, the only one of us that had an estate. I'm talking about grandparents and great-grandparents back all the way down. Usually, all we've left behind is bills. I didn't know how what to do, so we ended u sitting on the paperwork for months. We put it off. As his mother and best friend, I didn't want to interfere or ask questions. I felt it wasn't my place. I was so sure that he'd pull out of it. I never had a clue that he'd pass. He'd always tell me, 'mom I'm going to go home,' so that's what I thought would happen. If I'd know he was going to pass, I'd have certainly had someone look at the paperwork. It's just we never thought he'd need it. He ended up with Arty Erk because he had handled his finances, but still, he never had knowledge that it would end up this way. And what about Micheline Levine, his attorney?

Dilla had been with her for most of his career, since he'd been with the Ummah. Whaen Dilla started to make it, he interviewed with several attorney's and he felt the most comfortable with Scott Felcher, who employed Micheline. Dilla was big on going with the people he felt the most comfortable with.

I called her a little while back to let her know that Arty wasn't being fair with me and that he'd made a few comments that I felt were racist. We'd had a relationship in the past and whenever she'd had a disagreement with Dilla, I'd smooth it over, Dilla had a lot of respect for his elders but he brought her to tears a few times and refused to say that he was sorry, but I'd help bridge the gap. Yet she didn't seem to care when I expressed my displeasure with the situation.

What specific comments did you find racist?

When Dilla got sick, I'd been having health problems of my own, but since I had to take care of Dilla, I ended up neglecting my own health. I was feeling really ill and had very little activity in my lungs. I needed needed medication and I had bills. Not bills that would take a lifetime to settle but bills nonetheless.

At one point, Arty told me to call him back and in the meantime, he'd try to see what he could do. I waited and never got the return call. Still in the same poor shape, I called him and he said that he couldn't do anything and asked me, "Well, what did you expect to happen? Were you expecting a big windfall of money?" I said, "no, but you did tell me to call back and otherwise I wouldn't have done that."

At one point in the conversation, he told to me consider going to social services or getting state aid. My gut told me if I had not been a black mother, he wouldn't have said those words. But that wasn't the first time. In the past, he'd made comments about Dilla buying rims. He called me up one time to chastise me for Dilla having a lack of funds and told me that he wouldn't be in this predicament had he not spent money on rims for his truck. But Dilla made the money, he worked for it and he anted to spend it on what he wanted to spend it on. Erk doesn't know much about the community and how important it is what they see you in and how you dress, how you look in public.

I never told Dilla about that but I wish I had. He would've fired him right there. At the end of my last conversation with Erk, I told him that he didn't have to every worry about me calling him again in this lifetime. That as over a year ago and I called Micheline about five minutes late to let her know what he'd said and how I felt about it. I only talked to her once after that, about the guy we chose from Stones Throw to work on Dilla's remaining catalog.

Ultimately, they don't' want anyone who knows the business to deal with Dilla's stuff. They'd rather do it themselves and close themselves off from the community.

So what's the status of Dilla's kids at the moment?

They're doing fine. Both of the mother's are drawing social security and his daughters are living with them. Dilla wanted them to be taken care of and they are.

You've mentioned how close of a relationship you have with Dilla's artist friends? Who do you still keep in touch with?

Everyone calls me. Busta calls regularly. Erykah, Common, The Roots. All the top name artists used to come over during Christmas and New Year's and at various points during the year, so we came to be a family. It's a beautiful relationship that's never faltered, even the artists out in LA. Madlib is a perfect example. Before they'd met face to face, Dilla and him already had a great relationship. The thing is, Dilla didn't want to work with just anyone. There were times he'd gotten offers that would involve big money and he would be like 'I'm not feeling them,' and tell me that he knew better. I'd be sick about it, because it would be at times when he really needed the financial resources, but it wasn't about that, it was about quality. I mean he's still receiving awards and dedications worldwide to this day.

So what do the artist's themselves think of the tumultuous relationship you've had with the estate?

I can't name one of them who's happy about it. None of them want to see me having to grovel for money for medication. I've always been a businesswoman but I had to give it up to take care of Dilla.

What was your profession?

I ran a day care, I had always done that in a building at Conant Gardens. I'd always taken care of myself and never depended on Dilla.

What about the relationship with Stones Throw? You see a lot of mean-spirited comments and rumors in chat rooms that they've been less than upright in business matters regarding Dilla.

Stones Throw has always been wonderful. When I cam to LA to take care of Dilla, his medical bills were sky-high but the people from the label were there every day. The only time they didn't come was when I would call them and tell them to come a day later, because Dilla was too sick for visitors. They took care of the finances, they gave him advances for music that had barely been discussed. They've been great.

Dilla didn't have health insurance for his last two years, so every time he went in and out of the hospital, he would rack up massive bills, sometimes up to a quarter of a million dollars. But they would always try to give us help, even if they didn't have it. I know people say mean things about them but they just aren't true. They're totally honest and they loved Dilla, they stuck by him to the very end.

Why do you think the estate has been so brusque in dealing with you and the artist community?

I think it's simply a control issue. They don't want to worry about ma dukes saying anything. They don't have the time to be bothered, Time will tell. They've definitely done things that are unnerving, that's for sure.

What would you have liked to have seen happen?

I would've liked to be in harmony with them and for there to have been less bigotry, I would've liked to have seen activity. If you do work, people find out about it. Dilla wasn't about controversy, he would've liked things to have been peaceful. Dilla was about love in many formats and for his estate to have done the exact opposite is not having any respect for him or who he was.

Has it been difficult for you to be one of the main people in charge of protecting your son's legacy?

It's been a joy. Even in bad times when people want to slander me, people know the truth, everyone in the community knows. I was there at the beginning and people know that I loved and gave everything to my son. There was nothing I wouldn't have done for Dilla. If it takes 10 years for them to get over this merry-go-ground, it's going to be okay because Dilla wanted to help people who suffered.

Being in Detroit, it's overwhelming the talent that these kids have here. But there's no art appreciation, there's no type of outlet at all. We have very few recreations here. When you come to my home it looks like Beirut. We need these talented and responsible children to see a spark to see the possibility.

What do you thing about the current renaissance of Detroit hip-hop, with Black Milk, Elzhi, Phat Kat and others starting to break nationally and who pay such an obvious tribute to your son's music?

I think it was a wake up call for them. They were all so close. Phat Kat would come here every day and would just be hanging around outside. The inspiration has gotten stronger for them. They know they're not promised anything, Dilla knew when he was going to leave. He talked about different things for me to do when he was gone, but I didn't want to hear that. But he knew that he only had a certain amount of time left that he was blessed with. My greatest bit of advice is to tell artists to get a living will and to name for your executor someone who loves you through thick and thin. Don't take things for granted. I know Dilla's not the first one to get bad advice. It happens a lot in this industry but I hadn't a clue about it. This stuff just wasn't on my mind. All I want to do now is get the foundation up and running because that's what Dilla really wanted.

Is there any bit of your son's music that you hold most dear to you?

I know all of his music but Donuts means the most, because I was there. We had our schedules in the hospital and we'd rotate it around dialysis. It was hard because we'd have to do stuff in the wee hours of the night, with stacks of crates littering the room. We worked double-time and the doctor's were worried but they ultimately knew that it was necessary to keep his spirits up. It was wonderful to be a part of and it's special to me. I didn't even understand the way he arranged things at first. I hadn't given thought to the arrangement, with the "last song of the night." He knew his time was winding down and that album was his way of letting you know. It's like being taken along for a ride. Dilla would always say, 'are you ready for a ride,' and that was what he felt with that album.

Any other favorites?

I liked "Fuck the Police," a lot because Dilla had so much trouble with the police and it tormented him. He was all about being clean and crisp when he left home, his car was always immaculate and the police always assumed that he was dealing drugs or something. I remember the night the inspiration for the occurred. They were in the basement making music and they went to the gas station four doors from my home to get food. On their way there, the cops tried to tear them up, We ran down to the gas station and the cops were already stripping the car apart, trying to disassemble it. Dilla was furious. He hadn't done anything wrong. He hasn't driving a Caddy truck or a Lexus, he was just in a Ford Ranger that my husband had bought it for him because he worked at Ford. It was Dilla's first real car, before he'd made any money on his own and now the cops were belittling him. It hurt him so bad. I told him not to get so upset and that he should put his anger to good use and write a song about it. They didn't get much work done that night but it was business as usual the next day.

When did you first sense how musically gifted Dilla was?

At two months old, he could do perfect harmony, it was incredible. My husband would play jazz to put him to sleep every night and I was going to school for night classes and we thought it would sooth him. Meanwhile, he'd been harmonizing along with the basslines in perfect pitch. It was amazing, we'd tape it and play it for other musicians. We were a very musical family, my husband was always training people to sing.

At two and three years old, he'd start to go to the record shop every Friday and they would play all the new records for him. He'd buy a few then go to the park and spin records. He was only 2 and a half. Now ironically, it's an area where they have an artist haven.

What would you like people to remember about your son?

I'd like them to remember what his music was about. It was very simple: it's about love. Sometimes it was negative, sometimes it was positive. I didn't appreciate that until he had passed. Dilla loved people, he loved doing what he did, and he loved those he worked with.

So with all this in mind, what are you plans for the future?

I'm planning on founding the J Dilla Foundation in his honor. I suppose I'll just do it with my own name, God gave me one too. The artists will be informed that this is what Ma Dukes is doing in honor of him. No one can stop me from doing it and the work will still be the same. I just want his fans to know how much we appreciate him and love and cherish all the support.

The Ear of the Beholder

Rosanne Cash

I have a friend who has two grown children. She is estranged from her son, who has many egregious complaints about my friend, and vivid tales of childhood neglect and various other appalling maternal offenses. Her daughter, on the other hand, assures my heartbroken friend that the son has an overactive imagination combined with a need to blame everyone else for his own problems and that in fact, the stories of her failings as a parent never occurred. Who owns the truth?

In my own life, there was a Hollywood movie made about my family: my father's drug addiction, the spectacular dissolution of my parents' marriage, the genesis of the romantic relationship between my father and stepmother, my birth and the birth of my sisters, and my father's rise to fame. This was all covered in less than two hours. If you went through this film with a fine-toothed fact-checker, you would emerge safely on the side of a non-litigious wide release.

But is it the truth? Not mine. Certainly not my mother's, and to some degree, not even my father's. It's a pastiche, an impression. An amalgamation of facts strung together, even as a poetic narrative, is not necessarily the same thing as the truth.

In my last column, I wrote about the songwriting workshop I used to teach, and how some students were so attached to the facts that it hindered the quality of their writing. I encouraged them to use poetic license, and give up the facts if they had to, to improve their lyrics. One comment sent in by a reader struck me:

> . . . for those of us interested in becoming more honest with ourselves as we mature, I think it is more important to put away our creative fictions and cut to the soul of the matter when writing. Just because you are more interested in "rhyme scheme errors" than the integrity of the relationship between fact and expression, you shouldn't extinguish the passion for honesty that lives within your younger, more intuitive students.
>
> —Posted by Geoff Baker

Ouch. I have spent a lifetime in the service of creative fiction, as well as non-fiction ornamented by fiction, so let me elaborate even further. The "truth" (or "honesty") and the "facts" are not necessarily the same, they are not necessarily equal and one often requires the suspension of the other. This may not be the case in higher math or on Wall Street (or, actually, it may work there as well, but I'm clueless about that) but it is an immutable "truth" in art and music that facts are not necessarily the best indicators of the deepest human experience.

The table where you found the suicide note, the cup of coffee that turned cold because you were distracted in a painful reverie staring out the old wavy-glass window at the rain dripping off the eaves, the seashell left in the coat pocket from the last time you were at that favorite spot at the ocean, when it all came clear that you were at the right place with the wrong man, the letters, the photos, the marbles and jewels—all these physical, material, real-world artifacts carry poetic weight and should be used liberally in songwriting. These are the facts that convey truth to me.

The exact words he said, who was right or wrong, whether he relapsed on the 7th or the 10th, why exactly she does what she does, the depth and weight and timbre of the feelings, whether Love Heals Everything—these aren't facts, these are ever-changing blobs of emotional mercury, and when you are working in rhyme, it can be much more powerful and resonant to write about the shards of the coffee cup than about the feeling that caused him to throw it across the room. You are better off moving the furniture than you are directly analyzing the furniture maker. This is to say nothing of the fact that the lyrical content of songs is by definition wholly entwined with melody, rhythm, tone and possibly a backbeat, and these carry their own authority.

Recently, I wrote a song with Kris Kristofferson and Elvis Costello. It was a wild idea I had while I was lying around recovering from surgery this past winter. They are both friends—I've known Kris since my childhood—and Elvis and I had just written a song together by email. (He called it "Song With Rose" as a working title, and when it came time to record it on his new record, "Momofuku," he kept the eponymous title, which delighted me). I asked them separately if they would be interested in recording together, the three of us, and they were both game.

We started talking about this in February. We found that the only day in a six-month window when the three of us would be in New York at the same time, without obligations, was April 5th. I booked the studio, not knowing what we would do. As the date got closer, I started to get a little nervous and thought maybe my initial idea of recording old songs of ours together might not have the fresh energy and originality I was looking for. Elvis and John Leventhal, my husband and frequent collaborator and producer, kept mentioning that they hoped we could write something together that day, but that also made me anxious. It seemed too much pressure for one day.

I had a song that was incomplete, but a great idea, that I had started writing when I was halfway through recording "Black Cadillac." It never really worked, and last year John picked it up again, streamlined it musically and suggested some lyric changes—actually lyric deletions, as he thought it was too wordy. I pared the first verse down to this:

> *You want love*
> *But it's never deep enough*
> *You want life*
> *But it's never long enough*
> *You want peace*
> *Like it's something you can buy*
> *You want time*
> *But you're content to watch it fly*

I loved the song, but it was still incomplete and didn't seem to have a home. John thought this would be a great song to write with the gents, and so I sent the first verse by e-mail to Elvis and to Kris (by way of his wife, Lisa, as Kris doesn't do e-mail), to see if they would be interested in finishing it with us.

Elvis responded immediately, and within a couple days had e-mailed back a second verse, and some ideas for bridges. I loved his verse ("You want imagination but you cannot pretend . . . "), and we began a dialogue about where it should go. Nothing from Kris, who was touring in Europe.

We waited.

On April 4th, the day before the session, Lisa sent an e-mail saying, "Here are his thoughts so far . . . " and a verse from Kris that raised the hair on the back of my head and brought instant tears to my eyes. I sent it to Elvis, fingers shaking, and he wrote back within minutes, his excitement and exclamation points jumping off the screen. It was perfect.

It all came together seamlessly the next day, in a way that I've seldom experienced in 30 years of recording. It was like alchemy. It was eight hours of magic (and I never use that word). Elvis tinkered with his verses a bit, we divided up the vocal parts and the three of us stood in a circle with the three musicians—John, Zev Katz and Joe Bonadio—and recorded the song. It still doesn't have a proper title, or a home, but it is a thing of beauty. (Regarding the title, I suggested "Free Will," Kris suggested "Faith and Free Will," and Elvis was concerned that anything with "free will" would remind people of a movie about a whale; so right now we're calling it "April 5th," because that's when we recorded it.) A few people who have heard it have said that even though the lyrics are uplifting, even elegiac, the song makes them cry, and they are not sure why. I had the same experience, and I'm not sure why, either. There are no "facts" in these lyrics, no literal references to our lives, beyond our combined assimilated experience and unstated values.

We are so deeply limited by language, and so ennobled by it. Songs are the attempt to convey what is under and behind language, and so it is counter-productive, if not counter-intuitive, to clutch at exactitudes of circumstance that retreat further in meaning the more desperate we become to quantify them.

My friend Joe Henry says that songwriting is not about self-expression (ewwww), but about discovery. I am of entirely the same mind, which is why I recoil against the attempt to categorize "personal" songs of mine as diary pages and why I resist that niggling insistence on the facts. Self-expression without craft is for toddlers. Real artistic accomplishment requires a suspension of certitude. E.L. Doctorow said that "writing is an exploration. You start from nothing and learn as you go." He may not have been referring specifically to songwriting, but it applies. Great songwriting is not a poor man's poetry, or a distant cousin to "real" writing. It requires the same discipline and craft. Bright flashes of inspiration can initiate it, but it cannot be completed that way. (That is not to say that all songwriting is important and good, just as not all fiction is important or good. I don't think anyone would put "Like a Rolling Stone" or my dad's "Big River" (a truly great piece of American poetry wedded to a wicked, swampy backbeat) in the same category as The Archies' "Sugar, Sugar" (it is what it is).

But in the space where truth and fact diverge, a larger question arises: if the facts don't lead us to meaning, what does? Perhaps a willingness to live with questions, not answers, and the confidence to ascribe meaning where we find it, with our own instincts as guide. I should approach my writing as if I am meeting someone for the first time, and have no idea what he will say or what kind of mood he is in. If you already know entirely what you want to say, and want to document an "honest" rehash of what happened and why, then I still maintain that you are better off taking up jurisprudence.

I appreciate my readers' instinct to protect my songwriting students and their attempts to stay honest, but in songwriting, as in painting, photo-realism is only one style; it is not the litmus test for everything else. In many great songs a larger, universal modicum of truth is revealed and resonates on a personal level with the listener, even when the facts make no sense at all. Sometimes especially when the facts make no sense at all. And, if everything goes well, you can also dance to it.

Branded

Carrie Brownstein

Kanye West has inexplicably launched his own travel website; it's like Orbitz or Travelocity except that it's Kanye. Ostensibly, the point is that West is selling more than hotels and plane tickets; he is selling a lifestyle, namely, his.

On its own, the news of Kanye's online travel agency is benign, novel in its quirkiness, maybe even admirable as seen as part of a long line of West's creative and unique endeavors; but within the broader context of artists or people-turned-brands, West's new venture is not so much troubling as it is tiring. Maybe it's that it comes at a time when Madonna is once again ubiquitous, gracing the cover of half a dozen magazines. And Madonna is always extolling something—oxygen facials, peeing in the shower (kills fungus!), Pilates, adoption, Kaballah, children's literature, Britain. Madonna is so branded that it's hard to distinguish between her and, say, Proctor & Gamble; she's just some other company that shape shifts with the times, transforming her outward appearance and message to attract new buyers, all the while selling us on a new way to exist in the world. And the concept of artist as a brand is also overwhelming within the context of an election year—one in which we as consumers (I mean, voters) are already inundated with sales pitches of how we can best make America (that brand we live in) safer, cleaner, and stronger.

When bands become brands, the dynamic creates a very cynical way of viewing music; the inherent value shifts from an aesthetic or sonic one to a monetary one. If I am choosing between a U2 iPod or a regular one, a White Stripes camera or the non-White Stripes camera, my role as a fan has been commodified as well. Basically, I feel like a tool.

I'm not fooling myself—bands and fans and the music industry as a whole are a business, and a struggling one at that. And there has always been a bottom line. But when everything is branded it gives me the feeling like I'm doing all of my shopping at the mall; there is the illusion of choices, but mostly they are being made for me. And by being at the mall in the first place, I've already forfeited most of my options.

Much of music has always been about buying into an idea, a movement, a sphere of influence, an aesthetic, and a voice. As music fans, we're sometimes willing to let the collective voice of the audience speak for us, or for the music to represent a bit of who we are. But I'd be less willing to do that for a brand. Imagine putting brand stickers on your car, following brands around the country, asking for a brand's autograph, or trying to sleep with members of the brand. Frankly, it wouldn't be as fun. So, before Bright Eyes puts their name on a hybrid car or Feist comes out with a line of handbags, they should remember that their fans would likely be embarrassed to utter the words, "I'm with the brand."

Crowd Control

Wendy Lesser

Whenever a conductor lifts his arms, points his finger, or gestures with his head, he is actually controlling thousands of body parts. These include (among others) the right arms and left fingers of the string players, the hands and lungs of the woodwinds, the lips of the brass section, the wrists of the percussionists, and the eyes and ears of all the musicians performing under him. But the body parts also include the eyes, ears, lungs, and hands those of us out there in the audience: we too are watching his characteristic movements, listening for the notes, catching our breaths, bringing our palms together in applause. This control can never be perfect, in regard to either the bodies onstage or those off it, and that is a good thing, because robots can neither play nor appreciate excellent music. But to the extent a conductor's control approaches perfection, in a Zeno's Paradox–like fashion, without ever getting there, we in the audience stand to benefit. Listening to the Berlin Philharmonic perform under Simon Rattle, one has a sense of what that near-perfection might sound like.

I got my first hint of this the night before the fabled Berlin orchestra began its latest series of performances at Carnegie Hall. On that Monday night last November, Rattle served as the guest conductor for the Simón Bolívar Youth Orchestra of Venezuela, a two-hundred-strong group of energetic, extremely talented, somewhat raw young people who were performing Bartók's Concerto for Orchestra and Shostakovich's Tenth Symphony. This was only the second Carnegie concert of their lives (the first had been the previous afternoon), and from my box seat directly over the stage, I could actually see both the excitement and the nervousness in their faces; I also got a clear view of the filled-up Carnegie auditorium—the same view that was facing the musicians as they looked out—so I had some sense of what was causing that excitement and nervousness. Under their own young conductor, the phenomenal Gustavo Dudamel, they performed the Bartók vibrantly and thrillingly, though if pressed one would have to say that the loud, fast parts were better than the quiet, slow ones. This is natural for a young orchestra, so it was rather amazing that they could do something else when Simon Rattle took over in the second half. In his, and their, rendering of the Shostakovich symphony, even the delicate bits of near-silence and pensive andante were played beautifully.

If he could accomplish this with a group of relatively untested young musicians (the Bolívars range in age from sixteen to twenty), imagine how much more he could do with one of the greatest, if not *the* greatest, orchestras in the world. In the course of its one-week stay in New York, the Berlin Philharmonic played three full-evening concerts at Carnegie Hall, each one featuring a major Mahler piece matched to a much shorter, much more modern composition. In terms of the modern works, the progression was definitely upward, from Magnus Lindberg's serviceable *Seht die Sonne*, to Thomas Adès's impressive but finally ornamental *Tevót*, to György Kurtág's already classic, deeply moving

Stele. As for the Mahler works, it was a toss-up: few if any listeners could ever have heard more stirring, terrifying performances of the Ninth Symphony, the song-cycle *Das Lied von der Erde*, and the Tenth Symphony, so which you preferred depending largely on your prior feelings about the music.

Simon Rattle is, above all, a dramatic conductor. I don't mean just in the way he moves his own body (though that, too, is grippingly stageworthy), but in the way he thinks about and shapes performances. He can bring out the theatricality even in a Haydn symphony, and with a composer like Mahler—who specializes in the interior drama, the romantic-agonistic feeling inside or behind the music—Rattle is in his element.

As I could see during rehearsals, his method of heightening the drama often lay in toning *down* the musicians rather than stirring them up. This may seem counter-intuitive, but it is clearly right: those quiet parts of Mahler are where we listeners most often forget to breathe, where we feel our life seeping away from us or perhaps coming back to us in unrecognizable form. To produce this unearthly effect, Rattle repeatedly got his performers to play in the palest, most delicate tones. "I know everybody thinks his part is the most important here," he said during one rehearsal, "but that means it suddenly gets too loud." Elsewhere he warned them against speeding up too much: "I'm the one who likes this movement played *very* slow," he reminded them. And he would constantly test their sound—honed in the acoustically perfect auditorium of Berlin's Philharmoniker Hall—to make sure it worked in the Carnegie's different (if equally sound-friendly) environment. "This space is excellent for *pianissimo*," he told his players, "but it makes our *piano* sound too strong. So let's try that passage again, but more quietly." Sometimes he said these things to them in English, and sometimes in German (over the four years I've been watching him, Rattle's command of German has increased enormously, which makes it harder for a non-German-speaker like me to follow all the twists and turns of a rehearsal); but in every case the effect on the orchestra was immediately apparent, and he rarely had to get them to repeat a passage more than once. If he *did* have to go over something too often, he would realize that his instructions were becoming unhelpful. "First I tell you to play it slower, then I tell you to play it faster, and now you're completely confused. Just play the music," he said at one point, essentially asking them to fall back on their own tremendous musicianship. This, too, is the sign of a masterful conductor: understanding the limitations of his own control.

One of the things Rattle had occasion to mention to his musicians, during the course of their rehearsals, was the limits of his control over the audience. He had already alerted them, during their previous visit in 2006, to the fact that the New York audience would leap to its feet and rush for the subways immediately after the last note sounded. This is not normal behavior for music audiences anywhere else in the world, and it might be taken as downright rejection if the musicians were not warned about it in advance. (Even *with* the warning, the behavior still seems, and is, incredibly rude.) But this time he also had to mention the coughing. "Be careful how you play this bit," he said during Tuesday morning's rehearsal of the Ninth, "or you're likely to get two thousand people all coughing at once."

In the event, the coughing proved more of a problem than even he had expected. That Tuesday night, during a quiet passage of the Ninth's first movement, somebody—or perhaps several some-bodies—coughed so loudly that the flute player couldn't hear the harmonic change that was his cue, and as a result failed to enter on time. This in turn threw the rest of the orchestra off, so that they had to scramble to regroup. I didn't catch any of this with my own ear, and neither did anyone else I know; I only learned about it a day or two later from a member of the orchestra. But I did hear the remarkable speech Rattle gave as a result. In the brief space between the first and second movements, he turned around to the audience and addressed us in a soft-spoken, polite, but firm manner. "Ladies and gentlemen," he said, "this is a piece that requires enormous silence. It comes out of silence, and it goes back into silence. I hope you will join us in creating that magical atmosphere. And these"—he held up his own white handkerchief, used for mopping his brow between movements—"can be quite useful for that purpose."

I can think of only one comparable moment of direct address during all my years of attending performances, and that was at a dance concert many years ago at the New Victory Theater. Mikhail Baryshnikov was performing alone onstage (I think it might even have been the piece set to his own heartbeat), and an oblivious young woman in the first row was noisily eating a seemingly endless series of plastic-wrapped candies. I was sitting right behind her and was almost ready to murder her myself, when suddenly, without breaking his gestural sequence, Barysh-nikov said, "Stop that." He said it only once, and he said it just loud enough to be heard in the first few rows, but he terrified that girl into behaving herself.

Rattle's announcement had a similar effect on the whole of the Carnegie auditorium. There was not another cough during the remaining three movements of the Mahler symphony. This was annoying in itself (if the coughing was so obviously voluntary, why had they done it in the first place?), but it was also tremendously heartening: it seemed that if we could just borrow Simon Rattle for another month or two, he could probably whip these terrible New York audiences into shape. Rattle himself, at any rate, appeared to be enjoying his new-found powers, for he held the final silence at the end of the Ninth—a deep, scary, reverent silence—for longer than I have ever heard any end-silence held in Carnegie Hall. Only when he released his extended arms, letting them fall to his sides, did the audience feel free to burst into its thunderous applause.

I saw him do this with the final silences on the other two Mahler works as well (though he was foiled, in the case of the Tenth, by a loud cougher who had cannily been waiting for just such a silence to interrupt, and whose noise was taken by the rest of that unusually boorish crowd as its release signal). And then, in the orchestra's Sunday afternoon performance of *The Rite of Spring*, I saw him do something different.

The Berlin Philharmonic's rendition of Stravinsky's piece was actually part of a larger program called The Rite of Spring Project. The culmination of months of work on the part of music teachers, music advisors, an imported choreographer, and over a hundred New York City schoolchildren, the project involved dance as well as music, and student-played, student-written compositions as well as the professional performance. It was held in the far-uptown United Palace Theater, a former 1930s movie palace (now the home of Rev. Ike's congregation) which holds more than three thousand people within its huge, unbelievably rococo space. The audience that Sunday afternoon consisted of the usual Carnegie Hall types, vastly augmented on this occasion by the families of the participating schoolchildren, walk-ins from the 175th Street neighborhood, and a large sprinkling of other people lured in by the $15 ticket price.

At the break between the student-composed part of the program and the Stravinsky-composed part, an informally dressed Simon Rattle got up on the makeshift stage and spoke to the audience about what we were about to see and hear. He briefly summarized the plot of *The Rite of Spring* in a way that made it sound analogous to our own troubled times, and then remarked, "And if this sounds familiar . . . ," setting off a wave of collusive audience laughter. He then issued a warning, or guideline, or instruction, but he did it so delicately that everyone simply took it as a pleasantly offered joke. "*The Rite of Spring*, which lasts about half an hour, *sounds* as if it is ending several times before it actually does end," he said. "With opera, they say it's over when the fat lady sings. Well, in this, you'll know it's over when the moon rises and the tall girl dances herself to death." And with that, he made his way down to the floor-level orchestra pit and took up his baton. He didn't need to say another word; the applause came only when he wanted it, and then it wouldn't stop. The overwhelmed schoolchildren who had been dancing onstage seemed pleased but also slightly terrified—they didn't have their curtain calls thoroughly rehearsed, as professionals would have, so they looked a bit like a hundred deer caught in the headlights, and they just stood there looking like that until Simon Rattle climbed back up, took two of the central children by the hands, and led them all in their bows.

The Rise and Fall of the Festive Fifty
Tom Ewing

I love polls. I tell myself—sometimes it's even true—that I love the conversations they start more, but polls and surveys fascinate me: the hard currencies of percentages and decimal points; the nuances of rankings, rises and falls; the tempting, treacherous way an aggregate opinion emerges from a datamass. Growing up I even had a favorite poll—and I didn't feel like a lunatic, because it was a lot of other people's favorite poll, too: John Peel's annual Festive Fifty countdown.

The Festive Fifty was a listener survey—you sent in your three favorite tracks, Peel totted up the results, and he played the songs on the radio in order, during his end-of-year shows. As a kid getting into indie I played my C90s of the 1988 countdown until they snapped—my first time hearing the Fall, Sonic Youth, the Wedding Present, Pixies, My Bloody Valentine. As a grownup, with a job in market research and this music long sunk into the grain of my life, what amazed me looking at the Festive Fifty was how transparent it was as a poll, how open to fluke and freak results: Peel's whims and personal favorites would bubble up high on the list, next to popular records he'd probably never played. On the 1992 list, for instance, his introduction to Suede's

"The Drowners" was tinged with faint disapproval, while spiky Welsh-language group Datblygu met with undisguised delight.

Recently I found a torrent of every Festive Fifty from the first, in 1976, to 1991: sometimes just the records, but mostly broadcasts taken from old tapes like mine. Of course, the first one I played was 1988, and then I remembered how Peel himself had been more worried about what hadn't got in:

"I think you'd have to agree with me really that it's an ultra conservative Festive Fifty . . . I mean it's been mainly, kind of, young lads strumming guitars. A lot of good tunes, I don't deny that, but as I say—conservative. The only black records to get into there are Number 50, Public Enemy; Number 37, Shalawambe from Zambia, and number 28, Overlord X."

This wasn't the first or last time Peel said similar things, but when I heard that at the time, I took it very seriously. Peel's strength as a broadcaster, and one reason the Festive Fifty was so popular, was that you wanted his approval, and the disappointment in his voice here was obvious. Would his audience listen? The next year I winced slightly as only one "black record"—by De La Soul—made it into the chart.

Peel's argument looks somewhat shopworn now—it resurfaces almost every time connoisseur tastes find a collective voice, and reliably pushes buttons, as the subject of taste diversity is more than a little touchy. But the key word in Peel's complaint isn't "black," it's "conservative." Peel wasn't simply wringing his hands, he was annoyed at his listeners for ignoring much of the music that he himself had been playing them: His late-80s shows were full of hip-hop, African pop, and house music. His comment is a window on the frustrating relationship between a tastemaker and their audience. To understand the complaint, and the nature of that relationship, we need to look back to the early Festive Fifty polls.

The first Fifty, in 1976, simply asked listeners to choose their all-time favorite tracks. With Led Zeppelin on top, and Bob Dylan and Pink Floyd in the top five, it's a solid celebration of classic rock virtues, skewing a little to the thoughtful: Fond of visionaries, rewarding long songs and Y chromosomes. A closer look suggests a more varied audience: The crossover between Poco and Beefheart surely wasn't huge. But generally Peel's listeners in 1976 were a serious-minded bunch with an appreciation of rock's recent history and progression.

And then the meteor struck. Peel kept running the Festive Fifty as an all-time list between 1978 and 1982, but that 1982 poll is strikingly different from the 76 one: Not one single track survives from the earlier list. If you want evidence as to punk's "scorched-earth" effect in the UK, here it is. From a researcher's perspective, for an apparently settled list of preferences to change absolutely in six years would be astonishing in an individual; in a group it's unprecedented.

If, of course, it was the same group. Did Peel convert his listeners to punk, or build a new audience? He was already playing punk in 1976, though it doesn't show up on the first Festive Fifty— the hour-long special he devoted to it that December (also floating around on P2P) saw him embrace it fully, but by that time those first votes were in. The beloved Floyd and Zep tracks from the '76 poll slip gradually from the chart over the next few years: Other shows on the BBC's Radio 1 network covered rock, and Peel was the place to go for punk, so this gradual churn makes sense.

At any rate, by conversion or recruitment he had created a new audience, just as he'd created one for the hippy rock and folk he'd played on early 70s radio. Was the problem that he couldn't keep on creating audiences, or that he kept moving while they stood still? Peel's own excitement over punk, after all, was one out of many excitements: He found himself won over successively by rap, grindcore, techno, drum'n'bass, happy hardcore, and a multitude of global pop musics. But as his 1988 comment shows, precious little of it made any impact on the Festive Fifty, our only record of his audience's collective tastes.

Why couldn't he take his audience with him? First of all, for many people, he did. Few Peel listeners got into everything the man liked, but most of them were won over by something: In my case I'd have been a much later convert to electronic music without hearing the Orb on his show. Quantitative polls, even very interesting ones, often confuse "what people have in common" with "what people think": Guitar bands were the center of Peel's audience's taste but they weren't the totality.

Also punk, and the indie label movement it led to, needed Peel in a way the other musics he championed never did: Peel's shows were a litany of label names, contact addresses, and other details that helped give a scene its nervous system. Those networks were already in place for African music, or dance music—they had their own gatekeepers. One of the few African records that did make it into the Festive Fifty was the Bhundu Boys' "My Foolish Heart," from their fine 1987 album True Jit: Recorded with Western producers, it won Peel's sympathetic ear, but the existing "world music" fanbase despised its apparent commerciality and the group fragmented into failure and personal tragedy.

I wonder too if Peel underestimated how strong punk was: Its canon formation happened very quickly, and stuck. On the 1980 rundown there's a certain sardonic weariness in Peel's voice as he recites the consistent top five positions for "(White Man) in Hammersmith Palais," and the reason he stopped the all-time polls in 1982 was fairly obvious: He would otherwise be playing the same records forever.

It's crucial to point out, though, that Peel never showed the slightest sign of disliking his audience, even if he was sometimes wearied by their choices. The last Festive Fifty I downloaded is from 1991, and is unusual in that it was never broadcast as a whole: Peel's discontent peaked and he refused to run the "predictable," Nirvana-topped chart. I remember being immensely disappointed, even hurt, and I doubt I was alone: The Festive Fifty was back the next year, and the listeners showed their thanks by voting Bang Bang Machine's "Geek Love"—fearfully obscure and a firm Peel favorite—as number one.

The incident had shown the limits of Peel's patience, but also of his wrath. Peel in his later years was more like the conscience of British indie fandom than its guide: He played more electronica, metal, and worldpop than ever; his audience listened, and voted for Camera Obscura and Ballboy. Both sides seemed happy.

In British broadcasting culture this role might be described as "Reithian"—after the founder of the BBC, who believed broadcasting had a mission to "educate, inform, entertain": To bring people what they ought to know about, as well as what they wanted, in order that the one would gradually become the other. Reithian values are often now associated with a class-based cultural elitism, and are rather out of favor in a broadcasting environment that's both more market-driven and better attuned to niche and popular culture. Peel could plainly be seen as Reithian, but strongly rejected the idea that he was an elitist.

He certainly wasn't a populist—it's a myth that Peel's tastes were omnivorous, and he generally treated commercial pop as a circus, or a broad joke he could play straight man for. But for him elitism was a matter of perspective and style rather than taste:

Reading his interviews, what he abhorred was the idea that taste could be a mark of superiority as well as individuality. As for style, Peel's grew into a shambolic friendliness, embracing his mistakes and emphasizing his lovable domestic side—if he was an elitist, he was never condescending.

After Peel's death there was a general assumption—not much discouraged by the BBC—that there could never be another broadcaster like him. His unassuming style, pretty much unique among British DJs, is surely part of the reason, but it's also true that the wideband license Peel had to play anything he fancied was increasingly out of place on radio even before he died. The idea of Peel as unique, an inimitably great and generous public servant, keeps his memory alive but does his legacy no favors by suggesting his Reithian project can't be continued.

The enemies of that project are easy to finger: They include marketers and pollsters like me, keen to help the BBC and its commercial competitors segment and identify sustainable audience subgroups. But that's not the whole story: If John Peel were starting a career now, as a DJ or perhaps an mp3 blogger, it wouldn't just be marketers that would stop him finding an audience. The digital culture of personalization—your own last.fm station, your own tailored recommendations, your own Festive Fifties every day of every year—makes the idea of "education" by tastemakers like Peel seem even more antiquated. The sudden left turns and infuriating inconsistencies his shows offered would as likely be resented as embraced. It's probably easier to admire John Peel than it sometimes was to listen to him. But if he was sometimes disappointed in his audience—and if he often baffled them in turn—it was because he respected their intelligence rather than pampering their tastes. The renegotiation of that contract is what stands in the way of his successors.

Soul to Soul

Hall & Oates make the ladies scream

Rebecca Schoenkopf

Every year, I go to the BMI awards dinner. The music publishing company is one of two (along with ASCAP) that collects your royalties every time someone plays your song, so that if you are, for instance, Gary Wright, you can buy a house in Palos Verdes because 33 years ago you recorded "Dream Weaver."

Every year, the guy from Lifehouse gets a bunch of awards for being a top getter of lovely royalty cash, and no, I don't know why either, though Lifehouse's debut eight years ago was an enjoyable little collection of soft rock and pop that wasn't in the least offensive and was very catchy. Are they Jesusy? Is there some yooge base of loyal homeschooled kids that is buying every album? Do they love them as much as I loved Mr. Mister? Or more, considering I didn't bother with Mr. Mister's sophomore effort, even though I could have gotten it as one of my 12 tapes for a penny? I do not know, and I do not care to find out.

One year, Brian Wilson was being honored, but I hate the Beach Boys so I didn't stay, and one year Ike Turner was there, and I broke my finger. That year, my tablemate was Michigan

Congressman John Conyers, and I was so excited! Then I re-counted the time after 9/11 that airport security made him strip down because of his pacemaker, and he said that wasn't he but rather was John Dingell, and he didn't talk to me anymore after that.

This year, the big winner with all the hits was Polow Da Don, and I never came within a hundred yards of him to ask him what the hell "my London, London Bridge wanna go down," while a band called "Hinder" won Song of the Year for "Lips of an Angel," which is just grody and wrong and sorta Deliverance—as were they; some among them even had perms—and it was fun fun fun till my daddy took my T-bird away.

But it is not a BMI awards dinner without a) an open bar; b) industry types who won't schmooze you; and c) a guest of honor that makes the ladies scream. So after the filets and jumbo shrimp were et, lying in a sauce for which five sticks of butter had given their lives, it was time for Daryl Hall and John Oates to get their lifetime achievement awards. Eeeeeeeeeeeee!

I'm just kidding. I didn't really care. Except for this: In the trib-ute to H/O beforehand, in addition to a multimedistravaganza of Hall's leonine Nordicness and Oates's jheri-curl mullet and Mag-num mustache, the goodly folk at BMI interviewed some other goodly folk about H/O's Meaning and Import to the World of Rock. Del Bryant, the warm and genial president of BMI pro-claimed, "Hall and Oates are the most successful duo in the his-tory of rock!" which made my head spin—really? Maybe they've sold more records than Ike and Tina, but were they more suc-cessful than Simon & Garfunkel, say, or Captain and Tennille? (I couldn't think of any other duos except the Thompson Twins, so, really, maybe they were!)

The Wik tells me Simon & Garfunkel only had two No. 1 singles, while H/O had six, so by that metric, I mean, yeah, I guess,
but the Wik has put me in a grand funk and I think it is time to
change the subject. So I was already getting a small bit crotchety
when one of the folk interviewed in the tribute vid elbowed his
way into my reverie with, "John Hall has the greatest voice in the
history of soul."

I know!

That was when my head exploded all over the the guy sitting
next to me. He deserved it, though, as he couldn't be bothered to
stop BlackBerrying even during an ovation for Al Gallico, who'd
published "Stand by Your Man," "The Most Beautiful Girl," and
"Time of the Season," and who'd passed away May 15.

Also, I got some of my head on the centerpiece. It was very
messy.

The Greatest Voice in the History of Soul.

Go ahead. Read it again.

The Greatest Voice in the History of Soul.

Let's play a little game: I'll name people with greater voices in
soul history, and you nod in agreement.

Sam Cooke.

Marvin Gaye.

Otis Redding.

Aretha.

Lou Rawls.

Isaac Hayes.

Smokey Robinson.

Ray Charles.

Etta James.

Mahalia Jackson.

Stevie Wonder.

Curtis Mayfield.

A little someone I like to call "James Brown."

And everyone else in soul history who wasn't Daryl Hall.

Wasn't that a good game? It was!

But then a funny thing happened. I was berating the entire world in my head for overselling, for inciting this awful angry backlash—in me, anyway—when clearly they should have just said, "Okay, all the women in your 30s and 40s, now it's time to backward skate!" Why not just let us have our fun, goofy nostalgia? Why pretend Hall & Oates is anything more important than a good time? It's like calling Bret Michaels the greatest poet of his generation.

Touch my back stage pass / ride my lim-o-zine!

Soon, Babyface was onstage at the Beverly Wilshire singing "Sara Smile." (The guy from Lifehouse had sung "Every Time You Go Away," and some dude from Fall Out Boy who wasn't the one who married the Simpson girl sang "Rich Girl.") And as "Sara Smile" floated out above the audience, I walked to the back and shook my hips, just a little, in sort of a retarded-white-girl-sobering-up kind of way. Why, it wasn't a bad song at all! In fact, it was sort of . . . gorgeous!

I suspect it might have been because Babyface has a greater voice in the history of soul than Daryl Hall does, too. Also, Babyface wasn't on the Flashdance soundtrack—which it's possible I own on cassette, I'm just saying it is physically impossible to be the owner of the greatest voice in the history of soul if you sang "Maneater." I think Irene Cara would agree.

Hall and Oates themselves came out for a quick set that left everyone wanting more—"Maneater," "I Can't Go for That (No Can Do)" and "She's Gone," and I stopped being angry and let the love wash me clean. It was time for a backwards skate.

Pure Country
Ken Tucker

Leon Kagarise, who died in 2008 at age 71, was a Baltimore audio engineer who was also a pure amateur—an amateur photographer, amateur record-collector, and most of all a fan—who followed country musicians he admired when they performed at rural amusement parks, at a little outdoor open stage in Maryland, and a farm in Pennsylvania Amish country. The names are big—Johnny Cash, George Jones, Dolly Parton, Hank Snow—but the events are small.

The color photographs that Kagarise snapped with his Zeiss Ikon camera are candid, casual, and artless, yet they capture the artistry and image-creation of these musicians with serious, sometimes stunning, precision. There aren't any pictures in the new book that collects his work—*Pure Country: The Leon Kagarise Archives 1961-1971* (Process Media)—that will haunt or frighten you the way any number of photo collections of early rock and rollers such as Elvis, Jerry Lee Lewis, and others can. *Pure Country* is like leafing through a family scrapbook, if your family included June Carter standing in the woods late at night, glowing in a white shirtwaist dress with ruffles, red high heels and perfectly bobbed hair, looking at the camera as though she was ready to kiss it. You know that famous photo of a sneering, hopped-up Johnny Cash giving the camera the finger? Leon Kagarise didn't take that picture, or anything like it; in fact, Kagarise probably would have burned such a photo as soon as he developed it, abashed at its vulgarity. Yet his photo of Cash on page 53 of *Pure Country*—a Cash in right profile, onstage at the New River Ranch in Maryland, leaning into the audience strumming his guitar, his hair combed in a short, neat pompadour, his trademark black clothing on this evening a simple black business suit—captures Cash's smolder as well as any song he recorded.

A vanished world is summoned up in these photographs; a world in which men and women who sang about heartbreak, dissolute despair, unhappy marriages, and shameful affairs offered up hard lives as the norm and as no excuse to not say thank you to the fans and sign autographs for hours after a performance. Hank Snow's country-industry image was that of the genial Singing Ranger, the smiling Canadian who half-crooned, half-yodelled his melancholy as upbeat inspiration. But take a look at Kagarise's photo of Snow caught offstage in Sunset Park, PA, in 1964—his face uncharacteristically masked by big brown Ray-Ban sunglasses, his face a blank mask, his hairpiece looking like hard molded plastic atop an endless forehead—and you see Snow for the first time as a tough little sonofabitch who was struggling to keep racking up hits while Nashville was starting to ignore his hard-twang music in favor of "countrypolitan" string sections, even as he and the rest of the industry tried to comprehend what the Beatles and "All My Loving" and "I Saw Her Standing There" meant for the future, and Kagarise's photo suggested that that future required dark brown shades.

The washed-out colors of Kagarise's pictures of lesser-known acts like the Stonemen—a raucously funny, tremendously passionate family talent-show act—or the mountain-music boys Jim and Jesse, or the pious, curvy sex-angel Connie Smith . . . all of these images contain quiet explosions of contradictory messages: intricate harmonies about messy lives; formally-dressed artists taking pains to assure their audiences that they're no different from them. To look at Hank Snow in *Pure Country* is to hear him sing "I Don't Hurt Anymore" and know that the title sentiment is an artful lie: that he can still feel great hurt, and see that he knows the people listening to him has that hurt in them as well. Leon Kagarise seems to have been exhilarated every time he captured the complexity of the relationship between artist and audience, music and image, hurt and joy.

My Mentor, My Teacher

Stanley Booth

Stanley Booth remembers producer Jerry Wexler,
who died in August, 2008.

I met Jerry Wexler in New York City on Dec. 11, 1967, the day after Otis Redding had died. A self-described "vehement Jewish
atheist," he might have called our encounter a mitzvah. For me,
plunged into despair and confusion, after being in the studio with
Otis all the previous week, at Stax Records in Memphis, Tenn.,
as he recorded "Dock of the Bay," it was nothing short of a mir-
acle. Indeed, our meeting saved my life, as Jerry was to do, over
and over, in the 40-plus years of our friendship.

Yet on introduction, I had no idea who he was, though I certainly knew of his partners at Atlantic Records, Ahmet and Ne-
suhi Ertegun. I had been listening to the company's artists since
I was 12, thus I also knew its catalog—almost by heart.

That day in the studio in New York, Ahmet, wearing a Brooks
Brothers suit, leaned over the console with a man dressed in a casual blue jacket, as Vanilla Fudge's plaint "And you don't really love
me, you just keep me hangin' on" filled the air. "I like that record
a lot," I said, gladder than I could express to have something else

to think about. "It's got that heavy bass sound, but it's a cute lit-tle pop number." Noticing for the first time that I was in the room, the man in the blue jacket turned to me and then said to Ahmet, "Hey. He understands." That was Jerry. The next thing I knew, we were talking about Raymond Chandler and Dashiell Hammett, two of my literary heroes. He understood.

We got to know each other quickly and well. He seemed—though he would have scoffed at the notion—sent from God to be my guide through dark times; my mentor, my teacher, my rebbe.

In 1969, during a deranged Thanksgiving weekend in New York City, while I was on tour with the Rolling Stones—a tour that would end with the stabbing death of Meredith Hunter, at the hands of the Hell's Angels at The Altamont Festival, less than two weeks later—Jerry invited me to his house in East Hampton for their holiday dinner. His wife, Shirley, served an elegantly cooked goose. His mother and his children, Lisa, Paul and Anita, were there. Horribly sleep-deprived and underfed—and only slightly stoned—I feasted, and fell in love with his family. Magritte paint-ings floated on the walls. By dessert, I thought I was in heaven.

Hell followed, and continued, long after Altamont. Under contract to write a biography of the Stones, I worked with painful slowness back home in Memphis, and then got the idea that I could work better in Miami, where Jerry had a second house. On the verge of a break with Atlantic Records, he had moved there to set up Criteria Studios, thinking he could create a more leisurely existence; one that combined making records with play-ing golf. It was a disaster. The house band, the Dixie Flyers—mostly transplanted Memphians—was at one point reduced to digging up Sam the Sham's backyard by car headlights, trying to figure out where they had hidden their drugs. Jerry eventually threw up his hands, as if hearing Bob Dylan's "I'm goin' back to New York City, I do believe I have had enough" running through his head. I retreated back to Memphis.

In the summer of 1972, Jerry and I went to the Newport-New York Jazz Festival, where we heard Duke Ellington, Roland Kirk and other great players. It was a high point of our friendship. Then we joined the Stones, who were by this time signed with Atlantic, on tour, taking an ounce of cocaine along for the ride. Which was, considering the delay in writing my book, and my other problems, way too much. I fled.

1975 was better. Jerry introduced me to Etta James. Shortly thereafter, he broke with Atlantic for good, and began a career as an independent producer with the likes of Dire Straits, George Michael, Carlos Santana, Linda Ronstadt, and most famously, Dylan. As many have pointed out, when Dylan received his first Grammy for best male rock performance in 1979, he thanked God, then Jerry, in that order.

I, on the other hand, was in no mood for thanksgiving yet. In fact, I entered into a deeper period of freefall with the publication of "The True Adventures of the Rolling Stones" in 1984—a critical success and resounding popular failure—followed by "Rythm Oil: A Journey Through the Music of the American South" in 1991. Drugs were only part of my near-lethal lifestyle: I married and divorced three (or was it four?) times—the last, to a woman who tried to kill me. The marriage ended when I set her car on fire.

I was too ashamed to ever tell Jerry of her existence, even though we spoke on the phone at least every couple of weeks. He always had jokes to relay. I cannot remember a single one that is printable in this publication. What I can remember, are the conversations we began to have about new American films noirs. I hadn't had a TV in years, but bought one—and a VCR—when Jerry began to send me tapes of movies, including: Carl Franklin's "One False Move" and Quentin Tarantino's "Reservoir Dogs." Such gestures may seem small, but they're exactly the kind of thing I mean, when I say Jerry saved my life again and again.

In 1993, I began to climb out of this depressed and beastly— I use the word literally—mode of existence when, I joined the Roman Catholic Church. Jerry, who had split from Shirley and then wed a Greek woman—a relationship that also ended in divorce— was on his own path toward a happier and more stable existence. He married the novelist Jean Arnold. He continued doing a little producing: the B-52s, for example, of my home state of Georgia, to which I had relocated. My favorite phone call to Jerry was an annual one, made at an ungodly hour on Easter morning after my return from Mass: "Christ is risen!" I would shout gleefully into the phone. His favorite, and considering the circumstances, kindly rejoinder, was to turn on at full blast, Dusty Springfield's "Son of a Preacher Man," which he of course had produced and always seemed to have ready for my call.

The last time I spoke with Jerry, he seemed in bitingly good-humored remission from his final illness. I was in bed, nursing bruises from a recent tumble I'd taken—the indignities of aging!— and he asked me how I was. "Fine," I answered quickly, knowing the mortal seriousness of his own condition. "'Fine,'" he said, after discovering why I sounded a little the worse for wear. "You goyim are all alike."

Certain obituaries about Jerry have already made much, perhaps too much, of his failures as a family man during his most active years in the music industry, something over which he suffered extensive guilt. Jerry's daughter Anita, for example, had gone on the road with Doctor John, become addicted to heroin, and died of AIDS. What none of these written memorials has underscored, so to speak, is his profound generosity toward those he came to love. Like so many of us who have felt sharply our shortcomings as fathers and sons, he set about to create a family of friends, which he did primarily by telephone, as he advanced in years, and travel became difficult for him.

It was second . . . no, first . . . nature for him to love the people I loved. Indeed, Jerry was instrumental—again, so to speak— in the courtship of my ultimate wife, the poet Diann Blakely. Almost immediately upon hearing that we were corresponding—if only as fellow writers—with increasing intensity, he began to shower her with gifts. These included: immaculately typed weekly postcards featuring heroes like Furry Lewis; packets of articles written by, or about, him; adoringly autographed photographs of himself, alone or with friends; a lavishly inscribed copy of his life story; and boxed sets of Aretha Franklin, Ray Charles and other members of his pantheon. On learning that Diann was from Alabama, he confided to her that he considered his induction into her native state's Music Hall of Fame, one of the great honors of his life; and immediately sent her a videotape of the ceremonies. After months of such attentions, she was, predictably, smitten— with him, and, eventually, much to my great good fortune, with me.

"More Bass," said Jerry, when asked what he wanted written on his tombstone. No sound more closely approximates the rhythm of the human heart, especially in the Southern style he loved, with its one-TWO-three-FOUR backbeat.

"That Same Small Town in Each of Us."
Charles Taylor

"That same small town in each of us." That's how Don Henley described the vanishing American landscape in his 1989 song "The End of the Innocence." You could glimpse that town in the fantasy that closes Spike Lee's devastating movie "25th Hour." It's the small town as refuge to outcasts, fugitives, lovers, and vagabonds—in other words, the place where the sick, the tired, the poor really are welcomed, where Americans go to re-find America and to escape what America has become.

The video for Henley's song shows the images of American abundance we know from Norman Rockwell and from Life magazine in the '40s and '50s: big-finned cars; endless wheatfields; Fourth of July picnics where, for sheer size, the spread on the table competes with the flag fluttering from the porch. But photographed in black-and-white and often in slow motion, the pictures are already ghosts. The plenty of the land, the verve of the people, seem to drain away as we watch. The song has set us up for this desiccation, just as the shots of a brick wall papered with tattered campaign posters of a grinning Ronald Reagan, showing all the vitality of the undead, tells us which vampire has bled these images dry. The foreshadowing of this rot lies in the line that precedes "That same small town in each of us": "Somewhere back there in the dust."

And that's where the song implicates us. The line says we've discarded this notion of America. Not the false vision of small-town purity in Reagan's "shining city on a hill" speech, a boastful corruption of the sermon by John Wesley from which the phrase is taken. What we've left back there in the dust, through cynicism or disappointment or weariness, is the belief in America as shared enterprise, as a constant tension between hard reality and unrealized dream. The people and the towns in this video are under a spell. It's as if they are living among the replicas of America in a land where the very idea of America has become something childish we have to put aside in order to become adults.

Toward the end of the video, there's a shot that gathers up all the corruption that the images and the song have hinted at and reflects it back to us: A lovely young woman, stands outside a door on which, in script, is written the words "The Majestic." It could be a theater, a dance hall, or a cheap hotel. Her hair is done in an upsweep and she's got a modest stole atop her black sheath cocktail dress. The look on her face is ambiguous. She might be early for a date, or trying to pick up a customer for the evening, or for the hour. You can tell she doesn't expect a good time. She could be a few years past high school, or closer to thirty, but in either case what's left of her youth is falling away fast. For just a second, her eyes meet the camera and she comes alive with a slight smile that could be a come-on, or a shrug that acknowledges her situation, says, "You know how it is." It's a terribly seductive image, but looking at her, you don't know whether to feel encouraged or ashamed. Whatever is going on, you know, in your gut, that something has gone terribly, terribly awry. Pretty young women should not look this weary or this resigned.

Something has gone wrong in Michael Eastman's new book of photographs "Vanishing America" (Rizzoli, $39.95). Occasionally in these shots of main streets, beauty shops, gas stations, juke joints, drive-in retaurants, cheap-stay hotels and churches, you see a car or a pick-up truck. A neon "Open" sign is visible in the window of a St. Louis ice-cream joint. But there isn't a person visible in any of these photos. This is America as it might look post-neutron bomb. The buildings are still standing, but the people are gone.

Anyone who's taken a car trip anywhere in America in the last several decades has seen a downtown that looks like these pictures. What once were the type of modest, handsome department stores that catered to middle-class shoppers stand empty. Sometimes there are blocks of them. Maybe a few businesses have moved in—often antiques stores or travel agents. But they have the look of kids dressed up in their parents' Sunday best—the finery flops around them, always in danger of sliding off.

Mostly, the locations in "Vanishing America" don't even have that faded gentility. Eastman includes several shots of signs slowly peeling away from the brick walls they're painted on. But 618 Martin Luther King Drive in Savannah, a nondescript bar with garish cocktails painted on either side of the steel mesh door, looks like its dying in place as well. So does Kallison's Western Wear in San Antonio, Gordon's Toggery in Dubuque, Skippys and Floyds Barber Shop in Peoria, The Gospel Connection, a movie palace turned church in Saint Genevieve, Mississippi. These are all places in rehearsal for extinction, fading away like the forgotten Gold Medal flour sign on a wall in Guadalupe, California.

Eastman shoots from the same dead-ahead vantage point from which Edward Hopper composed many of his paintings. But Hopper's deserted Sunday morning sidewalks, late-night diner and drugstore windows were clearly in respite from the life that would surround them in the day and evening. Eastman's storefronts and abandoned buildings look so fragile you wonder if they'll vanish in the night, leaving you, the next morning, to wonder if they were ever there.

"Vanishing America" is a wake for what the country looked like before every place looked like every other place, when a drive through a new town or state meant risking a meal in a restaurant you didn't know instead of just looking for the next Olive Garden.

"My Blueberry Nights," the new movie from the Hong Kong director Wong Kar Wai (it came and went in a few weeks last in April and will hit DVD on July 1) works like Prince Charming's kiss on Sleeping Beauty. It's as if Wong believes he could breathe the color and life back into the kind of locations we see in the Henley video.

America has long served as a state of mind for foreign directors. What is Hitchcock's "North By Northwest" but a transplanted Britisher's comic fantasy of the vastness of America? The country is so big that Cary Grant (another Brit who found a home here) can run and run and run across it and still not get to the end. When, in the climax, he's dangling from Mt. Rushmore, it's a neat visual emblem of how small he feels against the bigness of the country. The immigrant grocery stores of the turn-of-the-century Lower East Side in Sergio Leone's "Once Upon a Time in America" are big enough for the Metropolitan Opera to move in (and the goings on are melodramatic enough to keep them occupied).

America is, for Wong, a coast-to-coast cornucopia of small enclaves: diners, bars, highways, downscale casinos, motels that offer the kind of populuxe decor that perks you up as much as the cup of coffee waiting at the restaurant across the parking lot. Sometimes the locations—a Memphis bar where the jukebox hasn't heard the news that Otis Redding is dead; a Manhattan diner in the midst of the evening dinner rush—are hopping. Other times, when the diner proprietor (Jude Law, charming in a way he's never been before) and his lovelorn late-night regular (Norah Jones, whose lips, seen in close-up, appear to be floating on the screen as the lips in Man Ray's painting "Lips (Heure de l'Observatoire)" float across the landscape of the canvas) are all alone past closing time, they seem the only lovers left alive. The elevated subway train might be hurtling overhead for no other reason than to shower flashes of light down on them.

Working for an American movie company with English-speaking stars who were pledged to other projects, Wong couldn't indulge in the months-long shoots that gave his last two films "In the Mood for Love" and "2046" (wonderful though they were) a kind of stately ponderousness. He's faster, looser here; his romantic wooziness is blithe instead of heavy-spirited.

There's something unsettling about the reviews that dismissed the film as Wong's fantasy of America. The movie is a romantic confection (if there were ever a movie that should be named after pie, it's this one) but it shows love for what the entrepreneurial America has left somewhere back there in the dust. Of course it's a foreigner's fantasy of America. The places Michael Eastman shoots in "Vanishing America" suggest that vibrant neighborhood bars and diners and motels and haberdashers could very easily become an American's fantasy of America.

Liner Notes for Reissue of *Let It Be*
Gina Arnold

Recently, a student at the university where I teach rhetoric and writing came up to me and-perhaps having heard from someone that I had once a vague interest in popular music-said, "I just heard a band I think you'd really like. Do you know the Replacements?" Do I know the Replacements? Are you kidding? I AM the Replacements, I wanted to reply-but of course I didn't, it would have sounded psycho. Did I know the Replacements? Jesus! Only the way you know all those little code words we now use to unlock our computers now: first pet, name of elementary school, favorite food. Did I listen to the Replacements? Not exactly: I glugged them down like Powerade after a particularly grueling marathon. Did I play them on my personal, pre-ipod, sound systems, in my car, in my dorm room, in my head? Sure: in the same spirit that a prisoner of war in a locked down cell sends out faint signals to the outside word . . . hoping they'll be heard, but feeling more certain they'll just become silent pings going off in an earless stratosphere. Did I go to see them when they came to town? When the Replacements came to town, the world stopped.

But that was the thing about the mats. You didn't just listen to them or like them or drop by a gig every now and again. You

simply were them. You wouldn't have said that about REM or
Sonic Youth or Husker Du or any of the other great bands of the
era, much as you loved them. You wouldn't have said it about
Springsteen, Madonna, or Prince. Unlike those acts, compelling
as they all were, was that once you fell into the Replacements vor-
tex, you had to take on their entire lifecycle, like that episode of
the *X Files* where hapless city workers are usurped by an amoeba
in the sewer or something.

And my question now is, why? What makes this music transcendent, when so much else from then is only worth the occasional spin on an oldies station, or has just faded into nostalgic
miasma? After all, few records make it past twenty years in the
crevices of our hearts without moldering into sentimental mush.
But the opening notes of "I Will Dare" from the Replacements acknowledged masterpiece *Let It Be* (1984) still has the power to set
my pulse racing in anticipation of the songs that follow. "16 Blue"
still seems like the truest assessment of adolescent angst yet
recorded-as is, I don't doubt, "Gary's Got A Boner" and "Tommy's
Got His Tonsils Out," in their own less poignant way. "Seen Your
Video" and "Answering Machine" still express something
primeval about the tyranny of technology over human emotion-
a subject so universal that it even allows for the fact that videos
are now disseminated by youtube and answering machines have
been replaced by texting. (The same can't be said for, say, Dorothy
Parker's famous story about waiting for the phone to ring, which
became outdated the minute that the answering machine came
into being.) As for "Unsatisfied . . . " well, suffice it to say that it
is the single most poignant rock song ever written, the really relevant mid-80s response to "I can't get no satisfaction" which lays
waste to that more famous paeon's self-obsession and entitle-

ment. The moment I heard "Unsatisfied," I found the underlying petulance of the Stones (and a number of other bands, not all of them English or from an earlier era) truly unbearable to listen to. Besides, when wrapped in that soaring anthem, Westerberg's words-his humility-felt so much more true. "Everything you dream of is right there in front of you but . . . liberty is a lie." The song slays me still, and it's not, I am sure, just, 'oh, I remember the day I was listening to this during some splendid moment of happiness,' either. I'm pretty damned sure that this is the LP-maybe the only LP-which will set you off even if you've never heard it before. It's a record that will make new memories for new listeners, not just make old memories come alive.

Music from the '80s is mostly unable to be appreciated without having been there. It's the soundtrack to an oldies dance, conjuring up visions of people with extremely silly haircuts. The Replacements music has avoided that fate, in part by just never becoming popular enough to be over familiar, but also because if you played a track like "Unsatisfied" in between many of today's hits, they'd fit right in. It's not that they were ahead of their time, either. They weren't. Like plenty of unique bands and artists they were out of time-on their own planet, unaware of all possible connections to back at planet earth. The planet was called Minneapolis, and lest the assessment of it as a place unconnected to earth sounds belittling or patronizing, recall that in the early 1980s-the time of high Reaganism-Minnesota was like the last liberal frontier. Cold, white, and pure of heart, it was the only state in America that didn't elect either Nixon or Reagan in the 1972 and 1984 elections (remember those 'don't blame me' bumper stickers?) It's where Laura Ingalls Wilder lived in "On the Banks of Plum Creek." It's the home of Prince. Those things may seem contradictory, but all of them speak to the location's deep seated isolation and its residential hardiness, not to mention a steadfast adherence to the core American value of independence, individuality, and the pursuit of happiness. In Minneapolis, in the early 80s, the herd mentality which the music industry bases its entire structure upon was strangely absent. There was a vacuum, and nature abhorred it. The void was filled by record stores like Oarfolkjokeopus, labels like Twin-Tone and bands like the Replacements.

Understanding Minneapolis may be the key to understanding the Replacements, and what makes them so great. After all, in 1984, the year that *Let It Be* (their third record) came out, popular music was still dominated by an overarching idea that only music from England mattered. This had of course been the case since the Beatles and the Rolling Stones came down the pike. Sure, the US had produced Dylan and the Beach Boys and Springsteen and the Ramones. We were also responsible for stuff like the Allman Brothers, the Eagles, and REO Speedwagon, all three of whom still very much dominated the airwaves at the time that the Replacements came of age. To most people who cared about music, even if you gave us Lou Reed, it pretty much seemed like every really great songwriter, auteur, and especially movement in rock came from England. America was the land of dreck. Hollywood, San Francisco, New York, and Chicago all had produced scenes, bands and genres which, in retrospect seem impossibly cheesy. Paradoxically, the mats obsession with cheesiness has produced something entirely lasting, something truly authentic.

It's true that in 1984, REM and a whole bunch of other indie bands from college towns had begun to change all that, at least amongst the college radio cognoscenti. But only the Replacements really rose above those bands obsession with rock history, and this is why. The Replacements were devotees of AM radio, and what they made of that music was authentic in a way that bands who attempted to mine (read: mimic) Woody Guthrie or Muddy Waters necessarily wasn't. The mats were more in touch with the kind of history expressed in songs like "Crocodile Rock" than "Rock Around the Clock"; they knew the chords to "Stepping Stone" but not to "Eight Miles High," and I doubt they had even heard of the Velvet Underground. Best of all, they were unashamed. By connecting to simple and unpretentious songs-whether it was the DiFranco Family's deplorable "heartbeat it's a love beat" or the Grass Roots "Temptation Eyes" (both of which they covered live and which are included on this CD)-they were able to tap a part of their listeners that had previously been denied to listeners like me. There is an ethics to memory, and certainly being forbidden to remember the pleasures of your childhood is no way to ensure that pleasure will be attainable in the future. The Replacements let us remember Kiss with fondness. They allowed us to be proud of our heritage.

Moreover, they had aura, in the most basic definition of the term, and that is why *Let It Be*, which represents the high point not of their songwriting or but of their own life as a band, is still exciting, relevant, and fun to listen to. You don't have to have 'been there,' the way you have to have been to appreciate so many other records of 1984. You can listen to the opening chords of the opening track "I Will Dare" today without having been born in 1984, and still get a short sharp jolt of adrenaline as you anticipate the rest of the song. Oh. My. God, you'll think. I love this! It's what we thought then, and it's what you will think now. You won't be able to help it. I guarantee it.

Today bands seem as if they were born with a preternatural knowledge of previous eras' music. MP3s and sampling have destroyed some of the prejudicial barriers we used to uphold so valiantly. No one cares what label an act is on; no one knows who their fans are out in cyberspace, and that's a good thing. At the same time, those barriers between genres did give the old music a lot of its context. Motown had the Civil Rights movement, the Dead had Summer of Love, and the Replacements had the less spectacular but (to them) just as desperate battle between the underground and the pop superstructure-one might almost say, the Reaganomic superstructure-which was bowing down the culture and still in some ways does today. It was a battle which the Replacements ultimately lost, but it is the fact that it is still audibly being waged on Let It Be which makes it so much more poignant than many another band. The pride of the warrior comes through on the record, no doubt, but it really came through live, at shows which are now celebrated as much for their shambolic nature and tenuous connection to professionalism as for their sheer power. The mats often sucked life, but in those days being embarrassing in public-daring to fail, if you will-was as radical as-well, as it still is, twenty three years later .

That part is unable to be captured-even on you tube-and you will have to take my word (and everyone else's) that they were both the best and worst band in the world, a band which forced you to come back and come back and come back again, in order to take part in the process of being a Replacement, or a Replacement fan. What I meant by saying that I *am* the Replacements is that I have lived the same deep experience that they did as a band-only without actually ever having picked up a guitar. Their history as a band had affected me as deeply as it did them: when they signed to a major in 1985, it was me who felt like I'd been stuffed into a stiff shirt and marched into a cubicle-scared, proud, excited and disgusted all at once. When their music was played on the radio or they made a rare appearance on SNL, it was if I'd just been proposed to, gotten married or promoted. When, in 1989, they broke up, I too went into shock. Figuratively speaking, I too lay around stunned on the couch and ate bon bons for a while-and then I moved on as well. But when I find myself in times of trouble, and no one's there to comfort me, there will be an answer, and that is *Let It Be.*

This Much I Know
Edwyn Collins

Interview with Michael Odell

I'm happy that my brain has retained some cherished memories. When you have a stroke you lose quite a lot. I can remember the tin bath that my mum used to bathe me in. I ca[TXB]n still see her washing me. I cherish that one.

I was doing a radio interview and I didn't feel well. I woke up in hospital and I was overwhelmed when I realised what had happened. It was eight weeks before I could bear to listen to music. [My wife] Grace brought me a CD compilation I'd made for the car. I listened to Johnnie Allan's "Promised Land" and I broke down. I was relieved . . . I could remember it.

As a boy I collected stamps. I had a Penny Black that was my pride and joy. I sold my collection at a Glasgow pawnshop and bought a semi-acoustic guitar. That changed my life.

I was a bit of a letdown to the Collins family. I was expected to be a lawyer, a doctor or an academic. My sister Petra became a judge. They found it hard to fathom my love of punk.

I didn't like macho punk like the Jam or the Clash. Orange Juice camped it up a bit. At our first shows, people would shout "Poofs! Poofs!" and I took that as a seal of approval.

I used to be an illustrator for the Glasgow Parks Department. I drew chaffinches and squirrels and moorhens for park leaflets. I'd take kids from Glasgow's East End around the nature trail. They'd say, "Are youse a punk sir?" and I'd say, 'Yes, I'm a nature punk."

I realised quite early that fashion could piss people off. I remember my granny seeing the Beatles on TV. She said, "Those boys need a haircut." It was offensive to her.

We were on Top of the Pops with 'Rip It Up'. The dance troupe was called Ruby Flipper and they did this routine where they mimed ripping up a piece of paper. Afterwards our manager was crying. He said, "The big moments are never as good as you think they're going to be."

That speck on the horizon? It could be your ship coming in. I didn't have a major record deal when "A Girl Like You" was a hit. I lived in a grotty one-bedroom flat. Because I owned the copyright that one song bought me my house.

After my stroke I'd lost all the songs I ever wrote. I could recognise them as mine when I heard them on a stereo but I couldn't remember any lyrics. That took ages, writing them out and relearning all the phrasing.

I had neurosurgery done after the second haemorrhage. They took a section of my skull away and put it in the fridge for six weeks with my name on it. When the swelling went down from the surgery they put it back. But I got MRSA so they had to take it out again. I got a titanium plate instead.

Dysphasia means I struggle to find words. I'm fighting to get language back. I used to have all the beautiful words but they've gone now.

I'm lucky to have survived. I used to share a flat with Grant McLennan of the Go-Betweens. Two years ago he had a heart attack and died. Why didn't he get a second chance and I did?

I'm happy again. I'm contented with life. Now Grace gets more grumpy.

Little things mean a lot now. I bought my uncle Sandy's house in Helmsdale, in Sutherland. It's been in the family since 1802. We don't have a TV there. We sit by the fire and I watch Grace sit like an old lady staring into the flames, sipping her sherry.

Six-Word Reviews of 763 SXSW Mp3s
Paul Ford

featuring K through S

I recently downloaded the SXSW 2008 torrent file, which contains nearly 48 continuous hours of music from 763 acts appearing this week at the South by Southwest festival in Austin, Texas (these bands elected to give away MP3s; they represent less than half of the total number of acts). I found myself wondering how to locate the songs worth hearing, and imagined that others were having the same problem.

Thus, the 763 reviews you'll find below. For brevity, I kept each to exactly six words.

I realize that I have potentially hurt the feelings of nearly 3,000 musicians, for which I apologize. By no means should you ever stop writing and recording music.

EXPLAINING THE ARBITRARY RATING SYSTEM
••••• Worthy of five circles.
•••• Worthy of four circles.
••• Worthy of three circles.
•• Worthy of two circles.
• Kill me.

SIX-WORD REVIEWS OF 763 SXSW MP3S

Paul Ford

NO.	TIME	ARTIST	GENRE	LOCATION	SONG	REVIEW	RATING
337	4:28	Kaddisfly	Rock	OR	Empire	Least favored intro:"This is the..."	•
338	2:57	KaiserCartel	Rock	NY	"Season Song (live)"	You know what audiences love? Whistling!	•
339	3:54	Kaki King	Experimental	NY	"Pull Me Out Alive"	Nicely glued together, with no surprises.	••••
340	2:53	Kalashnikov	Rock	PORTUGAL	"george bush bin laden one love one family"	A profound, heartfelt endorsement for war.	•••••
341	3:27	Kam	R&B	TX	"Surrender"	I'm never high enough for this.	•
342	3:36	Kanko	Latin Rock	TX	"patada"	Gritty, sincere, punk-pop in Spanish.	••
343	3:20	Karina Nistal	Electronic	TX	"Viviendo"	Dry-sounding basic electronica; Latina rapper.	•••••
344	3:43	Kate Tucker and the Sons of Sweden	Pop	WA	"Faster than Cars Drive"	Starbucks loves them; I understand why.	••••

IMPRESSIVE PROMO COPY

"Hello motherfucker!!! Kalashnikov's a legendary Portuguese band, pioneer of wartime rock 'n roll: music made for the battlefield. Born in Lisbon in 1996 they soon started to play in wartime scenarios to motivate men to slaughter. From Bosnia to Colombia, from Liberia to Tchetchenia, from Afghanistan to Tchetchenia, from Liberia to Iraq wherever there is war, you will hear the Kalashnikov sound."

#	Time	Artist	Genre	Location	Title	Comment	Rating
345	3:37	Kate Voegele	Rock	OH	"Only Fooling Myself"	13 ways looking at Sheryl Crow.	::
346	4:05	Kate Walsh	Singer-Songwriter	UK	"Your Song"	Just ask, honey, he'll do you.	•
347	4:15	KB Da Kidnappa	Hip Hop/Rap	TX	"Ghetto Raised Feat. Bushwick Bill"	Worth it for Bushwick Bill's appearance.	⋮
348	3:56	KbN	Electronic	TAIWAN	"0.7"	Taiwanese knob-twiddling perfect for soundtracks.	::
349	1:59	Ketchup Mania	Rock	JAPAN	"Namida Vacuum Sound"	Utterly predictable girly Japanese punk.	:
350	4:55	Kevin Shields	Experimental	CA	"Muscle Hair"	Like a dog fucking a blender.	•
351	4:08	Khan	DJ	GERMANY	"Strip Down"	KHAAAAAAN!!! The switch at 2:50—huh?	:
352	4:36	Kid Congo and the Pink Monkey Birds	Rock	DC	"The History of French Cuisine"	Opens goofy and gets even goofier.	⁙
353	5:11	Kid Dakota	Rock	MN	"10,000 lakes"	Haunting, yes—but haunting like Caspar.	::
354	4:04	Kidz In The Hall Hip	Hop/Rap	IL	"DRIVIN DOWN THE BLOCK"	Biz Markie descendants without the humor.	⋮
355	2:56	Killa Kela Hip	Hop/Rap	UK	"All Killa No Filla"	Reportedly his stuff is all beatboxing.	⋮

SIX-WORD REVIEWS OF 763 SXSW MP3S *(continued)*

Paul Ford

NO.	TIME	ARTIST	GENRE	LOCATION	SONG	REVIEW	RATING
356	3:34	Kim Fontaine	Acoustic	SK	"Coincidentally"	One hell of a rock voice.	•••
357	2:55	King of Prussia	Pop	GA	"Misadventures of the Campaign Kids"	Ideal for a boarding-school movie.	••
358	2:44	Kitty, Daisy & Lewis	Country	UK	"Mean Son of a Gun"	Amazing UK recreation of old country.	•••••
359	3:26	Knife World	Rock	MN	"SunBeam"	Oh great, they're yowling like cats.	•
360	5:30	Knuckle Yummy	Blues	TX	"Nice and Low"	Hang around for about three minutes.	•••
361	4:00	The Knux	Hip Hop/Rap	LA	"Cappuccino"	These brothers like coffee and vaginas.	•••
362	3:12	KOOPA	Rock	UK	"The Crash"	They seem to believe in this.	•
363	2:23	The Krayolas	Rock	TX	"Little Fox (Spanish)"	This right here goes waaaay back.	•••••

SOMETHING ELSE I GLEANED

Many people don't write songs for an audience. They write songs for Gray's Anatomy, for Zach Braff, and for Apple advertisements (Volkswagen if they're not ambitious). If I was in a band I would write a slow song with an 808, reverb, and a female vocalist, and call that song "Zach Braff's Eyes Reflected in My Nano." I would make sure it got to the right people. By which I mean Zach Braff, or one of the leechlike marketing creatures that feed from the skin of Steve Jobs under his mock turtleneck.

#	Length	Artist	Genre	Location	Song	Comment	Rating
364	3:24	Kreamy 'Lectric Santa	Punk	CA	"Workaholics Paradise (lost and found)"	Wow. That sure did redeem itself.	⁝⁝
365	4:02	Krief	Rock	QC	"What We Wanted"	Krief is the queef of grief.	•
366	4:07	Kush & Jah Bloodfiyah Angels	Reggae	CA	"Thick Smoke"	I honestly don't know from dub.	⦂
367	2:56	Ladyfinger	Rock	NE	"Too Cool For School"	Looks like Ladyfingers broke up. Sad.	•
368	3:15	Ladyfingers	Rock	NY	"Cure for the Common Cold"	Oh—wait, guess I was wrong.	•
369	3:32	Land of Talk	Rock	QC	"Speak To Me Bones"	Only 443 songs to go now.	⦂
370	2:30	Langhorne Slim	Rock	PA	"Restless"	Chorus works well; bass is nice.	⁝⁝
371	2:54	Lars Vaular	Hip Hop/Rap	NORWAY	"Eg e fra Bergen"	Answers the question: can Norwegians rap?	⦂
372	4:08	Laura Barrett	Singer-Songwriter	ON	"Robot Ponies"	Finally, a definitive robot pony song.	⁝⁝
373	3:42	The Law	Rock	UK	"Still Got Friday To Go"	America needs to establish rock tariffs.	⦂
374	3:43	Le Baron	Rock	MEXICO	"Inmovil (Wrong ID)"	There's a likeable melodic feel here.	⦂

SIX-WORD REVIEWS OF 763 SXSW MP3S *(continued)*

Paul Ford

NO.	TIME	ARTIST	GENRE	LOCATION	SONG	REVIEW	RATING
375	2:49	Le Concorde	Pop	IL	"International Flight"	Dinky, but appealing Matthew-Sweet harmonies.	••
376	3:17	Le Loup	Rock	DC	"we are gods! we are wolves!"	Neither is accurate. They are nerds.	•••••
377	8:49	Leslie Keffer	Experimental	TN	"Nascent Part I"	A solid punishing wall of noise.	•••••
378	4:34	Lexie Mountain Boys	Experimental	MD	"Punch Balls"	Merciless gloop; the title is accurate.	•
379	2:34	Lick Lick	Rock	TX	"Rolling Pin"	Pass a law to stop organ.	•
380	3:36	The Lifters	Rock	TX	"SHE'S A DEVIL"	But which devil? Choronzon? Memnoch? Azazel?	•
381	4:01	Li'l Cap'n Travis	Rock	TX	"Cherry Chapstick"	Summery tune content to drift along.	•••••
382	2:52	Limbeck Alt	Country	CA	"Let's Get Crazy"	Where is the crazy you promised?	••
383	3:10	Lindsay Jane	Singer-Songwriter	MB	"I Can't Rescue You"	Let's go cry in my dorm.	••

#	Time	Artist	Genre	Location	Track	Note	Rating
384	8:55	The Linus Pauling Quartet	Rock	TX	"Alien Abduction"	Fills that "nine-minute jam" hole.	••
385	3:12	Lions	Rock	TX	"No Generation"	Not affiliated with Lions Clubs International.	•
386	2:35	Lipstick Terror Latin	Rock	MEXICO	"The Epitome of A Catalyst Intervention"	The kids call this "neo-harcore."	•
387	4:04	Lissie	Singer-Songwriter	CA	"On My Chest remix"	Toured with Kravitz. That explain it?	••
388	7:14	little claw	Experimental	OR	"feeding you your new home"	Sucking is okay but enough already.	••
389	4:49	Little Freddie King	Blues	LA	"Walkin With Freddie"	Old blues guy from New Orleans.	•••••
390	3:01	Little Jackie	Pop	NY	"The World Should Revolve Around Me"	Imani Coppola ("Cowgirl Legend") alter ego.	••••
391	2:19	Little Teeth	Rock	CA	"japanese candy"	Vocals are very appealingly messed up.	••••
392	4:07	The LK	Pop	SWEDEN	"Stop Being Perfect"	Swedish electropop that goes "boop, boop."	••
393	0:26	Lobi Traore & Joep Pelt	World	THE NETHERLANDS	"I Yougoba"	Appealing 26-second blues from Mali.	•••
394	2:41	The Lonely H	Rock	WA	"Hair"	Seattle? They're still starting bands there?	•

SIX-WORD REVIEWS OF 763 SXSW MP3S *(continued)*

Paul Ford

NO.	TIME	ARTIST	GENRE	LOCATION	SONG	REVIEW	RATING
395	4:21	Longwave	Rock	NY	"No Direction"	Boldly preserving Flock of Seagulls's legacy.	••••
396	3:28	Look See Proof	Pop	UK	"Casualty"	Catchy in that Hard-Fi way.	•••
397	3:33	Lord T and Eloís	Hip Hop/Rap	TN	"Coup D'etat"	Aristocrunk. Because they love dem hose.	•••••
398	4:13	Lorrie Matheson	Singer-Songwriter	AB	"Gone"	Archetypal opening-band singer-songwriter performance.	••
399	5:40	Los #3 Dinners	Rock	TX	"Can't Stop...Gotta Rock!"	So badly infected with rock disease.	•••
400	3:57	Los Dynamite	Rock	MEXICO	"Ready Ready"	Debut album cleverly called "Greatest Hits."	•
401	4:18	Low Line Caller	Pop	TX	"Over-the-Counter Kids"	Happy to be in the background.	•••••
402	3:55	Lower Life Form	Hip Hop/Rap	TX	"Same Ol' Song"	Live-jazz-band-backed-hip-hop.	••••

FRATERNAL BANDS

The Breakup Society • Great Lakes Myth Society • World/Inferno Friendship Society • Beat Union

#	Duration	Artist	Genre	State	Song	Description	Rating
403	4:19	Loxsly	Rock	TX	"Lamprey Eels"	A warm indie bath with bubbles.	⁙
404	2:47	LUCA	Rock	AZ	"Damned"	They live on the second floor.	⁚
405	4:43	Lucero	Rock	TN	"The Mountain"	Appropriate organ use; thrashed-throat vocals.	⁙⁙
406	3:29	Lymbyc Systym	Pop	TX	"Fall Bicycle"	Laptop tropes—sudden cuts, linear dynamics.	⁙
407	3:12	Lyrics Born	Hip Hop/Rap	CA	"Hott 2 Deff"	Perfect for selling cars or Zunes.	⁙
408	4:51	LZ Love	Blues	TX	"Creepin'"	Blues-rock that's a little cheesy.	⁚
409	4:34	Mac Arnold & Plate Full O' Blues	Blues	SC	"Ghetto Blue"	A guy recalls the Chicago ghetto.	⁙
410	1:38	Madeline	Pop	GA	"I Do What I'm Told"	Plenty of court and spark here.	·
411	2:03	Magic Arm	Singer-Songwriter	UK	"Move Out"	Sparrows playing claves while they chirp.	⁚
412	2:54	Magic Bullets	Pop	CA	"Red Room"	He sings like he has hemorrhoids.	·
413	4:14	Magic Christian	Rock	CA	"Turn Up The Heat"	Bay Area Feelies-era British rock.	⁚

SIX-WORD REVIEWS OF 763 SXSW MP3S *(continued)*

Paul Ford

NO.	TIME	ARTIST	GENRE	LOCATION	SONG	REVIEW	RATING
414	2:32	Magic Wands	Rock	TN	"Black Magic"	I don't feel like clapping along.	•
415	3:37	Magnet School	Rock	TX	"Crush"	Because magnets have special education needs.	•
416	3:44	Magnolia Summer	Rock	MO	"The Slip That Leads Into The Fall (Live on KDHX)"	Singer will start crying any minute.	•
417	10:08	Mala Suerte	Metal	TX	"Non Serviam"	Sabbath played at one-fourth-speed.	•
418	2:38	Mannequin Men	Rock	IL	"Boys (They Don't Mind)"	Lots of good stuff in here.	•••
419	4:27	Marcia Ball	Blues	TX	"Louella"	A classy honky-tonk piano lady.	•••

I NOTICED

I wanted to like more of the rap here, but I became very tired. Everything was either about acquiring material goods (which includes women), or, alternately, about how all other rap is about acquiring material goods.

On hearing my nth predictable song about how hip-hop is predictable, it struck me that I was witnessing individuals engaged in a formalist exercise where the form itself is the only appropriate lyrical subject; thus rap is, in some ways, the blogging of music. (This is happening to "indie rock" in the Strokes/Killers/Libertines mold, as well.)

The best of it all is Akala, a grime artist from Britain, particularly when he delivers the line in his song "Electro Livin" (not included here, but from the same album) "We are sad for things we cannot have/But we are not sad for Baghdad." It reads as political naivete but he performs it with redeeming authority.

#	Time	Artist	Genre	State	Song	Comment	Rating
420	5:12	Mark Pickerel & His Praying Hands	Rock	WA	"Forest Fire"	Ex-Screaming Trees drummer's alt-country.	•••
421	3:14	Martha Wainwright	Singer-Songwriter	QC	"Bloody Mother Fuckin Asshole"	Great, commercial-proof lonely woman lament.	•••••
422	3:38	The Matches	Rock	CA	"Wake The Sun"	Not as good as their website.	•
423	5:01	Matt Barber	Singer-Songwriter	ON	"Easily Bruised (demo)"	Canadian feelings: fragile as robin's eggs.	•
424	3:18	Matt Caldwell	Country	TX	"Lonely Road"	The gears of Nashville are turning.	••
425	2:44	Matt Keating	Singer-Songwriter	NY	"St. Cloud"	Nice early 1990s singer-songwriter songcraft.	•••
426	3:46	Maya Azucena	R&B	NY	"Junkyard Jewel"	Great voice but the material's undifferentiated.	••
427	3:44	The Meatmen	Punk	MI	"Rock & Roll Juggernaut"	What a fantastic band this was.	•••••
428	3:50	Megaphone	Hip Hop/Rap	MA	"Danger Danger"	Spare production grows on you eventually.	•••
429	2:57	Meiko	Singer-Songwriter	GA	"How Lucky We Are"	Too much syrup on the pancakes.	•
430	4:16	Melissa Young	R&B	GA	"Just A Girl"	Tempo exactly one-third too slow.	•

SIX-WORD REVIEWS OF 763 SXSW MP3S *(continued)*

Paul Ford

NO.	TIME	ARTIST	GENRE	LOCATION	SONG	REVIEW	RATING
431	3:34	Midtown Dickens	Rock	NC	"The Job Song"	Barista-rock. They call it "adoracore."	•••
432	4:07	The Mighty Underdogs	Hip Hop/Rap	CA	"Gun Fight"	It sounds like an Eminem cover.	•••
433	4:31	Million Year Dance	Rock	TX	"Met With The Soul (Live)"	But the singer renamed himself "Tyagaraja."	•••
434	3:34	Minipop	Pop	CA	"Like I Do"	Picks up a little at 1:07.	••
435	4:13	Misha	Electronic	NY	"Summersend"	The vocals are very weirdly carbonated.	•••
436	3:05	The Mission District	Rock	QC	"Youth Games"	A Fountains of Wayne B-side.	•
437	3:48	Mission to the Sea	Acoustic	TX	"Sugar And The Queen Master 1 MP3"	Casual crooning combined with thumb piano.	•••••
438	4:20	Mitra	Metal	TX	"Crucifixed"	HAIL THE HOOF OF THE DEMOGORGON!	•
439	3:28	Mittens on Strings	Rock	IL	"Big Brother (Demo)"	This song could date my sister.	•••••

440	4:01	Miz Metro	Singer-Songwriter	NY	"Grand Solution"	No Doubt fans are growing up.	•
441	2:59	Mockinpott	Punk	MEXICO	"Japon 4"	Now it's Sunday, and I'm tired.	•
442	2:27	Model/Actress	Rock	CA	"The Nodder (Featuring David Yow)"	The terrible anguish of Max Headroom.	⋮
443	3:58	Moke	Rock	THE NETHERLANDS	"Here comes the summer"	Drums. Guitar. More guitar. Vocals. Guitar.	•
444	4:31	mom	Electronic	TX	"Skipping Stones"	Instrumental Iceland-lite stomp with glitches.	•
445	3:38	Mona De Bo	Rock	LATVIA	"Zarins"	Latvian take on badly recorded blues.	•
446	3:53	Monahans	Rock	TX	"I Run To You"	After the intro I expected more.	⋮
447	4:25	Monareta	Alt.	COLOMBIA	"MATANZA FUNK"	Extraordinary potential that refuses to arrive.	⋮
448	3:18	Mondo Topless	Rock	PA	"Take it Slow"	But do we need another Cramps?	•
449	3:26	Money Mark	Singer-Songwriter	CA	"Pick Up The Pieces"	Beasties collaborator out on his own.	⋮
450	4:45	The Most Serene Republic	Alt.	ON	"Present Of Future End"	Canada is now one giant band.	⋮

SIX-WORD REVIEWS OF 763 SXSW MP3S *(continued)*

Paul Ford

NO.	TIME	ARTIST	GENRE	LOCATION	SONG	REVIEW	RATING
451	4:11	Mostly Bears	Rock	AZ	"Melancholysim"	Prog rock composed with monster trucks.	••••
452	3:24	The Mother Truckers	Country	TX	"No Mercy"	Twangy rock that cheerily hops along.	•••
453	3:28	Mr. Lewis & The Funeral 5	Rock	TX	"My Girl, Suicide"	They accurately define themselves as "macabaret."	•••
454	3:51	Mr. Mike	Hip Hop/Rap	TX	"No More War"	Gunshot samples. Emcee's voice is deep.	•••
455	2:21	Muck and the Mires	Rock	MA	"Doreen"	Garage doesn't get much better, sadly.	•••
456	5:14	The Mullens	Rock	TX	"Esmerelda"	Esmerelda has made him very happy.	•
457	2:34	The Muslims	Rock	CA	"EXTINCTION"	Why is the bass so pleasing?	•••
458	4:07	My Dad is Dead	Rock	NC	"My Safe Place"	Cool this guy is still around.	•••
459	2:40	Mystery Palace	lectronic	MN	"Stepchild"	Bent circuits, buried vocals, works well.	•••

#	Time	Artist	Genre	Location	Song	Comment	Rating
460	2:53	Naked On The Vague	Punk	AUSTRALIA	"All Aboard"	"All aboard, the ship is sinking."	•
461	4:24	Naked Raygun	Punk	IL	"Treason"	This here is a Naked Raygun song.	••••
462	3:52	Nakia & His Southern Cousins	Rock	TX	"Playing The Cards"	Well-crafted "you suck" Appalachian rock.	•••
463	2:32	Nana Grizol	Pop	GA	"Voices Echo Down The Halls"	Athens, GA, ensemble...with yowling vocals.	••
464	3:38	Nancy	Rock	BRAZIL	"Doe Sangue"	Nothing like the classic comic strip.	•
465	5:05	Navruz World	World	UZBEKISTAN	"Mustakhzod"	About time Uzbekistan represented in here.	••••
466	2:02	Necropolis	Punk	OH	"Van v Art"	"Like a trip to the dentist.	•
467	2:45	Neimo	Rock	FRANCE	"Johnny 5"	Last 45 seconds are well-produced.	••
468	4:25	Neptune	Rock	MA	"Grey Shallows"	Sounds more like Uranus! LOL JK.	••
469	3:10	New Bloods	Punk	OR	"Oh, Deadly Nightshade"	All over the place and cheerful.	••••
470	3:17	Nicole Atkins	Singer-Songwriter	NJ	"Maybe Tonight"	Perfect for a 70s variety show.	•••

SIX-WORD REVIEWS OF 763 SXSW MP3S *(continued)*

Paul Ford

NO.	TIME	ARTIST	GENRE	LOCATION	SONG	REVIEW	RATING
471	2:08	Night Of Pleasure	Punk	OH	"Caesar's Palace"	Things must fucking suck in Ohio.	•
472	4:25	Nik Freitas	Rock	CA	"Sun Down"	All that's missing is Mr. Garfunkel.	•••
473	2:59	Nina	Rock	MEXICO	"Daisy Duke"	Van Halen, but in another language.	•
474	3:33	No Kids	Pop	BC	"For Halloween"	I'm out of synonyms for perky.	••
475	3:23	Noah and the Whale	Singer–Songwriter	UK	"2 Bodies 1 Heart"	Unfortunately it's not about Siamese twins?	•
476	3:16	Norton	Pop	PORTUGAL	"(Your) Balcony"	The Postal Service wouldn't deliver locally?	•
477	1:56	Nosaprise	Hip Hop/Rap	TX	"Standing Here"	Noble attempt by a YOUNG emcee.	••
478	3:59	Nouveau Riche	Rock	PA	"Sick"	All that packaging means no flavor.	•
479	3:30	Nouvellas	Rock	NY	"Satisfied"	Crunchier guitar and this'd be great.	••••

#	Length	Artist	Genre	Location	Title	Comment	Rating
460	2:53	Naked On The Vague	Punk	AUSTRALIA	"All Aboard"	"All aboard, the ship is sinking."	•
461	4:24	Naked Raygun	Punk	IL	"Treason"	This here is a Naked Raygun song.	••••
462	3:52	Nakia & His Southern Cousins	Rock	TX	"Playing The Cards"	Well-crafted "you suck" Appalachian rock.	•••
463	2:32	Nana Grizol	Pop	GA	"Voices Echo Down The Halls"	Athens, GA, ensemble...with yowling vocals.	••
464	3:38	Nancy	Rock	BRAZIL	"Doe Sangue"	Nothing like the classic comic strip.	•
465	5:05	Navruz World	World	UZBEKISTAN	"Mustakhzod"	About time Uzbekistan represented in here.	••••
466	2:02	Necropolis	Punk	OH	"Van v Art"	"Like a trip to the dentist.	•
467	2:45	Neimo	Rock	FRANCE	"Johnny 5"	Last 45 seconds are well-produced.	••
468	4:25	Neptune	Rock	MA	"Grey Shallows"	Sounds more like Uranus! LOL JK.	••
469	3:10	New Bloods	Punk	OR	"Oh, Deadly Nightshade"	All over the place and cheerful.	••••
470	3:17	Nicole Atkins	Singer-Songwriter	NJ	"Maybe Tonight"	Perfect for a 70s variety show.	•••

SIX-WORD REVIEWS OF 763 SXSW MP3S *(continued)*

Paul Ford

NO.	TIME	ARTIST	GENRE	LOCATION	SONG	REVIEW	RATING
471	2:08	Night Of Pleasure	Punk	OH	"Caesar's Palace"	Things must fucking suck in Ohio.	•
472	4:25	Nik Freitas	Rock	CA	"Sun Down"	All that's missing is Mr. Garfunkel.	•••
473	2:59	Nina	Rock	MEXICO	"Daisy Duke"	Van Halen, but in another language.	•
474	3:33	No Kids	Pop	BC	"For Halloween"	I'm out of synonyms for perky.	••
475	3:23	Noah and the Whale	Singer-Songwriter	UK	"2 Bodies 1 Heart"	Unfortunately it's not about Siamese twins?	•
476	3:16	Norton	Pop	PORTUGAL	"(Your) Balcony"	The Postal Service wouldn't deliver locally?	•
477	1:56	Nosaprise	Hip Hop/Rap	TX	"Standing Here"	Noble attempt by a YOUNg emcee.	••
478	3:59	Nouveau Riche	Rock	PA	"Sick"	All that packaging means no flavor.	•
479	3:30	Nouvellas	Rock	NY	"Satisfied"	Crunchier guitar and this'd be great.	•••

#	Time	Artist	Genre	State	Song	Note	
480	1:55	The Nymphets	Punk	QC	"Wednesday Morning"	At least their website is cool.	•
481	5:45	The Oaks	Alt.	FL	"2. Masood"	Introspective, wanders, apparently inspired by Afghanistan.	⋮
482	2:10	The Octopus Project	Rock	TX	"Truck"	Everybody! There's a party in Marioland!	⋮
483	3:43	O'Death	Rock	NY	"Down To Rest"	Banjos are everywhere. Poi Dog Ponderous.	•
484	4:49	Oh Juliet	Rock	LA	"Hunting The Canyon"	Another meal at Hard Rock cafe.	⋮
485	2:23	Oh No! Oh My!	Rock	TX	"Walk In the Park"	Tastes like Frosted Flakes with Splenda.	⋮
486	3:47	Oh Susanna	Singer-Songwriter	ON	"Greyhound Bus"	"Kiss my ass. Eat my dust!"	•
487	4:48	Ola Podrida	Alt.	NY	"Cindy"	I'm in a prison of music.	⋮
488	3:34	The Old Ceremony	Rock	NC	"Stubborn Man"	How are things with you, reader?	•
489	4:28	Olga	Americana	LA	"Your Love Don't Work Like Mine"	I am overwhelmed by press releases.	•
490	3:44	Oliver Future	Rock	CA	"Signing Off"	The cats are fighting right now.	⋮

SIX-WORD REVIEWS OF 763 SXSW MP3S (continued)

Paul Ford

NO.	TIME	ARTIST	GENRE	LOCATION	SONG	REVIEW	RATING
491	5:11	The Optimysticals	Experimental	NC	"Pitch Control"	Best part: 1:30 of bird sounds.	•
492	4:06	Orion Rigel Dommisse	Singer-Songwriter	PA	"Fake Yer Death"	It's so depressing, so very depressing.	•
493	3:27	Ouija Radio	Rock	MN	"RED EYE FLY"	Red eye removal renders this obsolete.	•
494	2:15	The Pack A.D.	Blues	BC	"All Damn Day Long"	Vocalists seem very prone to blues.	•
495	3:44	Paddy Casey	Singer-Songwriter	IRELAND	"Fear"	The ideal anthem for college freshwomen.	•••
496	2:20	Paint It Black	Punk	PA	"Past Tense, Future Perfect"	An angry Minor Threat from Philly.	••
497	4:21	Papa Chuk	Hip Hop/Rap	TX	"Way 2 Reel"	Whoa, you can hear the Robitussin.	••
498	3:16	Papercranes	Rock	FL	"Treasure"	Remember Aleka's Attic? Here's the singer.	••

SOUND BANDS
Sounds Under Radio • Nameless Sound Collection • The Soundtrack of Our Lives • Axel K Soundsystem • Atlas Sound • The Sound of Urchin • The Hush Sound

#	Time	Artist	Genre	Location	Title	Description	Rating
499	3:38	The Parisians	Rock	FRANCE	"Why Choose One Side"	French—which makes this "Freedom Rock."	••
500	5:26	Parkas	Rock	ON	"Filthy Rich Kids"	Their tour video looks pretty fascinating.	••
501	3:11	The Parlor Mob	Rock	NJ	"Carnival of Crows"	My fist's too tired to pump.	•
502	4:02	Parts & Labor	Rock	NY	"Fractured Skies"	The Island of Misfit Toys Orchestra.	•••••
503	3:09	Pataphysics	Rock	TX	"Jesus Grow a Handle Bar Mustache For Me"	Wants to be weird; just quirky.	•
504	2:56	Patricia Vonne Alt	Country	TX	"Missing Women"	Former model seeks Paula Cole mantle.	••
505	3:18	Pattern is Movement	Rock	PA	"Right Away"	The travels of organ-grinder monks.	•••
506	4:42	Patty Hurst Shifter	Rock	NC	"Life Is Mostly Waiting"	Opened for the Drive-By Truckers.	•
507	3:03	Paul Collins Beat	Rock	NY	"Don't Wait Up For Me"	Ex-Nerves drummer can write songs.	••••
508	3:42	Paul Kelly	Singer-Songwriter	AUSTRALIA	"God Told Me To"	Australian sings about divinely inspired murderer.	••
509	9:33	Paul Metzger	Experimental	MN	"Bright Red Stone"	Nearly ten minutes of experimental banjo?	••

SIX-WORD REVIEWS OF 763 SXSW MP3S *(continued)*

Paul Ford

NO.	TIME	ARTIST	GENRE	LOCATION	SONG	REVIEW	RATING
510	4:22	Paul Thorn	Rock	MS	"A Long Way From Tupelo"	Good song about a car breakdown.	•••
511	5:45	The Paul White Quintet	Jazz	TX	"Inabanaga"	My old jazz teacher'd love this.	••
512	8:30	Pedro Menendez Ensemble	Jazz	ARGENTINA	"Kolndombe"	Introspective, engaging minor–key Argentinian jazz.	•••••
513	2:10	Peel	Rock	TX	"Oxford"	I'd have gotten this from Oink.	•••••
514	0:49	Peelander-Z	Punk	NY	"Me Gusta Lucha Libre"	50 seconds of Spanish hardcore. Thanks!	••••
515	2:23	Peggy Sue & The Pirates	Singer-Songwriter	UK	"Television"	Punk-skiffle about television addiction. Huh?	••
516	4:49	The People's Revolutionary Choir	Rock	UK	"Do You Feel Like I Do?"	Pink Floyd Strawberry Fields all over.	•••
517	3:39	The Perpetrators	Blues	MB	"Baltimore"	Makes me feel like a victim.	••
518	3:15	Pete Robbins & Centric	Jazz	NY	"Candy To The Crowd"	Something satisfying about the middle here.	•••

#	Time	Artist	Country		Song	Comment	
519	5:23	Phantom Limb Alt	Country	UK	"Dont Say A Word"	Band from Bristol yearns for swamps.	⋮
520	3:20	Phil and the Osophers	Rock	NY	"International Introvert"	Best drumming since maybe the Shaggs.	⁝
521	4:15	Phonograph Alt	Country	NY	"Normal Illinois"	Don't have that damn Brooklyn sound.	⁝
522	3:14	Phosphorescent	Rock	NY	"A Picture Of Our Torn Up Praise"	Sounds like a crumbling palace, brothers.	⋮
523	3:35	Pidgeon	Rock	CA	"California is for Fuckers"	I agree entirely with the title.	⋮
524	2:54	Pierre Aderne	World	BRAZIL	"Mina do condominio"	Another soft-voiced Brazilian. Nice percussion.	⁝
525	3:15	Pig Out	Electronic/Dance/DJ	NEW ZEALAND	"Disco Bag (Radio Edit)"	You can have too much cowbell.	⋮
526	3:42	The Pigeon Detectives	Rock	UK	"I'm Not Sorry"	They're big in Britain, of course.	⋮
527	3:39	Pigeon John	Hip Hop/Rap	CA	"Weight of the World"	Indie emcee has a bouncy flow.	⁞
528	3:58	The Pillows	Rock	JAPAN	"Ladybird girl"	They have a cute bear logo.	⋮
529	2:15	Pink Nasty	Pop	KS	"Away Message"	Grows on me like dark moss.	⋮

SIX-WORD REVIEWS OF 763 SXSW MP3S *(continued)*

Paul Ford

NO.	TIME	ARTIST	GENRE	LOCATION	SONG	REVIEW	RATING
530	4:10	Pink Reason	Punk	OH	"Holding On"	Works like a broken Slurpee machine.	⋯
531	4:03	Pinstripe	Rock	UK	"Closest Thing to Heaven"	Yet more packaged adolescent British rock.	·
532	4:58	Pissed Jeans	Rock	PA	"People Person"	Claims adjuster's secret noise side-project.	⋯
533	3:17	Pistolera Latin	Rock	NY	"Mentirosos"	Whoa—"as featured on 'Democracy Now'".	⋯
534	7:09	Plants and Animals	Alt.	QC	"Faerie Dance"	I'm tired of long swooning songs.	⋮
535	4:42	The Playing Favorites	Pop	CA	"Indigenous"	Left off the Reality Bites soundtrack.	⋯
536	5:19	Pleasant Grove	Rock	TX	"heart contortionists"	Vocals and guitars don't line up.	·
537	3:47	porterdavis	Blues	TX	"Come Closer"	Earnest goes to Austin: the band.	⋮
538	3:04	Portugal The Man	Experimental	AK	"Sugar Cinnamon"	They're from Alaska and genuinely weird.	⋯

539	3:30	Postman	Hip Hop/Rap	THE NETHERLANDS	"Downhill"	Gangsta rap from Amztadam, da Nethalands.	⋯
540	2:51	Power Pill Fist	Electronic	PA	"Vile"	I miss Pigface so much sometimes.	•
541	4:20	PPT	Hip Hop/Rap	TX	"Dallas"	Click to add title, beautiful lady.	•
542	2:52	The Presidents of The United States of America	Rock	WA	"Lump"	I have always hated this song.	•
543	2:20	Pretty and Nice	Rock	MA	"Grab Your Nets"	From the Charles, not the Thames.	•
544	3:13	Project Jenny, Project Jan	Electronic	NY	"320"	Initially—totally retarded. Then just retarded.	⁙
545	5:59	Pterodactyl	Rock	NY	"Esses"	Vocal shenanigans and layered loopty glunk.	⋮
546	5:28	Pyeng Threadgill	Jazz	NY	"It's Late"	Purely confident of her vocal chops.	⋮
547	2:41	The Quebe Sisters Band	Country	TX	"So Long To The Red River Valley"	Ideal for A Prairie Home Companion.	⋮
548	3:59	Question	Hip Hop/Rap	TX	"Ridin So Slow"	Love song from man to car.	⋮
549	6:10	Ra Ra Riot	Rock	NY	"Dying Is Fine"	Another Arcade Fire indie-rock brigade.	⋮

SIX-WORD REVIEWS OF 763 SXSW MP3S (continued)

Paul Ford

NO.	TIME	ARTIST	GENRE	LOCATION	SONG	REVIEW	RATING
550	4:32	Radio Moscow	Blues	IA	"A Mistreating Queen"	Blues bands kind of blur together.	••
551	3:47	RadioRadio	Rock	OK	"Marathon"	List many influences, but neglect Duran.	•••
552	4:40	Rana Santacruz Latin	Rock	NY	"Cajita De Barro"	Pink-moon–pleasant Mexican folk rock.	••••
553	3:32	The Rascals	Rock	UK	"Lying Under The Second Seal"	They opened for the Arctic Monkeys.	•
554	4:01	Ravens & Chimes	Rock	NY	"This is Where We Are"	Vocals too urgent by a half.	•••
555	4:37	Ray Bonneville	Blues	TX	"I Am the Big Easy"	New Orleans has inspired many songs.	••

AWESOMENESS VS. CUTENESS

It's easy to quantify male vocalists: they are either douchebags, or, if they play guitar as well, double dog douchebags. But I also found myself dividing the female vocalists — and there are surprisingly many, which is a promising development — into two camps.

First, there are twee little things who will sing about forest sprites and make you collages when you have the flu. Then there are the tougher ones who wear glitter and make eye contact. The question I asked myself, to divide between the awesome and cute, was: would this woman (1) help you to get an abortion? Or (2) just write a song about it? The ones who would drive you to the clinic without judging you, in my opinion, make better vocalists. I could be wrong but I think Martha Wainright, and the women from Creature, would go with you.

#	Artist	Genre	Location	Title	Comment	Rating
556	The Reaction	Punk	CA	"Right Now"	Please return to the basement immediately.	•
557	Rebekah Higgs	Singer-Songwriter	NS	"Parables"	Neat arrangement, catchy—just too much.	••••
558	Receptors	Electronic/Dance/DJ	VA	"Receptors–"	Can they win the boss level?	•
559	Reckless Kelly	Country	TX	"Nobody's Girl"	Southern rock, Skynyrd descendants, excellent chops.	••••
560	Record Hop	Rock	TX	"Maths"	Mind keeps wandering. No there there.	••
561	The Red Romance	Pop	NY	"Don't Cry"	A grand museum of lyrical cliches.	•
562	The Redwalls	Rock	IL	"Summer Romance"	This song should be about elves.	•••
563	Renee Sebastian	R & B	NY	"Please Break My Heart"	I wish Sade made more albums.	•••
564	Restlesslist	Electronic	UK	"Butlin Breaks"	Soundtrack for a Sergio Leone videogame.	••
565	Reykjavik!	Rock	ICELAND	"Flybus!"	They sound very little like Bjork.	•••
566	Richard Julian	Singer-Songwriter	NY	"If you Stay"	Part Elliot Smith, part Randy Newman.	••••

SIX-WORD REVIEWS OF 763 SXSW MP3S *(continued)*

Paul Ford

NO.	TIME	ARTIST	GENRE	LOCATION	SONG	REVIEW	RATING
567	7:03	Richard Oppenheim Septet	Jazz	TX	"Peacocks Walked"	Jazz ragas reinterpreting Ferlinghetti's "Coney Island..."	::::
568	3:49	Right on Dynamite	Rock	NY	"Won't Let It Go"	They're having more fun than me.	·
569	3:28	The Right Ons	Rock	SPAIN	"Do Your Thing, Babe"	"Too Hot to Handle" from Spain.	·
570	2:13	Ringo Deathstarr	Rock	TX	"Some Kind of Sad (demo)"	They call this "nugaze." Oh man.	::::
571	3:19	Riz MC	Electronic	UK	"People Like People"	This man is very, very brave.	·
572	4:11	Rob G	Hip Hop/Rap	TX	"Reppin My Block"	Stand up for your block, Rob!	·
573	2:48	Robin & Linda Williams	Bluegrass	VA	"Things I've Learned"	Yep, I'm in the jailhouse now.	::::
574	3:46	Rock & Roll	Rock	FRANCE	"Made It To New York"	"Rock & Roll." What. They're named.	·
575	3:08	The Rodeo Alt	Country	FRANCE	"Winterlands"	Paris indie country with lush strings.	:::::

#	Length	Artist	Genre	Location	Title	Notes	Rating
576	3:59	Romance Fantasy	Rock	NV	"Blackheart"	Classic live rock sound, great vox.	⋯
577	2:16	Ruby Jane	Bluegrass	MS	"Track 02"	This fiddler was born in 1994.	⋅⋅
578	2:56	The Russian Futurists	Electronic	ON	"Let's Get Ready To Crumble"	Percussion feels like it belongs elsewhere.	⋅
579	4:11	Ryno & Slim Gutta	Hip Hop/Rap	TX	"Can You Handle It"	Pretty goofy song about ass tapping.	⋅
580	3:43	Sabaton	Metal	SWEDEN	"Primo Victproa"	Swedish metal, so thus utterly hilarious.	⋯
581	3:21	The Sadies Alt	Country	ON	"Anna Leigh"	Alt. country. It grows like kudzu.	⋯
582	4:12	Sahara Smith	Singer-Songwriter	TX	"Circuitry"	This singer was born in 1988.	⋅⋅
583	4:42	Saint Bernadette	Rock	CT	"Love Is A Stranger V2-1"	Enjoyed the vocals quite a bit.	⋯
584	3:36	Salvador Santana Band	World	CA	"Imacallya"	Melting-pot dance from all over.	⋯
585	3:21	Samara Lubelski	Pop	NY	"Taste The Candy"	This song is risky for diabetics.	⋅
586	4:00	San Saba County Alt	Country	TX	"5th Time Around"	Very parsimonious with those chord changes.	⋅⋅

SIX-WORD REVIEWS OF 763 SXSW MP3S (*continued*)

Paul Ford

NO.	TIME	ARTIST	GENRE	LOCATION	SONG	REVIEW	RATING
587	1:40	Satin Dolls	Rock	MEXICO	"Vuelve"	Even more Mexican new wave pop?	::
588	3:42	Say Hi	Rock	WA	"Northwestern Girls"	Small arcades, exploding in the sky.	::
589	4:56	Scale The Summit	Rock	TX	"Shaping The Clouds"	Adrian Belew rolls in his grave.	.
590	2:37	Scary Mansion	Singer-Songwriter	NY	"Sorry We Took All Yr Money"	Like a big bucket of regret.	::::
591	3:59	Scavone	Hip Hop/Rap	NY	"Arrestin' Me"	He hates when police confiscate weed.	::
592	4:42	Scissors for Lefty	Rock	CA	"Nickels and Dimes"	Typewriter sound effects inspire my rage.	.
593	3:45	Scott H. Biram	Rock	TX	"Been Down Too Long"	Ridiculous Hellbilly that turns very smart.	::::
594	2:29	Screamin' Cyn Cyn & The Pons	Punk	WI	"Set The Table"	They strive to annoy, succeed entirely.	::::

MARTHA WAINRIGHT
She wrote a song called "Bloody Mother Fuckin Asshole" and while I enjoy it on its own merits, I enjoy it more knowing that it will be difficult to use this song to sell Volkswagens.

#	Length	Artist	Genre	Location	Title	Comment	Rating
595	3:08	Search/Rescue	Rock	WA	"Fireflies"	The blessed vocalist never starts screaming.	•••••
596	2:35	The Second Grace	Singer-Songwriter	ITALY	"Antananarive"	Over-precious folksy drum-loop love.	•
597	4:40	Secret Shine	Rock	UK	"Lost Memory"	Reverb is the sixth band member.	••
598	3:08	The Service Industry	Pop	TX	"Job Of Quality"	Song about people who won't pay.	••••
599	3:41	Services	Electronic	NY	"Presenter"	Such a promising, promising beginning here.	•••
600	5:53	Sexto Sol feat. Vernon 'Spot' Barnett	Rock	TX	"Samba Pesada"	Sort of an indie-rock Santana.	•••
601	4:06	Shame Club	Rock	MO	"How Far"	An awful case of severe guitardation.	•
602	3:03	Shawn Sahm and the Tex-Mex Experience	Rock	TX	"Why Don't Ya"	Like a moldy carnival corn-dog.	•
603	2:27	Shellshag	Punk	NY	"Shut Up"	It's cruel to slow punk down.	•
604	3:19	Shina Rae	Electronic/Dance / DJ	TX	"Touch"	Fast fourier transforms are not enough.	•
605	6:14	Shir Khan	Electronic	GERMANY	"Office Boy (Shir Khan Rmx)"	Berlin's very own Fetter Junge Dunn.	•••

SIX-WORD REVIEWS OF 763 SXSW MP3S *(continued)*

Paul Ford

NO.	TIME	ARTIST	GENRE	LOCATION	SONG	REVIEW	RATING
606	5:03	Sholi	Experimental	CA	"November Through June"	An oiled machine that rolls along.	::
607	3:04	Shootin' Pains	Experimental	TX	"Half Pint"	"Goat Fuckin Psycho-Ameracommunist Folk Rock"	:::
608	3:17	Shooting Spires	Rock	NY	"Right"	Brooklyn is a heaven for beards.	::
609	2:56	The Show Is the Rainbow	Experimental	NE	"Swatting Flies"	Lunacy; holds up to multiple listens.	::::
610	5:32	Shri	World	UK	"Mela"	Distorted Indian weirdness; 1990s-feeling samples.	:::
611	4:30	Sia	Pop	UK	"Electric Bird"	As seen on (perfect for) TV.	::
612	3:43	Sian Alice Group	Rock	UK	"Motionless"	Dynamics barely vary until maybe 2:00.	.
613	2:19	Silje Nes	Singer-Songwriter	NORWAY	"Ames Room"	Twinkle dinkle little software editing suite.	.

BLACK BANDS

Black Diamond Heavies • Black Earth • Black Helicopter • Black Joe Lewis & the Honey Bears • Black Mike and Chemistry • Black Moth Super Rainbow • Black Mountain • Black Pus • Black Tide • Black Tie Dynasty • Black Top Demon • Black Tusk • Blackholicus • Blacklist

#	Time	Band	Genre	State	Song	Comment	Rating
614	3:56	The Silos	Rock	NY	"Behind Me Now"	Guitar solos, so many guitar solos.	•
615	2:28	Simply Saucer	Punk	ON	"She's A Dog"	1978: Canadians mix Stooges and Floyd.	⋮
616	2:34	The Singles	Rock	MI	"Summer"	They ride around on a tritecycle.	•
617	4:09	Sissy Wish	Pop	NORWAY	"Ya Ya"	Norway has an answer to Robyn.	⋮
618	3:53	Sleep	Hip Hop/Rap	OR	"Say Goodbye"	Oregon rapper has much to say.	:
619	2:58	Sleepercar Alt	Country	TX	"Wasting My Time"	I appreciate the focus on craft.	⋮
620	5:32	The Sleepover Disaster	Alt.	CA	"Cathedral"	These folks are the shoegazer's shoegazers.	:
621	3:32	Slykat	Hip Hop/Rap	TX	"Wild as What"	Slykat has a penis for you.	•
622	4:02	Snowbyrd	Rock	TX	"St. Mary's Nights"	Makes me lean to the right.	:
623	3:22	Snowglobe	Rock	TN	"Waves Rolling"	Some Flaming Lips, some Beach Boys.	⋮
624	3:17	Socratic	Rock	NJ	"Just Turn"	More like Nietzschean eternal recurrence, amirite?	•

SIX-WORD REVIEWS OF 763 SXSW MP3S *(continued)*

Paul Ford

NO.	TIME	ARTIST	GENRE	LOCATION	SONG	REVIEW	RATING
625	3:19	Soiled Mattress & The Springs	Experimental	NY	"Jackpot"	Like what you've done to jazz.	••••
626	2:35	Solid Gold	Rock	MN	"Bible Thumper"	It was gloomy in the disco.	•••
627	3:56	Something Fierce	Punk	TX	"Teenage Ruins"	Lots of guitar and chorus, etc.	•
628	3:31	Something With Numbers	Rock	AUSTRALIA	"Apple Of The Eye"	I'm seriously hitting my limit now.	•
629	3:12	Son Lux	Rock	NY	"Break"	Keeps trying stuff to great effect.	•••••
630	3:24	"Son Of Dave"	Blues	UK	Devil Take My Soul	Sampled blues crashing into themselves recursively.	•••

ON NODDING

Even with the most peculiar songs ("Break" by Son Lux, say) there is some innate sense of structure that caused me to nod my head, perhaps just a little, as I listened, and with certain songs ("Rich Girls," by The Virgins) it was hard not to jump up out of the chair. Working through the nearly 48 hours of music in this collection I found myself craving that stimulus like a rat trained on cocaine. And when a song that produced that feeling was over I felt a sense of despair — once again I would be thrown into an hour or more of music that would generate no interior response. I wanted to go back and listen to the good songs over and over but that was a pleasure denied for later.

#	Time	Band	Genre	State	Song	Notes	Rating
631	2:40	Songs for Moms	Punk	CA	"1906"	Cheerful punk ladies, moving right along.	::
632	3:35	Sonya Kitchell	Singer-Songwriter	MA	"Let Me Go"	Song slowing down? Just add organ.	::
633	3:19	The Sound of Urchin	Rock	NY	"Shake The Magic Eight Ball"	The guitar goes higher—then higher.	:
634	4:42	SouthBound	Hip Hop/Rap	TX	"Another World"	Twin brother rappers: Sandman and Lowkey.	.
635	4:05	Spear of the Nation	Hip Hop/Rap	CA	"Clap!"	Falls apart at 1:06. Odd synth.	::
636	2:45	Spiral Beach	Pop	ON	"Made Of Stone"	Why do bands call themselves "kaleidoscopic"?	::
637	3:15	Spottiswoode & His Enemies	Rock	NY	"That's What I Like"	Spottiswoode likes all kinds of ladies.	::::
638	2:35	Spring Tigers	Pop	GA	"Economix"	They do not transmit their enthusiasm.	.
639	2:58	Squincy Jones	DJ	TX	"Grindom"	Here's a word I hate: "turntablism."	::
640	3:34	Stalkers	Punk	NY	"Let's Get It Together"	More fucking rock from fucking Brooklyn.	::
641	2:45	Standing Nudes	Rock	NY	"When I Arrive"	Guitar sounds like a Jews harp.	::

SIX-WORD REVIEWS OF 763 SXSW MP3S *(continued)*

Paul Ford

NO.	TIME	ARTIST	GENRE	LOCATION	SONG	REVIEW	RATING
642	2:28	Stanton Meadowdale	Rock	TX	"Came Feel The Same"	Not bad, but not exactly thrilling.	∷
643	3:03	Steel Train	Rock	NJ	"I Feel Weird"	Post-September 11 Arcade anguish pop.	∷∷
644	3:25	Stephanie Dosen	Singer-Songwriter	TN	"Vinalhaven Harbor"	A song like curling Victorian wallpaper.	∷∶
645	5:04	Stephen Kellogg & The Sixers	Rock	MA	"4th Of July"	Hard-luck story ladened with twang.	∷∶
646	4:01	The Steps	Rock	TX	"Belle"	Another band that likes Stooges, Faces.	•
647	3:18	Steven Wray Lobdell	Blues	OR	"All Mystics are Numbered"	Described as "Carnatic Rock"; think Can.	∷
648	4:57	The Story Of	Pop	TX	"After Just a While"	Early genesis vibe——consequently tooоо looooong.	∷∶
649	2:11	The Strange Boys	Rock	TX	"Nothing"	Like a garage-sale mix tape.	∷∷∶
650	3:07	The Strugglers Alt	Country	NC	"Morningside Heights"	The R.E.M. in him is powerful.	∷∷∶

#	Time	Artist	Genre	Location	Song	Note	
651	3:09	Studemont Project	Hip Hop/Rap	TX	"Left on Teetshorn"	Imagine if Joe Meek produced rap.	⋮
652	3:59	The Subjects	Rock	NY	"The Hounds of War"	I can't figure out this song.	⋮
653	3:24	The Submarines	Pop	CA	"You, Me and the Bourgeoisie"	Mr. Blue Sky with some clouds.	⋮
654	3:49	Susan Cowsill	Singer-Songwriter	LA	"I Know You Know"	Her evil middle name is "Wishes."	⋮
655	4:03	Sussie 4	Electronic	MEXICO	"Remote Control"	Starts out Burial, becomes early Ministry.	⋮
656	2:36	Swampmeat Alt	Country	UK	"Sister Mary"	Perfect music for humping an alligator.	⋮
657	4:53	Sxip Shirey	Experimental	NY	"My Own Dirge"	Beatbox breakbeats with harmonica for melody.	⋮
658	3:24	Sybris	Rock	IL	"Oh Man!"	Sybris—good name for a spaceship.	⋮
659	0:57	SYME	Rock	NORWAY	"No Spark, No Heart"	I refuse to take this seriously.	·

American Dreamers

Pete Seeger, William F. Buckley, Jr., and public history

William Hogeland

The eighty-nine-year-old musician and activist Pete Seeger, who is largely responsible for connecting folk music to the American left, joined the Communist Party in his twenties. Seeger has been candid, if at times self-serving, about his early support for Stalin, but the recent PBS "American Masters" documentary on Seeger is so disingenuous, when it comes to his and the Party's activities, that it gives an impression of 1930s communism as a program for nothing more than peace, equality, and down-home music. The young Seeger comes across as a cheerleader not for Stalin's Russia, but only for the sorts of social reforms any progressive might advance today.

Equally misleading in its portrayal of an unsettling early position has been press coverage of the career of William F. Buckley, Jr., who died in February. Buckley made his name by providing intellectual leadership to those who did much, in the 1940s and '50s, to punish Seeger, other former Party members, fellow-traveling liberals, and certain bystanders. Appreciations of Buckley's contribution to conservatism blur not his embrace of McCarthyism—some of his admirers remain fairly proud of that—but his support for white Southern efforts to prevent black citizens from voting.

Buckley and Seeger share, along with fake-sounding accents and preppie backgrounds, a problem that inspires forgetfulness, falsification, and denial in their supporters. Fired by opposed and equally fervent political passions, both men once took actions that their cultural progeny find untenable.

But these two men—their careers strangely linked in the hunt for communists, the struggle for equal rights, and the emerging "culture wars" of the postwar era—are worthy of consideration without air-brushed reminiscence. Their names alone may evoke, for those who lived through it, the anxiety and turmoil that marked American cultural and political life during the Cold War. Mutual hostility between Seeger types and Buckley types devolved on fears of imminent, world-ending invasions; plans for preventing evil from ever recurring on a mass scale; and stark disagreements over what is legitimately American. When the Soviet Union was annexing its neighbors, filling gulags, and making swaggering predictions of world dominance, and the United States was toppling elected leaders in favor of authoritarians and hounding domestic dissenters, all amid the stockpiling of nuclear weapons, the division among Americans could feel, to those on both sides, like the last battle for humanity's soul. What Seeger and Buckley's youthful actions meant in their time, deliberately obscured by today's lionizers, continues to mean something crucial now.

Pete Seeger inherited communism from his father, a decisive event in the history of American vernacular music that has no place in the "American Masters" documentary. Charles Seeger, an arch-WASP bohemian born in 1886, taught musicology at Harvard and Berkeley. During his time in California, he formed an alliance with the Industrial Workers of the World, or Wobblies, an especially lively labor-organizing effort, which planned global working-class takeover through one, vast, general strike. Soon, like many others, he was connecting his radicalism to the more tangible success of the Marxist revolution in Russia. He joined the Communist Party and started a radical group called, in the exciting new lingo, the Composers Collective, which encouraged pieces by left composers like Aaron Copland and Marc Blitzstein and published a magazine called *Musical Vanguard*.

American leftists like Charles Seeger did not interpret the expression "international communism" to mean "Soviet dictatorship and expansion." They saw the young Soviet state as the first in a series of concerted revolutions through which workers would take ownership of the means of production and humankind would advance toward a future without the awful poverty that was destroying the lives of so many laborers, blacks, and poor people in America and elsewhere. American communists wanted to build a homegrown movement that would bring together factory laborers, dirt farmers, mineworkers, fruit pickers, and sharecroppers. They hoped to shatter elite privilege, end race discrimination, and distribute fairly the wealth of the United States and the world.

Charles Seeger also wanted to connect Marx-Leninism to his own discipline. The Wobblies were famous for singing on picket lines, but Seeger was trained in the high classical tradition and called for modernist concert pieces—in a Soviet official-culture vein—celebrating the workers' collective virtue. He wrote articles on music theory for *The Daily Worker*, the paper through which the Party updated communists and sympathizers on Communist International, or Comintern, policy. By the late 1920s, and especially in partnership with his second wife, the composer and musicologist Ruth Crawford Seeger, he began seeing in traditional American music an art form already owned by the masses. Folk music, Seeger thought, existed outside the corruption and alienation of bourgeois culture; it needed only integration with Party ideology to become a means of worker empowerment. By the late 1930s—when his son Pete was becoming a politically passionate Harvard student, and the Great Depression was deepening American leftists' desire for change—the elder Seeger was discovering much of value in old ballads, work songs, blues, and traditional dance music, still thriving mainly in the south.

The American folk revival was not, however, the exclusive province of the left. In Europe, folk collecting and the promotion of traditional arts had long been emblematic of nationalist patriotism. In the U.S., an early promoter of folk music was the inveterate reactionary Henry Ford, who saw the music as unsullied by the immigrant and urban cultures he despised and the salaciousness he associated with jazz and vaudeville. American folk music and dance—which Ford believed, fancifully, to be essentially Anglo-Saxon—would be the musical component of the hygienic culture he wanted to promote among workers in factory towns—places where, for the supposed good of the workers and company efficiency, everything from labor to education to recreation was to be controlled and supported by the owner. To that end, Ford spent a great deal of money encouraging the first fiddlers' contests, community sings, and square dances from which an important strain of the American folk revival emerged.

Fired by opposed and equally fervent political passions, both men once took actions that their cultural progeny find untenable.

For leftists, too, folk music was free of corruption, but that meant free of Ford-style mass production, which was, in their view, oppressive in a way that Soviet mass production was not. Old songs and tunes—which some of today's folkies still imagine being handed down from time immemorial in backcountry communities—seemed to embody the inherently cooperative spirit of the people, a natural sense of union. To them, radio pop seemed aesthetically vapid and socially regressive.

Yet most of the music heard in homes in the southern backcountry actually had roots in commercial pop—the medicine and minstrel shows, Tin Pan Alley, Victorian parlor sheet music, ragtime and jazz, and, by the 1930s, downmarket "race" and "hillbilly" seventy-eight-rpm recordings and clear-channel broadcasts of "barn dance" radio shows. The genius of people living in neglected parts of country often lay in adapting pop music to cheap, sometimes handmade instruments and whooping it up. One can only wonder what the bottleneck-guitar-picking sharecropper or the fiddling miner, steeped in a fecund mixture of tradition and commercialism old and new, might make of the arrival of a left-wing academic, complete with notepad and giant tape recorder, eager to preserve southern music's supposed purity.

That strange relationship between homemade music and left politics was further complicated in the 1930s by changes in both the U.S. government and the Comintern. In 1935 Stalin announced "The Popular Front"—a worldwide coalition of communism with liberal politics that the Party had formerly excoriated. A goal was to restrain the rise of Nazi-allied fascism at any cost. *The Daily Worker* started encouraging communists to collaborate with liberals. Many leftists—some of whom were disaffected by Stalin's nationalism and dictatorship in Russia—found a place in the New Deal government. Among them were Charles Seeger and Alan Lomax, a left-wing folklorist who gave Pete Seeger a job at the Library of Congress.

But the coalition of communists and liberals did not last. In 1939 Stalin made a nonaggression pact with Hitler and repealed the Popular Front, leading many to flee the Party in disgust at the alliance with fascism. In this new ideological environment, Pete Seeger's career blossomed. Having traveled in the South and become adept at five-string banjo, the younger Seeger put his music to the service of the new Party line, which now opposed New Deal liberalism and U.S. war against Germany. In 1940 and '41, with the approval and guidance of Party elders (against whose dictates Seeger sometimes chafed), the group that would become known as the Almanac Singers, most notably featuring Seeger on banjo and Woody Guthrie on guitar, yoked "people's songs" to the Party agenda in a way that neither the philosophy of Charles Seeger, nor the musicians of the Southern backcountry, ever could. As stars of Party-inspired organizing, playing for strikers and at New York rent parties, the Almanac Singers invented the music that leftists had failed to find among the actual folk.

The Almanacs gave the old songs new lyrics, celebrating unions and mocking FDR as a warmonger. (In his book *Where Have All the Flowers Gone*, Seeger is refreshingly self-deprecating about his "peace" verses' doggerel and thin satire.) They began the vogue for wearing work clothes—overalls, jeans, denim shirts—to denote membership in the people. According to Joe Klein, in his definitive biography of Woody Guthrie, they adopted fake Southern accents and concocted biographies of hard travel. Most importantly for American music, The Almanacs invested their sound, which was far smoother than the real thing, with a mood of authenticity that the real folk never aspired to. Heads thrown back and mouths wide open, strumming and "singing out" with rousing, clean-cut intensity, they conjured a communist American future that was a fantasy of the rural American past.

Seeger was playing a rent party in June of 1941 when somebody rushed in with the news: Germany had invaded Russia. The pact was broken. Another reversal of the Party line immediately ensued. To the relief and bemusement of the Almanacs, they were now required to sing against Hitler. But they were also required to ally with Churchill, whom the Party had been calling an irredeemable imperialist. In his book, Seeger recalls his hilariously rushed conversation with Guthrie about how to adjust to supporting Churchill. "'Why, Churchill said "All support to the gallant Soviet allied!"'"Is this the same guy who said twenty years ago, "We must strangle the Bloshevik infant in its cradle!"?"Yep. Churchill's changed. We got to!'" Seeger, Guthrie, and the Almanacs started writing and singing pro-war songs full of glib jingoism that may have surpassed, for sheer dumbness, their anti-war ditties: "Round and round Hitler's grave / Round and round I go."

For six months, the group rallied the U.S. to enter the war, per the Party line. Then, with the bombing of Pearl Harbor in December and the declaration of war, they began singing rah-rah songs for victory. Soon Seeger was in the Army and Guthrie was a merchant mariner and the pre-war phase of Seeger's career, and of the American folk revival, came to an end.

The major theme of the documentary is the lifelong connection between Seeger's music and his social activism. Yet it erases that connection's formative moment—formative not only for Seeger, but also for leftist politics and American music. Even a passing reference to Charles Seeger's radicalism would seem pertinent to Pete Seeger's early development as both artist and activist. Truly disastrous, though, are the few moments that purport to deal with Pete Seeger's communism. We see footage of Hitler, and then see Seeger, in a recent interview, recalling collegiate arguments over what to do about Nazism. Some argued for pacifism, Seeger says, but "communists said the whole world should quarantine the aggressor. And I thought they were right." Snippets of Seeger's interviews then get stitched into a hasty and vacuous summary of his Party activities. Over a still of an "International of Youth" pamphlet, which gives way to a shot of Harvard's gates, Seeger's voiceover runs: "I ended up joining the Young Communist League, and let my marks slip, and I lost my scholarship to Harvard. Few years later,"—now over a still of young Seeger playing for a dance, with a group singing "Solidarity Forever" in the background—"just before World War Two, I think I—" cutting back to Seeger being interviewed "—actually joined and became a card-carrying member." Over footage of communist picketers, he says: "I was against race discrimination, and Communists were against race discrimination. I was in favor of unions, and Communists were in favor of unions."

That's pretty much all the film has to say about the role of communism and global politics in Seeger's early music and career. The Almanac Singers are introduced over stills of handbills for their performances (one reads "leading American Balladeers in a program of songs for peace"), followed by a still of the group itself, with Seeger saying in choppy voiceover: "The goal of the Almanacs—if anybody asks us—'we want to build a singing labor movement.' But we'd barely got started on that job before

World War Two broke out." Then, over a still of people reading about the Pearl Harbor attack in newspapers, and a faint, crackling voiceover saying "Remember Pearl Harbor," Seeger says, "All the idea of strikes and everything [a cut or a mumble], 'after the war is won, then we can think about that.'"

In the edit, there is no mention of the Party's decisive role, which had Seeger singing against the war, then had him singing in favor of it, well before Pearl Harbor. Lost with all salient fact is any feeling for the high political emotion of the period. Nor is there any mention of Stalin or the pact, although Seeger himself has not been afraid to discuss these issues before. When he says, for example, that the communists wanted to quarantine Hitler, he is probably reviving an argument he made in his book: the great powers were actually hoping Hitler would knock out communist Russia; when ambassador Litvinov asked, in the late 1930s, for a plan to bottle Hitler up, the liberal democracies turned their backs. While some might take a more critical view of Stalin's hope for quarantine, in the book Seeger is making a point with a basis in fact. An authorized biography by David King Dunaway (who appears as a talking head in the film) presents the young Seeger as unhappy about the pact but taking a "wait-and-see attitude." As recently as last year, in a widely published letter to the conservative Ronald Radosh, Seeger discussed his delusions about Stalin.

In the film Seeger's comments become meaningless. His declaration that strikes would have to wait until after the war only makes sense in a context that the film cannot give, as doing so would reveal Seeger's tailoring his music to Communist Party instructions. When FDR asked U.S. labor unions for a wartime no-strike pledge, the non-communist part of organized labor gave it.

Significant for Seeger's career is that the Comintern sent word to the radical end of the labor movement to support the no-strike pledge too. Seeger might have had something interesting to say about ambiguities in Party labor policy. Dunaway's biography suggests that he found the Party's support for the no-strike pledge frustrating: strikers were a key Almanacs audience.

Like Charles and Pete Seeger, Buckley looked to the Soviet Union as the fulfillment of an idea—one that he called satanic.

What Seeger has said before about the Almanacs' anti-war stance, the knee-jerk relationship to Party prescriptions, and his own support of Stalin are all absent. Cleansing the story of anything possibly upsetting or even nuanced, the filmmakers must be hoping to certify Seeger, despite former Soviet attachments, as an unimpeachably great American cultural figure of the kind often celebrated on PBS "American Masters." Gained at the cost of falsehood, certification not only does no good, it weakens our grasp on the truth. There probably will not be another well-funded, closely researched, carefully edited, widely broadcast documentary on Pete Seeger, complete with interviews. This one has failed each of the astonishing things it purports to celebrate: the folk revival, American activists' passions, the past century's idealisms, and the long, strange career of Pete Seeger. The film degrades our understanding of the man, his ideas, and his era.

William F. Buckley, Jr., who died this year at eighty-two, enjoyed a busy and influential career as the most famous galvanizer of American conservative thought. Buckley made *The National Review*—the magazine he founded, edited, and published—a kind of think tank for postwar conservative ideology. In its pages, he and his ideological compatriots championed strictly limited government, assertive law enforcement, rollback of the welfare state, free markets, and ceaseless war on communism at home and abroad. As a result, friends and foes alike have credited him lately with ending liberalism's intellectual hegemony, which prevailed in the U.S. political establishment from FDR's accession in 1932 until 1968, the bitter end of the Johnson administration.

The young Buckley's hopes lay partly in knocking out the then-vibrant liberal wing of the Republican Party. As George Will, one of the many leading conservative writers who once worked at *The National Review*, eulogized him in *The Washington Post*: "Before there could be Ronald Reagan's presidency, there had to be Barry Goldwater's candidacy. It made conservatism confident and placed the Republican Party in the hands of its adherents. Before there could be Goldwater's insurgency, there had to be *National Review* magazine."

The acceleration of conservatism involves an irony: in the magazine's widely quoted inaugural essay, Buckley described the publication standing "athwart history, yelling Stop." He wanted to stop the modern tendency of government to engage in what he called "radical social experimentation" in the form of such things as the New Deal and the United Nations, which he saw as products of a moral relativism that had become monolithic in the halls of American power. What he most wanted to stop was tolerance for what he considered modern error's extreme form, the Marx-Leninist view of humanity's advancement, through philosophically discernible stages, toward a condition of perfect equality fostered by an all-powerful state. Like Charles and Pete Seeger, Buckley looked to the Soviet Union as the fulfillment of an idea— one that he called satanic.

Buckley often referred to the Soviet empire by a single word, "gulag." On TV in the 1960s and '70s he'd purr the second syllable, eyebrows shooting past his hairline to show-stopping effect. By then, almost everybody was looking at the Soviet Union in moods ranging from concern to fear and loathing. Pete Seeger quit the Communist Party in the late 1940s. Even he and much of his prewar cohort had grown painfully aware of the awful oppression imposed on Russians and more and more Europeans. The Iron Curtain, as Churchill dubbed it, had fallen; the nuclear buildup had begun; Soviet tanks had rolled. International communism now meant, flagrantly, Soviet takeover of the world, including, in the famous words of President Khrushchev, the grandchildren of Americans. Today, Khrushchev's words may seem defensive braggadocio. Few took them that way at the time.

To Buckley and likeminded others, the socialist threat to American liberty lay not only in massive programs like Social Security, but also in the New Deal practice of giving government jobs to semi-secret communists and more open "fellow travelers"—the Alan Lomaxes and Charles and Pete Seegers and, more seriously, their counterparts in sectors involving national security. After the war, communists were officially included among subversives seeking to bring, in the words of the McCarran Act of 1950, "totalitarian dictatorship" to the United States. Party members and others had long been eagerly accepting instructions for domestic revolution from a police state with which the U.S. now verged on what seemed a war for the future of humanity. Having quit the Party was no defense, hence the famous question "are you now or have you ever been? . . ."

Despite his avowed reservations about Senator Joseph McCarthy, the young Buckley gave strong support, as did much of the liberal establishment (in Buckley's view weakly and perhaps insincerely), for what McCarthy and the House Un-American Activities Committee defined as a hunt for Russian spies, Party members, and communist sympathizers in government, entertainment, the arts, and business.

Buckley's inaugural essay for *The National Review* ascribed such great and entrenched power to liberalism, and such frailty to nascent conservativism, that even small successes could be greeted with shouts of astonished joy. And few would now deem conservative successes small. While welfare and entitlement programs that Buckleyites attacked appear likely to survive, the ambitious young Buckley of the 1950s turned out to be on, and to play a part in determining, what some consider the winning side of history.

But in one area—the civil rights movement—Buckley conservatives were decisively not on the winning side. "Why the South Must Prevail" is the title of a 1957 editorial by Buckley addressing efforts to enforce federal laws ensuring blacks the ability to vote. The piece argued in part:

The NAACP and others insist that the Negroes as a unit want integrated schools. Others disagree, contending that most Negroes approve the social separation of the races. What if the NAACP is correct, and the matter comes to a vote in a community in which Negroes predominate? The Negroes would, according to democratic processes, win the election; but that is the kind of situation the White community will not permit. The White community will not count the marginal Negro vote. The man who didn't count it will be hauled up before a jury, he will plead not guilty, and the jury, upon deliberation, will find him not guilty. A federal judge, in a similar situation, might find the defendant guilty, a judgment which would affirm the law and conform with the relevant political abstractions, but whose consequences might be violent and anarchistic.

The central question that emerges—and it is not a parliamentary question or a question that is answered by merely consulting a catalogue of the rights of American citizens, born Equal—is whether the White community in the South is entitled to take such measures as are necessary to prevail, politically and culturally, in areas in which it does not predominate numerically? The sobering answer is Yes—the White community is so entitled because, for the time being, it is the advanced race.

At the time, Buckley had been editing *The National Review* for only two years, having founded his magazine at twenty-nine. Though the editorial is unsigned, there can be little doubt that it is his work: editorial policy was his domain; more tellingly, its idiosyncratic blend of elegance and provocation was already becoming a Buckley trademark.

The *National Review* would reject the very term "civil rights movement" as "ludicrous," insisting instead on "the Negro revolt" as late as 1964. Not only did the effort to keep blacks from voting fail, Buckley's carefully articulated justification for illegally denying them the vote failed too, so utterly that today's Buckleyites, celebrating the great sweep of the man's pervasive influence, can't seem to recall a thing about it.

The *New York Times* obituary did mention, briefly, that Buckley supported the segregationist South on the grounds of white cultural superiority. More typical of mainstream assessment was the long summation of Buckley's career in *Newsweek*, which said only that Buckley "tolerated" segregation and supported white southerners' "protesting." That characterization, misleading in its vagueness, softens the conservative position on integration—the defining issue of the day, along with the Cold War. Readers of recent articles on Buckley's career could be forgiven for having no idea that *The National Review* described Martin Luther King Jr. as a "rabble-rousing demagogue" who taught "anarchy and chaos" and identified integration with Soviet communism.

The more textured, less temperate discussion of Buckley's politics developed online, where some bloggers and commenters loudly celebrated Buckley's death as the end of an evil phony, whom some called, among other things, a racist, citing part of the '57 editorial. Buckley fans responded that the civil-rights position was a glaring exception to a tough, not bigoted program; that the position amounted to states-rights advocacy, not racism; that Buckley later took a more enlightened view (*Newsweek* said that too); and that he'd acknowledged and taken responsibility for his error. Many defenders cited Buckley's answer to a question in a 2004 *Time* interview: "Have you taken any positions you now regret?" Buckley's answer: "Yes. I once believed we could evolve our way up from Jim Crow. I was wrong: federal intervention was necessary."

There Buckley admits to having been wrong about a position far different from the one he took in "Why the South Must Prevail," quoted above, which asserts a right—even a duty—of southern whites to preserve Jim Crow, on the basis of the white race's supposedly greater advancement. While Buckley's essay may therefore strike readers today as typical of 1950s racist objections to civil-rights legislation, its impact lay in how sharply it departed from the typical, which can be revisited in a statement by Robert Byrd, today a U.S. Senator and in 1945 a twenty-eight-year-old member of the Ku Klux Klan: "Rather I should die a thousand times," young Byrd said, in the cadences that have lately made him a darling of anti–Iraq War liberals, "and see Old Glory trampled in the dirt never to rise again, than to see this beloved land of ours become degraded by race mongrels, a throwback to the blackest specimen from the wilds." That comment appeared in a letter to the segregationist Senator and former Governor of Mississippi Theodore Bilbo, also a Klansman, who wrote a book entitled Take *Your Choice, Separation or Mongrelization*, and filibustered an anti-lynching bill by invoking the "blood of the raped and outraged daughters of Dixie." (A period ditty sung by Pete Seeger was called "Listen, Mr. Bilbo"—"Well, you don't like Negroes, you don't like Jews, / If there is anyone you do like, it sure is news.") Wearing white sheets and following Exalted Cyclopses and Grand Wizards, the Klan did not make sustained arguments in polished prose. As anti-intellectual as they were anti-black, Jim Crow supporters could be readily dismissed by educated liberals and made unappealing allies for educated conservatives.

Until the arrival of Buckley. His 1957 essay, a masterpiece of intellectual agility and verbal confidence, sounded like *The New Republic*, not *The Fiery Cross*. The essay's occasion was the recent success of Senate conservatives in preventing passage of legislation that would have required federal judges, not juries, to render verdicts in prosecutions of political operatives who failed to count black votes. The law was meant to hamper white juries' tendencies to free such defendants regardless of evidence. A striking feature of the essay is Buckley's outright support for jury nullification. Even more daringly he identifies a right for white southerners, when in the minority, to "take such measures as are necessary to prevail." He presents that right as beyond the law, which he associates with "political abstractions," and beyond even the Constitution, which he calls not adequate to cope with issues raised by Jim Crow and the struggle against it.

Buckley is making the kind of "natural law" argument for rights transcending charter and legislation that late-18th-century Americans made against the British Parliament's incursions on their liberties. It was a case that Bilbo and Byrd, sunk in hysteria and ignorance, needed a Yale man to make for them. Instead of denying or glossing over the consequence of the bill's defeat, Buckley announces it: "The effect of it is—and let us speak about it bluntly—to permit a jury to modify or waive the law." Buckley calls the supposed fact that whites are morally entitled to prevail by any means necessary a "sobering" one, admits that it is "unpleasant to adduce statistics" proving the white race superior (and does not actually do so), and appeals to the better angels of southern nature, closing with a veiled threat that, if the South does not behave as Buckley expects it to, his support may have to be withdrawn:

> [The South] must not exploit the fact of Negro backwardness to preserve the Negro as a servile class. It is tempting and convenient to block the progress of a minority whose services, as menials, are economically useful. Let the South never permit itself to do this. So long as it is merely asserting the right to impose superior mores for whatever period it takes to effect a genuine cultural equality between the races, and so long as it does so by humane and charitable means, the South is in step with civilization, as is the Congress that permits it to function.

That is the evolution Buckley was calling for in 1957: not that "we could evolve our way up from Jim Crow," as he said in 2004, but that "the Negro" might, during some period determined and overseen by the superior race, evolve upward from the backwardness that had made Jim Crow not only permissible but necessary.

While this early entry is characteristic of Buckley's lifelong approach to argument, his fans and protégés cannot claim and celebrate it, because its most important theme—about which Buckley is also blunt, and which bears on his conservatism as a whole—comes down to the three-part statement that undergirds the essay and that few conservatives today would want to affirm:

The claims of civilization supersede those of universal suffrage . . . If the majority wills what is socially atavistic, then to thwart the majority may be, though undemocratic, enlightened . . . sometimes the numerical minority cannot prevail except by violence: then it must determine whether the prevalence of its will is worth the terrible price of violence.

Civilization over democracy, even at the calculated, possibly tragic price of violence, taken up more in sorrow than in anger and then fought to the finish. That is the stance with which Buckley began creating a persona that may be unique in our cultural history. Buckley ordained himself the leisure-class warrior-philosopher, roused to militancy by ubiquitous barbarism, defending on behalf of conservatism not mere intellect but the highest cultural sophistication and refinement. That persona would make him not only a conservative leader but also a household name. On his TV show "Firing Line," which ran from 1966 to 1999, he did the eastern establishment one better, at once a parody and epitome of upper-crust manner, with an over-the-top hot-potato drawl that made FDR sound salt-of-the-earth. Buckley's perfectly phrased insults and languorous polysyllabery made him the pop-culture model of intellectual, cultural, and verbal advancement, an unflappable connoisseur, guardian of the best ever thought and said by man. Delighting in the joys of rationality, beauty, hierarchy, imagination, humor, and awe, as expressed especially in the music of Bach, he seemed called from his fig tree by an Athenian sense of citizenship, battling to push back both the mob and the weak-willed mob-enablers who were ruining the civilization that had produced his own gorgeousness.

Hence a contradiction, which seems to have become evident to Buckley early on: Southern workingmen out to prevent "mongrelization" made poor exemplars of advanced culture. Soon he was letting go of his hopes for the white south.

At a famous 1965 Oxford Union Debate with James Baldwin, for example, fighting what was already a rearguard action on civil rights, Buckley took the opportunity to argue against wholesale condemnation of American civilization for failing to live up to what Buckley now called its highest ideals. He averred that everybody agreed that race prejudice is evil; accused the civil-rights movement of no longer seeking equality but the regression of the white race (though he also continued to call slow progress on equal rights necessary); announced that if the issue must come to race war, he was prepared (echoing Churchill for his Oxonian audience) to fight it on the beaches, in the hills, in the mountains; and suggested, for a laugh, that what he really objected to was any uneducated southerner, black or white, being allowed to vote. That joke distilled an unusual mix of states-rights populism and upperclass prerogative put forth at length, that same year, by James J. Kilpatrick in *The National Review*: federalism will be destroyed unless states are free to impose voting qualifications, but those qualifications must discriminate equally, not on the basis of race.

It is unfortunate that each side, in accusing the other of bad faith, so often seems to be right.

It is not clear what requirements Buckley thought poor blacks and poor whites below the Mason-Dixon line should fulfill, or be denied access to the franchise. What is clear is that Buckley's later thinking on integration was not, as his defenders claim, a turnabout on race but a retreat to a more logically consistent snobbism. *The National Review* lost its all-out fights against school integration and the Voting Rights and Civil Rights Acts, but race long remained a defining conservative issue. Among many examples is a 1969 column in which Buckley hymned the research of Arthur Jensen on race and IQ, which showed blacks testing lower than whites on abstract reasoning skills, a finding from which Buckley deduced a racial imperviousness to improvement by education. In the 1970s *The National Review* persistently defended apartheid South Africa on the same basis that it had once defended Jim Crow.

A legacy of Buckley's development on race is today's conservative opposition to programs like affirmative action. Nobody today bases that opposition on a duty to preserve white privilege and prevent anarchy; opponents jump through hoops to show dedication to equality and democracy. Yet criticism of affirmative action, however altered its tone, is a direct inheritor of the ideological contributions Buckley made to conservatism in the 1950s. Today's position represents a fallback, not a break, from Buckley's early ideas, which were never renounced, only defeated. The important issue is not the possible persistence of racist ideas in Buckley's own thinking, but modern conservatives' huge—and hugely convenient—erasure, when it comes to race, of the intellectual origins of modern conservatism.

Seeger and Buckley were romantics. When they were young, and without regard for consequence, they brought charisma, energy, and creativity to dreaming up worlds they wanted—possibly needed—to live in. Because they made those worlds seem so real and beautiful that other people wanted to live in them too, they became larger-than-life characters, instantly recognizable a long way off, not quite real close up, and never quite grown up even when old. Hence their decisive influence. Seeger gave American folk music a purism in no way essential to it, a function of New England abstemiousness in Seeger's own makeup, which also connected him to Soviet communism. The Soviet Union is gone, but our music will never shake the purism. Seeger once said, with wit and accuracy, "I'm more conservative than Goldwater. He just wanted to turn the clock back to when there was no income tax. I want to turn the clock back to when people lived in small villages and took care of each other." Those yearnings began in his father's dreams for the future, but it was a dream about the past that made him Pete Seeger. In Buckley's dream, somebody is going to live in the castle above the village—better for everybody that it be he. That each in his own way dreamed southward, with fateful results, made them romantics in a special American tradition.

An important difference between Seeger and Buckley is that Seeger suffered for his beliefs. The film's innocence about his Stalinist provocations aside, he bravely risked jail by refusing to answer some of HUAC's questions; he was blacklisted, his career ruined for a long time. The film shows his concerts being angrily picketed by Young Americans for Freedom—Buckley's organization. Yet even in Seeger's persecution lies a telling reminder of what the two men shared: a sense that there are certain rights of which only the questing individual himself can be arbiter. When refusing to give names to HUAC, Seeger chose not to rely on his Fifth Amendment right against self-incrimination, claiming instead a transcendent liberty, that of association, which he could not prove but believed was natural, pre-existing any claims made by a committee of federal government.

Liberals may concur in calling Seeger's Stalinism romantic, if unfortunate (although "American Masters" viewers are not supposed to; the Stalinism is not supposed to exist). But liberals may also feel that "romantic" softens the virulence of Buckley's race ideas, letting him off too easily. Buckleyites, for their part, cannot call segregationism romantic, since they have left its central importance out of their story—and they are likely to feel that the adjective understates the evil done by Seeger's Soviet loyalties. Each side in this story has become adept not only at falsifying its own narrative but also at picking apart the other's fallacies to expose venal motives. It is unfortunate that each side, in accusing the other of bad faith, so often seems to be right.

Buckley's and Seeger's shared attraction to extremes did have the effect of condoning awful crimes: lynching of blacks and murder of civil-rights workers on the one hand, Stalin's mass murder on the other. Sorting out kinds and degrees of awfulness is as problematic as determining whether condoning those crimes also contributed to them. (The men themselves remained professionally innocent.) More important is that the two were far from alone. For if their dreams were not our dreams too, we would never have heard the names Pete Seeger and William F. Buckley, Jr.

Hard Rock Park

Carrie Brownstein

Last month, Hard Rock Park opened in Myrtle Beach, S.C. It's a rock 'n' roll theme park, complete with a Led Zeppelin roller coaster called the Ride, whose hairpin turns are synchronized to Robert Plant's wails in "Whole Lotta Love." I can't think of another ride that would inspire the question, "Daddy, what does 'I want to be your backdoor man' mean?" Sounds like a good time for people of all ages!

As far as I'm concerned, the park creators have overlooked a few obvious attractions.

TONGUE TWISTER

Visitors to the park ride on a giant replica of Gene Simmons' tongue. A voice emanating from the tongue keeps bragging about how long it is and how it never gets tired.

SMILE! YOU'RE ON CAMERA

Visitors make their own sex tape with a washed-up rocker of their choice, such as Motley Crue's Tommy Lee—or, to be more accurate, a carny who looks like him. You get to keep the video as a keepsake. Pay extra, and the theme park will leak the video onto the Internet.

STEVEN + STEVIE'S CAR WASH

Visitors drive go-karts through a car wash that uses only scarves. Steven Tyler's scarves do the washing; Stevie Nicks' scarves dry you off. Customers leave feeling refreshed and mostly clean. Adults only, due to the sensual nature of scarves.

ALL-ACCESS TOUR BUS

Park-goers get to feel what it's like to be on tour. For eight hours, you are trapped in a bus with a broken toilet. There are beer bottles everywhere, and the "fresh fruit" that someone decided to bring onto the bus has gone bad. Old episodes of Full House play on the DVD player while your lighting tech has sex in a bunk that's not his. When the Tour Bus ride is over, everyone showers in a bathroom in the club's backstage area. Whoops! We forgot the towels.

ROADIE: THE RIDE

Visitors lug around an amp everywhere they go. Park employees yell, "Put it there. Wait, no, put it there instead." Fun for the whole family.

MEET YR IDOL

This attraction lets fans line up for hours to get a close-up glimpse of their idols. The park makes the line rainy and cold or

100 degrees and sunny. Then, when you finally reach the front of the line, impersonators of the biggest names in music give you the brush-off and mock you as you try to get an autograph, take their picture, or tell them how their music changed your life.

BASS SOLO, THE MUSICAL

Sad, bitter, underappreciated bass players get to play you that one solo that never made it onto the album or into the live act. Performance Time: three hours.

OTHER NOTABLE
MUSIC WRITING OF 2009

Nitsuh Abebe, "Erykah Badu: New Ameriykah Part One: 4th World War," *Pitchfork Media*, June 6, 2008

Harry Allen, "Louder Than A Bomb," *Vibe*, August 2008

Eric K. Arnold, "The Demise of Hyphy," *San Francisco Weekly*, February 20, 2008

Andy Beta, "Black Dice: Through the Looking Glass," *Self-Titled*, May 2008

Mark Binelli, "The Future According To Radiohead," *Rolling Stone*, February 7, 2008

Mark Brown, "Reliving the ranch" and "Lennon's visit had the staff on their toes," *Rocky Mountain News*, January 25, 2008

Keith Cameron, "A man of many lives...Bob Mould," *The Guardian*, February 15, 2008

Jon Caramanica, "My Music, MySpace, My Life," *The New York Times*, November 9, 2008

Raquel Cepeda, "The N-Word Is Flourishing Among Generation Hip-Hop Latinos," *Village Voice*, October 22, 2008

Laura Checkoway, "Inside 'The Miseducation of Lauryn Hill,'" *Rolling Stone*, August 26, 1008

Nate Chinen, "Jazz World Confronting Health Care Concerns," *The New York Times*, February 21, 2008

Kimberly Chun, "Whatever!?," *San Francisco Bay Guardian*, January 2, 2008

Joshua Cohen, "Purist of the Self," *Harper's*, July 2008

Kandia Crazy Horse, "Singing the cyber blues," *San Francisco Bay Guardian*, May 7, 2008

Jonathan Cunningham, "Man-Child in the Promised Land," *Broward Palm Beach New Times*, March 6, 2008

Jeremy Denk, "An Interview with Sarah Palin," *Jeremydenk.net*, October 22, 2008

John Doran, "Kanye West, Sensitive Soul," *The Quietus*, June 24, 2008

J. Freedom du Lac, "Stuck In a Groove," *Washington Post*, August 29, 2008

Alison Fensterstock, "Sissy Strut," *Gambit Weekly*, August 12, 2008

Pete Freedman, "Dallas Hip-Hop: Swagger Like Us," *Dallas Observer*, November 27, 2008

Caryn Ganz, "Madonna: Hard Candy," *Rolling Stone*, May 1, 2008

Gary Giddins, "Player Pianoman," *Jazz Times*, July/August 2008

Michael Gonzales, "White Boy Music, " *Blackadelic Pop*, February 27, 2008

Ian Harrison, "Nick Sanderson - An Obituary, An Appreciation, " *The Quietus*, June 18, 2008

Rob Harvilla, "Why Chinese Democracy's Fine Print Is Way More Fun Than the Record Itself," *Village Voice*, November 26, 2008

Geoffrey Himes, "T Bone Burnett & the Skyliner Band," *Texas Music*, July 2008

Colin Irwin, "Power to the People," *Guardian UK*, August 10, 2008

Aaron Jentzen, "Record Breaking," *Pittsburgh City Paper*, May 7, 2008

Lenny Kaye,"Les Paul: American Master"*eMusic*, 2008
Monica Kendrick, "At the Church of the Empty Bottle," *Chicago Reader*, February 14, 2008
Chuck Klosterman, "Chuck Klosterman reviews Chinese Democracy," *The Onion A.V. Club*, November 19, 2008
Josh Kun, "Born In America, Heart In Mexico," *The New York Times*, July 20, 2008
Hannah Levin,"Getting the Gits," *Seattle Weekly*, June 25, 2008
Andra Lisle, Dave Bartholomew," *Wax Poetics*, Issue 30, 2008
Jennifer Maerz, "Luie Luie stands out as a genuine oddball in a world of faux freaks,"*SF Weekly*, April 23, 2008
Chairman Mao, "Hipster Boogie," *XXL*, September 2008
Michaelangelo Matos, "It's a Hit," *The Stranger*, September 16, 208
Anne Midgette, "A Conductor Comes to a Coda," *Washington Post*, June 29, 2008
Phillip Mlynar, "Knockout!," *Hip Hop Connection*, July 2008
Evie Nagy, "The Feminine Mystique," *Bust*, April/May 2008
Lucy O'Brien,"The unforgettable Ms. Cole," *Guardian UK*, September 26, 2008
Andrew Parks,"Daddy's Little Girl," *Decibel*, July 2008
David Peisner, "Faking the Band," *Spin*, November 2008
Brian Raftery, "Weird Al: Forefather of the YouTube Spoof,"*Wired*, September 22, 2008
Alex Rawls, "Hurricane Bobby," *Blurt*, September 2008
Chris Roberts, "Black Sky Thinking: The Joy Division Industry," *The Quietus*, April 10, 2008
Lisa Robinson, "It Happened in Hitsville," *Vanity Fair*, December 2008
Ron Rosenbaum,"The Opera's New Clothes," *Slate*, October 24, 2008

Kelefa Sanneh, "Savoring a Moment in the Sun, Despite a Court Date," *The New York Times,* February 26, 2008

Allison Stewart,"Too Much of a Good Thing? Nah!," *Washington Post,* December 16, 2008

Ned Sublette, "The American Legacy of Mongo Santamaría," *American Legacy,* Summer 2008

John Swenson,"The Songs Remain the Same," *OffBeat,* December 2008.

Gianluca Tramontana,"The House of Rock," *OffBeat,* May 2008.

LC Weber,"Where In the World Is Jay Electronica?," *The Smoking Section,* October 29, 2009

Jonah Weiner,"Lil Wayne: There Is None Higher,"*Blender,* July 2008

Christopher R. Weingarten,"Grow Up Like a Rock Star,"*Village Voice,* January 15, 2008

Chris Yuscavage, "I-N-D-E-P-E-N-D-E-N-T." *Vibe,* August 2008

Joseph Ohegyi, "B.O.B. Dylan,"*Joseph Loves It* blog (http://josephlovesit.blogspot.com/), March 30, 2008

V/A "They Love Kevin Jonas! The Pop Critic, Not So Much," *Washington Post,* August 13, 2008

LIST OF CONTRIBUTORS

Former rock critic **Gina Arnold** is now a PhD candidate in Stanford University's program in Modern Thought & Literature. Her dissertation is entitled *Rock Crowds & Power*.

When he's not pumping out reams of questionable gibberish for the fine folks at *Decibel, Revolver, Rock Sound* and *Alternative Press,* **J. Bennett** is busy being tall, charming and handsome. He is also the author of *Get In The Ring,* a six-volume compendium on the history of cockfighting. Comrade Bennett would like to dedicate his piece in this anthology to Jim Goad.

Stanley Booth TK

Carrie Brownstein is a writer, musician, and actor. She was a member of the critically acclaimed rock band Sleater-Kinney. Brownstein's writing has appeared in the *New York Times, The Believer,* Slate, and numerous book anthologies on music and culture. She writes a music blog for National Public Radio called *Monitor Mix* and is a contributor to NPRs *All Songs Considered.* Along with Fred Armisen (Saturday Night Live), she is one-half of the comedic duo, Thunder-Ant. She also has a feature role in the upcoming independent film, *Some Days Are Better Than Others,* directed by Matt McCormick.

Brownstein lives in Portland, Oregon where she is working on her first book of non-fiction to be published by Ecco/Harper Collins.

Rosanne Cash is a Grammy Award-winning singer and songwriter. Her fourteen albums, released over the last twenty-five years, have charted eleven #1 singles. Her most recent album, *Black Cadillac*, was released in January 2006 and received a Grammy nomination for Best Contemporary Folk/Americana Album. Her first book, *"Bodies of Water"* (Hyperion, 1995) received widespread critical acclaim, as did her children's book, *"Penelope Jane: A Fairy's Tale"* (HarperCollins, 2000). Her essays and fiction have appeared in *The New York Times, Rolling Stone, The Oxford-American, New York Magazine*, and various other periodicals and collections. Rosanne Cash lives in New York City with her husband, John Leventhal, and her children. She recently signed to Manhattan Records and has just completed her debut CD for the EMI-based label, *The List* which will be released in October. A new book of non-fiction will be published by Viking in June 2010.

Jace Clayton is a writer and musician based in Brooklyn. His essays have appeared in *The Washington Post, Abitare, n+1*, and he is a regular contributor to *Frieze, The Fader*, and *The National*. Clayton performers internationally as DJ/rupture, and blogs at *www.negrophonic.com*.

Joshua Clover is the author of four books, including two books poetry, one on *The Matrix* (British Film Institute, 2005), and the culture history, *1989: Bob Dylan Didn't Have this to Sing About* (University of California, 2009).

Edwyn Collins TK

Josh Eells has written about music and culture for *Rolling Stone, Spin, The New York Times, New York Magazine*, the *Austin American-Statesman*, and *Blender*, where he was an editor. He lives in Brooklyn.

Tom Ewing writes regularly about pop music at *Pitchfork* and at *freakytrigger.co.uk*, where he is halfway through his quixotic project of reviewing every UK #1 single. In real life he works in social media, and feels confident he will soon work out what that actually means.

Paul Ford is Associate Editor, *Harper's Magazine,* Contributing Writer, *The Morning News (TheMorningNews.org),* and author of the novel *Gary Benchley, Rock Star.*

Barry Gifford's most recent novels include *The Imagination of the Heart* and *Memories from a Sinking Ship.* The omnibus *Sailor & Lula: The Complete Novels,* will be published in April 2010. You may visit him on the web at *BarryGifford.com.*

Vanessa Grigoriadis is a contributing editor at *Rolling Stone, New York Magazine,* and *Vanity Fair.* She won the National Magazine Award for Profile Writing in 2007. After she spent many weeks researching Britney Spears' collapse for the article in this volume, she tried hard to ignore celebrity culture forever.

William Hogeland is a historian, novelist, dramatist, and critic. His essays on music have appeared in *The New York Times, The Atlantic Monthly, The Oxford American,* and *Slate.* He is the author of a work of narrative history, *The Whiskey Rebellion,* and a collection of essays, *Inventing American History.* He recently contributed the chapter on insurrections to the forthcoming *Blackwell's Companion to American Military History.*

Jonathan Lethem is the author of seven novels. A recipient of the MacArthur Fellowship, Lethem has also published his stories and essays in *The New Yorker, Harper's, Rolling Stone, Esquire,* and the *New York Times,* among others.

Wendy Lesser is the founding editor of *The Threepenny Review*. She is the author of seven books of nonfiction and one novel, as well as the editor of two anthologies of essays. She was educated at Harvard, Cambridge, and UC Berkeley, and has received awards and honors from the Guggenheim Foundation, the American Academy of Arts & Letters, the National Endowment for the Humanities, the Cullman Center for Scholars and Writers, the American Academy in Berlin, and numerous other institutions. Her next book will be about Shostakovich and his fifteen string quartets.

W. David Marx is a writer and editor living in Tokyo, Japan. His writing on music, fashion, and culture has appeared in *GQ, Harper's, NYLON,* and *The Fader*. Marx is Founder and Chief Editor of web journal *Neojaponisme.com* and a former editor of *Tokion* and the *Harvard Lampoon.*

James Parker is the author of "Turned On: A Biography of Henry Rollins"(Cooper Square) and a contributing editor at *The Atlantic.* He lives with his wife and son in Brookline, Massachusetts.

Michael Pisaro is a composer and guitarist, a member of the Wandelweiser Composers Ensemble, and founder and director of the Experimental Music Workshop. Recordings of his work are available on Edition Wandelweiser Records, Compost and Height, Nine Winds, cathnor, Another Timbre, Confront and other labels. He is Co-Chair of Music Composition at the California Institute of the Arts near Los Angeles.

Ann Powers is the chief pop critic at the *Los Angeles Times*. She is the author of "Weird Like Us: My Bohemian America" and, with the artist, of "Tori Amos: Piece by Piece."

David Ramsey is a writer and schoolteacher in New Orleans.

David Remnick, editor of *The New Yorker* since July 1998, began his reporting career at *The Washington Post* in 1982. He is the author of several books, including "King of the World" and "Lenin's Tomb," for which he won the Pulitzer Prize for nonfiction and a George Polk Award for excellence in journalism. He became a staff writer at The New Yorker in 1992 and has since written over a hundred pieces for the magazine.

Jody Rosen is the music critic for Slate, the author of *White Christmas: The Story of an American Song* (Scribner, 2002), and the compiler of *Jewface* (Reboot Stereophonic, 2006), an anthology of turn-of-the-century Jewish novelty recordings. He lives in Brooklyn.

Rebecca Schoenkopf is the author of *Commie Girl in the OC* and a veteran of California's alternative weeklies, most recently as editor-in-chief of *LA CityBeat*. She is a godless socialist feminist and single mother. She would like to bake you a pie.

Jesse Serwer is the music editor for *Jamrock* magazine and a freelance journalist. His work regularly appears in *Time Out New York*, *XXL*, *Wax Poetics* and *XLR8R* and at his own site, www.jesseserwer.com.

John Jeremiah Sullivan was born in Louisville, Kentucky, and now lives in Wilmington, North Carolina, with his wife, Mariana Johnson, and their daughter, Maria. He is a contributing editor at *Harper's Magazine* and a correspondent with *GQ*. His first book was *Blood Horses* (Farrar Straus & Giroux), and he is finishing another, about a lost episode in the history of early America.

Nick Sylvester lives in Brooklyn, New York. He is the web writer for *The Colbert Report*, a satirical news program on Comedy Central, and the drummer of the punk band Mr. Dream.

Charles Taylor's work has appeared in *Salon, The New York Times, The New Yorker,* the *Newark Star-Ledger, Newsday, Dissent, The Nation, Lapham's Quarterly* and other publications. A member of the National Society of Film Critics, he has contributed to several of the group's anthologies. Taylor has taught journalism at the New School, the Columbia School of Journalism, and New York University. He lives in Brooklyn and thinks Taylor Swift rocks.

Yuval Taylor is the co-author, with Hugh Barker, of *Faking It: The Quest for Authenticity in Popular Music.* As editor, his books include *Growing Up in Slavery, The Future of Jazz, The Cartoon Music Book* (with Daniel Goldmark), and *I Was Born a Slave.* His writings have been published in *The Guardian, The Antioch Review,* and *African American Lives.* He is senior editor at Chicago Review Press, and is co-writing, with Jake Austen, a book about black minstrelsy.

Ken Tucker is Editor-At-Large for *Entertainment Weekly.* He is also the pop-music critic for National Public Radio's "Fresh Air With Terry Gross," and a regular contributor to the *Best American Poetry* blog (http://thebestamericanpoetry.typepad.com/). His music reviews have appeared in *The New York Times, Esquire, Rolling Stone, The Village Voice, Spin, Creem, Circus,* and *The SoHo Weekly News.*

Aidin Vaziri is the pop music critic for the *San Francisco Chronicle.* He has written for *Rolling Stone, NME, Playboy, All Music Guide* and *Amazon.* In 1991, he risked serious injury at a Guns N' Roses concert at the Pantages Theatre in Los Angeles. "Who cares about a broken arm when you've just touched Axl Rose?" he says.

Jeff Weiss is a Los Angeles-based writer and regular contributor to the *Los Angeles Times* and *LA Weekly.* His work has also appeared in the *NME,* the *Village Voice,* and *New York Magazine*'s Vulture Blog, among others. His essay, "Soulja Boy: Cranking The Chain" was selected for last year's Best Music Writing, thus validating the allowance money he squandered on hip-hop magazines throughout the 1990s.

CREDITS

"Notes to reissue of Replacements, Let It Be" by Gina Arnold. First published in the album reissue Replacements, Let It Be, April 22, 2008. Copyright (c) 2008 Rhino Entertainment Company, a Warner Music Group Company. All Rights Reserved. Reprinted by permission of Rhino Entertainment Company.

"Shit Magnet" by J. Bennett. First published in Self-Titled, October 31, 2008. Copyright © 2008 J. Bennett

"My Mentor, My Teacher" by Stanley Booth. First published in Newsweek, Aug 26, 2008. Copyright © 2008 Stanley Booth.

"The Ear of the Beholder" by Rosanne Cash. First published in the New York Times, May 22, 2008. Reprinted with permission.

"Confessions of a DJ" by Jace Clayton. First published in n+1, Fall 2008. Copyright © 2008 Jace Clayton.

"TERRORFLU" was first delivered at the Experience Music Project Pop Conference and first printed in Lana Turner: A Journal of Poetry and Opinion. No copyright is claimed or recognized regarding these words in this order, or etc.